Lecture Notes in Computer Science 9320

Commenced Publication in 1973
Founding and Former Series Editors:
Gerhard Goos, Juris Hartmanis, and Jan van Leeuwen

More information about this series at http://www.springer.com/series/7409

Yuhua Luo (Ed.)

Cooperative Design, Visualization, and Engineering

12th International Conference, CDVE 2015
Mallorca, Spain, September 20–23, 2015
Proceedings

 Springer

Editor
Yuhua Luo
University of Balearic Islands
07122, Palma de Mallorca
Spain

ISSN 0302-9743   ISSN 1611-3349 (electronic)
Lecture Notes in Computer Science
ISBN 978-3-319-24131-9   ISBN 978-3-319-24132-6   (eBook)
DOI 10.1007/978-3-319-24132-6

Library of Congress Control Number: 2015947944

LNCS Sublibrary: SL3 – Information Systems and Applications, incl. Internet/Web, and HCI

Springer Cham Heidelberg New York Dordrecht London

Printed on acid-free paper

Springer International Publishing AG Switzerland is part of Springer Science+Business Media
(www.springer.com)

Preface

This year's, CDVE 2015 conference returned to its Mediterranean home – Mallorca, Spain. The 12th International conference on Cooperative Design, Visualization and Engineering, CDVE 2015, was held during September 20–23, 2015 by the Mediterranean Sea at Alcudia, Mallorca.

The papers in this volume reflect the fact that we are ready and confident to answer the challenge from a completely new computing landscape. The popularity of cloud computing, social media, and big data has been the driving force behind research and development in our CDVE community.

A number of papers address the topic of big data and its relation to cooperative work. They focus on information modeling, intensive task management, and how to use cloud technology to foster cooperation, etc.

Dealing with social network issues is the topic of another group of papers in this volume. They cover creating programming languages to automate cooperative processes, social network information visualization, and the ranking of cooperative research teams by analyzing social network data.

Using mobile devices for cooperation seems to be another trend in the papers. The application areas are especially wide, which show the great potential of mobile devices in supporting cooperative applications. There are papers concentrated on mobile e-learning, online interaction for museums, mobile e-commerce, and even the cooperative monitoring of the delivery of fresh products. Each application area may have its own specific issues to address in order to optimize the efficiency, usability, and effectiveness of the cooperation.

Crowd sourcing is again one of the major topics among the papers. There are interesting papers about applying crowd sourcing to architecture design, making client decisions in e-commerce, etc. In fact we should continue to explore this new way of cooperation and expect more achievements in this direction.

In the field of cooperative engineering, there are many research results reported, such as in the collaboration for product design, operation, and process control, enabling networked enterprises to realize interoperability, etc.

With respect to the theoretical analysis and modeling of group behavior, there are reports based on the analysis of real case data, using Baysian networks to model team behavior. The study shows that using Baysian networks in analyzing and modeling team performance from a psychological perspective is feasible. We believe that this achievement will contribute to enriching the theoretical study of cooperative team work.

To see the great progress made in the fields of cooperative design, visualization, and engineering has been a great pleasure. I would like to thank all of our authors for submitting their papers and presenting their hard work. They are at the frontier of technological advancement for the benefit of society.

I would like to thank all of our Program Committee members, volunteer reviewers, and Organization Committee members for their continuous support of the conference. My special thanks go to my colleague, the Organization Committee Chair, Dr. Sebastián Galmés Obrador, and my university – the University of the Balearic Islands – for their constant support and encouragement of this conference. The success of this year's conference would not have been possible without their generous support.

September 2015   Yuhua Luo

Organization

Conference Chair

Yuhua Luo   University of the Balearic Islands, Spain

International Program Committee

Program Chair

Dieter Roller   University of Stuttgart, Germany

Members

Jose Alfredo Costa	Jessie Kennedy	Manuel Ortega
Peter Demian	Harald Klein	Niko Salonen
Carrie Sturts Dossick	Jean-Christophe Lapayre	Fernando Sanchez
Susan Finger	Francis Lau	Weiming Shen
Sebastia Galmes	Pierre Leclercq	Ram Sriram
Halin Gilles	Jang Ho Lee	Chengzheng Sun
Matti Hannus	Jos P. van Leeuwen	Thomas Tamisier
Shuangxi Huang	Kwan-Liu Ma	Xiangyu Wang
Tony Huang	Mary Lou Maher	Nobuyoshi Yabuki
Claudia-Lavinia Ignat	Toan Nguyen	

Reviewers

Jose Alfredo Costa	Jean-Christophe Lapayre	Juan Carlos Preciado
Peter Demian	Pierre Leclercq	Guofeng Qin
Selim Erol	Jang Ho Lee	Dieter Roler
Susan Finger	Jos P. Leeuwen	Niko Salonen
Takayuki Fujimoto	Jaime Lloret	Fernando Sanchez
Sebastia Galmes	Lakhoua Najeh	Yilun Shang
Halin Gilles	Toan Nguyen	Weiming Shen
Tony Huang	Manuel Ortega	Thomas Tamisier
Shuangxi Huang	Carlos Pampulim	Xiangyu Wang
Harald Klein	Roberto Pérez	Nobuyoshi Yabuki

Organization Committee

Chairs

Sebastia Galmes   University of the Balearic Islands, Spain
Tony Huang   University of Tasmania, Australia

Members

Tomeu Estrany   Alex Garcia   Guofeng Qin
Takayuki Fujimoto   Jaime Lloret

Contents

Cooperative Team Work Analysis and Modeling: A Bayesian Network Approach

Pilar Fuster-Parra[✉], Alex García-Mas, Jaume Cantallops, and Francisco Javier Ponseti

Universitat Illes Balears, Carr. Valldemossa km. 7.5, Palma de Mallorca, Spain
{pilar.fuster,alex.garcia,jaume.cantallops,xponseti}@uib.es

Abstract. The purpose of this study was to discover the relationships among 18 psychological features in a *cooperative team* in order to analyse work team performance. A Bayesian network (BN) has been built from a dataset of 403 soccer semi-professional players, taking into account prototypical sportive teams with respect to other workteams, regarding its psychological features, such as *leadership, cohesion* or *group roles*. The BN shows three conditionally independent features according to the local Markov property: two cohesion dimensions and the cooperative style of management/coaching; and features such as *players satisfaction, experience, social integration* in the team, and the *workplace specificity*, i.e., the players' positions, which were located at the bottom in the BN show a clear dependence. The BN was used to make inferences achieving: (1) The social side of the cohesion has a low likelihood influence on the performance; (2) All psychological leadership styles (positive and/or negative) have some influence on the performance, the years remaining in the same team, and the player's position; (3) The positive leadership style is not a required condition for the performance or for the player's satisfaction, but a consequence of the other psychological variables.

Keywords: Cooperative group · Collaborative work · Team processes · Human performance · Cohesion team building · Workplace · Bayesian networks

1 Introduction

Work teams are a fact well known today [30] even when taking into account the associated psychological factors [5] analysis. However, it is more difficult to find studies that relate the equipment they need to cooperate with the effective performance of them [18]. Some psychological factors of collaborative teams have been studied more than others in terms of performance, such as cohesion [1] or facilitators group and blockers roles [16]. Features such as the specificity of the jobs [23] (or playing positions, in this case), generating performance expectations, perceived collective efficacy, motivational climate generated by the manager [27] and leadership styles, the coach, which are not usually studied, are here considered.

© Springer International Publishing Switzerland 2015
Y. Luo (Ed.): CDVE 2015, LNCS 9320, pp. 1–10, 2015.
DOI: 10.1007/978-3-319-24132-6_1

Bayesian networks (BNs) [25,33], well suited to reason with uncertain domain knowledge, can be applied to aid teams by providing cooperative and collaborative work' characterization estimates. BNs have been proven to be a strong tool to discover the relationships between variables that attempts to separate out indirect from direct association [17], and can capture the way an expert understands the relationships among all the features [15]. Contrary to deterministic understanding of the *causality* phenomenon [29], BN modeling lie within the data mining and machine learning literature [11,20]. The network structure is a directed acyclic graph (DAG) where each node represents a random variable [4,26] and the arcs may represent causality [38]. BNs combine graph theory and probability theory to represent relationships between variables (nodes in the graph) [17,18]. BNs have recently been used to analyze team performance related to different types of cooperation between team members and various motivational climates generated by teams coaches in sports performance [19], and achieving different results from those obtained by classical statistics.

Several studies have indicated the relationship between leadership behaviors and efficacy [7,40] and, how both features can influence team performance [10,24]. Moreover, some authors have used players satisfaction with participation [3] and each player's satisfaction with their role within the team [2] since both aspects can be more determinant than group size. In this regard, the greater each player's satisfaction with their participation and role is, the higher the group's confidence in its abilities is, and therefore, it might lead to a better team performance [2]. Different conceptual frameworks have defended that collective efficacy is one of the most important variables related to performance and success in sports [2,6]. Finally, it is important to note that Coaches' conduct, instructions, indications, social support, positive reinforcement, etc. can play an important role in the daily team functioning and can influence team performance [34,35].

The paper is organized as follows. Section 2 presents the Materials and Methods given the process to obtain the cooperative team model. Section 3 presents an analysis of the cooperative team model through a BN. Section 4 presents a discussion. Finally, Sect. 5 concludes the paper.

2   Materials and Methods

2.1   Participants

The participants were male semi-professional football players from 20 teams who participated in the Third Division of a Spanish soccer League. A sample of 403 between the ages of 18 and 39 years with a median age of 24 years (IQR $= 27 - 21.5$) was used.

2.2   Instruments and Material

The following instruments have been used:

1. **Leadership Behaviors.** Coach leadership behaviors were assessed using an adapted Spanish version of the Leadership Sport Scale (LSS) [13]. This is a 40-item instrument designed to measure the following five dimensions of leadership: democratic behaviors,autocratic behaviors, training and instruction, social support, and positive feedback.
2. **Group Environment Questionnaire.** The Spanish version of GEQ [6, 22], was used to assess team cohesion. This inventory of 18−items comprises the following four factors: Group Integration-Task; Group Integration Social; Individual Attraction to the Group- Task; and Individual Attraction to the Group-Social. These four factors are grouped into the two main factors of social cohesion and task cohesion.
3. **Collective Efficacy.** To assess collective efficacy, the *Cuestionario de Eficacia Colectiva en Fútbol* (CECF, The Football Collective Efficacy Questionnaire) [28], was adapted. This inventory of 26-items refers to some offensive and defensive situations, which are grouped into a single factor.
4. **Work Experience, Satisfaction and Expectations.** Were measured trough an ad hoc questionnaire containing the following questions, from would have to play a lot less,would have to play a lot more.
   (a) *Work Experience*: "How many times have you played in this team?".
   (b) *Satisfaction*: "Do you feel that you are important to your team during the game?" which has been previously used [28].
   (c) *Expectations*: we asked players and managers to predict what position they believed they would occupy in the standings at the end of the season.
5. **Performance.** To calculate the performance ratio, we evaluated how the team viewed its prospects (average of all players and coach expectations) at the beginning of the season as well as the final ranking [28].
6. **Specificity Workplace.** The positions of the players on the pitch were divided into 4 groups: goalkeeper, defender, midfielder and striker.
7. **Participation.** "Are you satisfied with your participation in the games?".

2.3   Learning Bayesian Networks

To learn a BN implies two tasks: (i) structural learning, that is, the identification of the topology of the BN, and (ii) parametric learning, that is the estimation of numerical parameters (conditional probabilities) given a network topology.

Structural Learning by Model Averaging. The structure was learnt from the collected data set. The problem of discovering the causal structure will increase with the number of variables [8,14]. Furthermore there are many structures that are consistent with the same set of independencies.

To obtain the structure, two options are either to select a single *best* model or obtain some *average* model, which is known as *model averaging* [9,21]. The *bnlearn* [31,37] package of R language [39] was used to obtain the structure. Our model was learnt by *tabu* algorithm. The final model was obtained repeating several times structure learning, a large number of network structures were

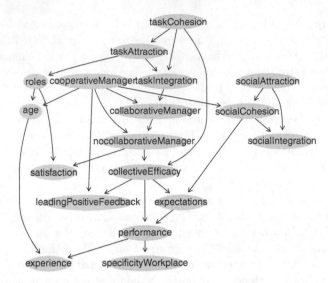

Fig. 1. Structure obtained by *model averaging* over 1000 networks built with tabu learning algorithm from *bnlearn* package in R language using a threshold = 0.95.

explored (1000 BNs) to reduce the impact of locally optimal (but globally sub-optimal) networks on learning. The networks learned were averaged to obtain a more robust model. The averaged network structure was obtained using the arcs present in at least 95 % of the networks, which gives a measure of the strength of each arc and establishes its *significance* given a *threshold* (95 %) (see Fig. 1).

Parameter Learning by Model Averaging. The conditional probability distributions are called the parameters. Parameter learning was perform by the *bn.fit* function and *bayes* estimator using a non-informative prior. A conditional probability distribution was obtained for each node of the BN.

2.4 Validation

The BN was validated using a 10-fold cross-validation for BN. In Table 1, the area under the ROC curve (AUC), and the percentage correctly classified for the different features is shown.

3 Cooperative Team Work Model

The cooperative team model (see Fig. 1) shows three main top psychological features embedded in the dynamic functioning of the cooperative team studied. First of all, we have two variables related with the concept of cohesion: the *social attraction* among the teammates, and the *collaborative cohesion* addressed to the tasks needed to accomplish the team's aims; and secondly, we found -as

Table 1. AUCs and accuracy for the different variables.

Variable name	State	Low	Moderate	High	AUC	Accuracy
Age	18–22				0.8743	63.7700
Age	23–26				0.7210	63.7700
Age	27–39				0.8339	63.7700
SpecificityWorkplace		0.5228	0.5620	0.5955		64.2680
Experience		0.8649	0.8352	0.9510		76.4268
Roles		0.8407	0.7781	0.8161		74.6898
Satisfaction		0.7474	0.7273	0.7278		73.6973
SocialAttraction		0.8832	0.8887	0.9132		82.6303
TaskAttraction		0.9212	0.8233	0.8930		74.6898
SocialIntegration		0.8703	0.8132	0.8361		75.9305
TaskIntegration		0.9716	0.8990	0.9171		84.3672
SocialCohesion		0.9845	0.9607	0.9721		89.3300
TaskCohesion		0.9933	0.9577	0.9676		87.5931
CollectiveEfficacy		0.8467	0.7258	0.8137		73.6972
CollaborativeManager		0.7940	0.7141	0.7560		64.0198
CooperativeManager		0.9121	0.8460	0.8566		80.1489
LeadingPositiveFeedback		0.8342	0.7206	0.7306		71.7122
NocollaborativeManager		0.6474	0.6444	0.7807		50.1241
Expectations		0.6891	0.6796	0.7280		58.5608
Performance		0.7408	0.6659	0.6717		52.1092

the third top variable- the *cooperative style of coaches or managers*. The bottom probabilistic dependant variables are divided in two different categories: (1) Psychological: the social integration of the team members, added to their satisfaction with the team tasks, and the manager's positive style of leadership; and (2) The team features: the members' experience, and their specific position inside the team structure and organization (Workplace specificity). The rest of intermediate probabilistic variables are related in two ways too: (1) The first one is oriented to precede the team's performance (which in its turn is the most important variable regarding the likelihood of the duration and the time pertaining to the same team), and (2), The social integration of the team members, which seems to be relatively "isolated" form the rest of variables.

3.1   Analysing Cooperative Manager Team

We choose at each state the variable and the state that most increases the likelihood of the *Cooperative Manager* variable in a *High*, *Low*, and *Moderate* states respectively. A summary is shown in Fig. 2. Step by step instantiations: successive instantiations are represented in the horizontal line, in step 1 is represented the marginal probability value. On the left: step 2 = *age* = 27 − 29; step 3 = *leadingPositiveFeedback* = High; step 4 = *nocollaborativeManager* = High; step 5 *socialCohesion* = High; step 6 = *roles* = High; step 7 *collectiveEfficacy* = Low; step 8 *taskIntegration* = High; step 9 *collaborativeManager* = High; step 10 *socialAttraction* = Moderate. On the middle: step 2 = *age* = 27 − 29; step 3 = *leadingPositiveFeedback* = Low; step 4 = *nocollaborativeManager* = High; step 5 *socialCohesion* = Moderate; step 6 = *roles* = High; step 7*collectiveEfficacy* = High; step 8 *taskIntegration* = Moderate; step 9 *collaborativeManager* = Low; step 10 *socialAttraction* = Moderate. On the right: step 2 = *age* = 23 − 26; step 3 = *leadingPositiveFeedback* = Low; step 4 = *nocollaborativeManager* = Moderate; step 5 *socialCohesion* = Moderate; step 6 = *roles* = High; step 7 *collectiveEfficacy* = Low; step 8 *taskIntegration* = High; step 9 *collaborativeManager* = Moderate; step 10 *socialAttraction* = High.

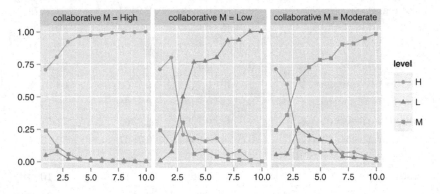

Fig. 2. Likelihood variations for cooperative manager variable once the variables of its Markov blanket are instantiated. In level label H, L, and M stands for High, Low, and Moderate respectively.

The global Markov property was applied to maximize and minimize likelihoods values of cooperative manager feature. The global Markov property states that any node X is conditionally independent of any other node given its Markov blanket (a Markov blanket of X in a BN is the set of nodes consisting of X's parents, X's children, and other parents of X's children). The features instantiated were in the Markov blanket of cooperative manager feature, therefore given its Markov blanket, cooperative manager is independent of the remaining features as the global Markov property states.

3.2 Analysing Performance Team

We choose at each state the variable and the state that most increases the likelihood of the *performance* variable in a *High*, *Low*, and *Moderate* states respectively. A summary is shown in Fig. 3. The step by step instantiations, i.e., successive instantiations are represented in the horizontal line. Step 1 represent the marginal probability value. On the left: step 2 = *specificityWorkplace* = High; step 3 = *experience* = High; step 4 = *collectiveEfficacy* = High; step 5 *expectations* = Low; step 6 = *age* = 27–39. On the middle: step 2 = *specificityWorkplace* = High; step 3 = *experience* = Low; step 4 = *collectiveEfficacy* = Low; step 5 *expectations* = Low; step 6 = *age* = 27–39. On the right:step 2 = *specificityWorkplace* = Medium; step 3 = *experience* = Moderate; step 4 = *collectiveEfficacy* = Low; step 5 *expectations* = High; step 6 = *age* = 18–22.

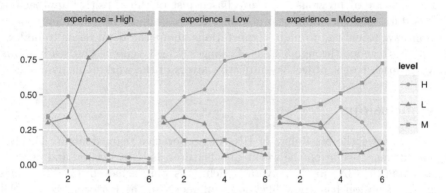

Fig. 3. Likelihood variations for performance variable once the variables of its Markov blanket are instantiated. In level label H, L, and M stands for High, Low, and Moderate respectively.

Again, as the features instantiated constitute the Markov blanket for team's performance, therefore given its Markov blanket, team's performance is independent of the remaining features as the global Markov property states.

4   Discussion

The local Markov property (any node X is conditionally independent of any other node given its Markov blanket) shows the preeminence of two variables on the dynamic performance of the equipment: cooperation or coach- manager and team cohesion. It has been noted in previous works [32], but in our study the relationships between the remaining features are established. Five bottom variables have been found: the positive style of coaches / managers; social integration in the workteam; satisfaction with the role inside the team; the specific workplace and lastly, the experience, i.e., time staying in the same team. There may be a distortion of objectivity due to the team affective attraction, which possibly affects the trust the members have on the team capabilities [12].

In previous findings, the satisfaction of the teamworkers seems to be related to the acceptance of roles [16], however in our study appears to be more related to the attraction of the task or team's objective, and also with the different aspects of the manager, including the "negative" ones. It is true that this fact is in some way anticipated by the concept of entrapment or sportive commitment [36], but not so clearly and objective. Finally, workplace specificity (i.e., positions, in our case) seems to be one of the most conditionally dependant variable. In order to reach the highest likelihood value of the cooperative management style for the coach we make instantiations on the BN. The best age range was the oldest one (27−29) years old, very far from the youngest ones in sport); the two next changes needed were the combination of two opposed styles of coaching to high value: the positive leading and the non-collaborative management style (as opposed to some amount of previous literature based just of the "Positive approach"); after the fifth step the value of probability reaches almost its maximum: social cohesion have to change to high. Expectations about the team needs to be low. This value is reached through 5 steps of changes (Fig. 3, center). Our study shows a new approach to the objective-subjective layers of the workteams dynamics.

5   Conclusions

The study shows the feasibility of BNs in cooperative team domain. The BN offers a different insight on the workteams features, both structural and psychological. From the BN analysis several conclusions were achieved: (1) The social side of the cohesion has a low likelihood influence on the performance; (2) All psychological leadership styles (positive and/or negative) have some influence on the performance, the years remaining in the same team, and the player's position; (3) The positive leadership style is not a required condition for the performance or for the player's satisfaction, but a consequence of the other psychological variables.

Acknowledgement. This research was funded by the Spanish Ministry of Science and Innovation (PI13/01477).

References

1. Beal, D.J., Cohen, R.R., Burke, M.J., McLendon, C.L.: Cohesion and performance in groups: a meta-analytic clarification of construct relations. J. Appl. Psychol. **88**, 989–1004 (2003)
2. Beauchamp, M.R.: Efficacy beliefs within relational and group contexts in sport. In: Jowett, S., Lavallee, D. (eds.) Social Psychology in Sport, pp. 181–193. Human Kinetics, Champaign (2007)
3. Boixadós, M., Cruz, J., Torregrosa, M., Valiente, L.: Relationships among motivational climate, satisfaction, perceived ability, and fair play attitudes in young soccer players. J. Appl. Sport Psychol. **16**, 301–317 (2004)
4. Butz, C.J., Hua, S., Chen, J., Yao, H.: A simple graphical approach for understanding probabilistic inference in Bayesian networks. Inf. Sci. **179**, 699–716 (2009)
5. Cannon-Bowers, J.A., Salas, E.: Teamwork competencies: The interaction of team members knowledge, skills, and attittudes. In: O'Neil, H.F. (ed.) Workforce Readiness: Competencies and Assessment, pp. 151–174. Erlbaum, Mahwah (1997)

6. Carron, A.V., Eys, M.A.: Group Dynamics in Sport. Fitness Information Technology, Morgantown (2012)
7. Chen, G., Bliese, P.D.: The role of different levels of leadership in predicting self and collective efficacy: evidence for discontinuity. J. Appl. Psychol. **87**, 549–556 (2002)
8. Chickering, D.: Optimal structure identification with greedy search. J. Mach. Learn. Res. **3**(3), 507–554 (2002)
9. Claeskens, G., Hjort, N.L.: Model Selection and Model Averaging. Cambridge University Press, Cambridge (2008)
10. Cohen, S.G., Bailey, D.E.: What makes team work: group effectiveness research from the shop floor to the executive suite. J. Manage. **23**, 239–290 (1997)
11. Cooper, G.F., Herskovits, E.: A Bayesian method for the induction of probabilistic networks from data. Mach. Learn. **9**(4), 309–347 (1992)
12. Costa, A.: Work team trust and efectiveness. Pers. Rev. **32**, 605–672 (1994)
13. Crespo, M., Balaguer, I., Atienza, F.L.: Análisis psicométrico de la versión española de la escala de liderazgo en el deporte de Chelladurai y Saleh en la versión de entrenadores. Rev. Psicol. Soc. Apl. **4**(1), 5–28 (1994)
14. Daly, R., Shen, Q., Aitken, S.: Learning Bayesian networks: approaches and issues. Knowl. Eng. Rev. **26**(2), 99–157 (2011)
15. DeFelipe, J., López-Cruz, P.L., Benavides-Piccione, R., Bielza, C., Larrañaga, P., et al.: New insights into the classification and nomenclature of cortical GABAergic interneurons. Nat. Rev. Neurosci. **14**, 202–216 (2013)
16. Eys, M.A., Carron, A.V., Beauchamp, M.R., Bray, S.R.: Role ambiguity in sport teams. J. Sport Exerc. Psychol. **25**, 534–550 (2003)
17. Fuster-Parra, P., García-Mas, A., Ponseti, F.J., Palou, P., Cruz, J.: A Bayesian network to discover relationships between negative features in sport: a case study of teen players. Qual. Quant. **48**(3), 1473–1491 (2014). doi:10.1007/s11135-013-9848-y
18. Fuster-Parra, P., García-Mas, A., Ponseti, F.J., Leo, F.M.: Team performance and collective efficacy in the dynamic psychology of competitive team: a Bayesian network analysis. Hum. Mov. Sci. **40**, 98–118 (2015). doi:10.1016/j.humov.2014.12.005
19. García Mas, A., Fuster-Parra, P., Ponseti, J., Palou, P., Olmedilla, A., Cruz, J.: Análisis de las relaciones entre motivación, el clima motivacional y la ansiedad competitiva entre jóvenes jugadores de equipo mediante una red Bayesiana (2015). doi:10.6018/analesps.31.1.167531
20. Heckerman, D., Geiger, D., Chickering, D.M.: Learning Bayesian networks: the combination of knowledge and statistical data. Mach. Learn. **20**, 197–243 (1995)
21. Hojsgaard, S., Edwards, D., Lauritzen, S.: Graphical Models with R. Springer, New York (2012)
22. Iturbide, L.M., Elosua, P., Yanes, F.: Medida de la cohesión en equipos deportivos. Adaptación al español del Group Environment Questionnaire (GEQ). Psicothema **22**, 482–488 (2010)
23. Jirotka, M., Gilbert, N., Luff, P.: On the social organisation of organisations. Comput. Support. Coop. Work **1**, 95–118 (1992)
24. Keshtan, M.H., Ramzaninezhad, R., Kordshooli, S., Panahi, P.M.: The relationship between collective efficacy and coaching behaviours in professional volleyball league of Iran clubs. World J. Sport Sci. **3**(1), 1–6 (2010)
25. Koller, D., Friedman, N.: Probabilistic Graphical Models: Principles and Techniques. The MIT Press, Cambridge, London (2010)

26. Glymour, C.: The Mind's Arrows: Bayes Nets and Graphical Causal Models in Psychology. The MIT Press, New York (2003)
27. Lameiras, J., Almeida, P.L., García-Mas, A.: Relationships between cooperation and goal orientation among male professional and semi-professional team athletes 1. Percept. Mot. Skills **119**(3), 851–860 (2014)
28. Leo, F.M., Sánchez-Miguel, P.A., Sánchez-Oliva, D., Amado, D., García-Calvo, T.: Incidence of cooperation, cohesion and collective efficacy on performance in football teams. Revista Internacional Ciencias Deporte **7**, 341–354 (2012)
29. Ligęza, A., Fuster-Parra, P.: AND/OR/NOT causal graphs - a model for diagnostic reasoning. Int. J. Appl. Math. Comput. Sci. **7**, 185–203 (1997)
30. Mathieu, J., Maynard, M.T., Rapp, T., Gilson, L.: Team effectiveness 1997–2007: a review of recent advancements and a glimpse into the future. J. Manage. **34**, 410–476 (2008)
31. Nagarajan, R., Scutari, M., Lèbre, S.: Bayesian Networks in R: with Applications in Systems Biology. Springer, Berlin, Heidelberg, New York (2013)
32. Olmedilla, A., Ortega, E., Almeida, P., Lameiras, J., Villalonga, T., Sousa, C., Torregrosa, M., Cruz, J., Garcia-Mas, A.: Cohesión y cooperación en equipos deportivos. Anales de Psicología **27**, 232–238 (2011)
33. Pearl, J.: Causality: Models, Reasoning and Inference. Cambridge University Press, Cambridge (2000)
34. Raedeke, T.D.: Is athlete burnout more than just stress? a sport commitment per-spective. J. Sport Exerc. Psychol. **19**, 396–417 (1997)
35. Riemer, H.A.: Multidimensional model of coach leadership. In: Jowett, S., Lavallee, D. (eds.) Social Psychology in Sport, pp. 57–73. Human Kinetics Publishers, Champaign (2007)
36. Scanlan, T.K., Russell, D.G., Beals, K.P., Scanlan, L.A.: Project on elite athlete commitment (PEAK):II. a direct test and expansion of the sport commitment model with elite amateur sportsmen. J. Sport Exerc. Psychol. **25**, 377–401 (2003)
37. Scurati, M.: Learning Bayesian networks with the bnlearn R package. J. Stat. Softw. **35**(3), 1–22 (2010)
38. Spirtes, P., Glymour, C., Scheines, R.: Causation, Prediction and Search. Adaptive Computation and Machine Learning, 2nd edn. The MIT Press, Cambridge (2001)
39. R Development Core Team. R: a language and environment for statistical computing. [Computer Software]. R Foundation for Statistical Computing, Vienna, Austria (2012). ISBN 3-900051-07-0, http://www.R-project.org/
40. Watson, C.B., Chemers, M.M., Preiser, N.: Collective efficacy: a multilevel analysis. Pers. Soc. Psychol. Bull. **27**, 1057–1068 (2001)

Extending CIAM Methodology to Support Mobile Application Design and Evaluation: A Case Study in m-Learning

Miguel A. Redondo[1(✉)], Ana I. Molina[1], and Christian X. Navarro[2]

[1] Escuela Superior de Informática, Universidad de Castilla – La Mancha,
Paseo de la Universidad, 4, 13071 Ciudad Real, Spain
{Miguel.Redondo,AnaIsabel.Molina}@uclm.es
[2] Facultad de Ingeniería Arquitectura y Diseño, Universidad Autónoma de Baja California,
Ensenada, México
cnavarro@uabc.edu.mx

Abstract. Traditionally, the development of systems supporting group work has been considered a complex task because multiple aspects have to be considered. As a consequence, it is necessary to apply methodological processes in order to reach successful and usable systems. CIAM is a methodological approach for developing groupware user interfaces by modeling aspects of collaboration and interaction. CIAM addresses the joint modeling of collaboration and human-computer interaction aspects, guiding the engineers through several modeling stages, starting from the analysis of the context of the group work until obtaining an interactive task model. In its initial proposal, CIAM does not deal directly with evaluation mechanisms and processes of the artifacts produced when this methodology is applied. In addition, CIAM is not primarily focused on the mobile computing paradigm. Thus, the objective of this paper is to describe how CIAM is being improved in order to provide more complete support for modeling and evaluation of collaborative applications based on mobile computing and especially the modeling of applications supporting Mobile Learning (or m-Learning).

Keywords: Collaborative mobile systems · Group interaction in mobile systems · Cooperative learning · Mobile usability

1 Introduction

The development of systems supporting group work is a complex task because multiple aspects have to be considered [1]. As a consequence, it is necessary to apply methodological processes in order to reach successful systems. CIAM (*Collaborative Interactive Applications Methodology*) is a methodological approach for developing groupware user interfaces by modeling aspects of collaboration and interaction [2, 3]. CIAM addresses the joint modeling of collaboration and human-computer interaction aspects, guiding the engineers through several modeling stages, starting from the analysis of the context of the group work until obtaining an interactive task model [4, 5]. The final user interface

© Springer International Publishing Switzerland 2015
Y. Luo (Ed.): CDVE 2015, LNCS 9320, pp. 11–18, 2015.
DOI: 10.1007/978-3-319-24132-6_2

is obtained from the interaction model, applying a semi-automatic method supported by the CIAT-GUI tool [6].

In its initial proposal, CIAM does not deal directly with evaluation mechanisms and processes of the artifacts produced when this methodology is applied. Furthermore, the notation used for this methodology is not primarily focused on the mobile computing paradigm.

Therefore, CIAM has been enhanced in order to support the modeling of collaborative applications based on mobile computing and especially the modeling of applications supporting collaborative Mobile Learning (or m-Learning) [7]. For this, we have proposed a framework for design and evaluation of mobile applications [8]. This framework serves as a basis for an evaluation tool that allows for the analysis of m-Learning applications characteristics and representing results into a radar chart. In addition, mechanisms and tools to highlight strengths and weaknesses are incorporated [9].

Thus, the objective of this paper is to describe this framework and how it has been integrated with CIAM in order to provide a more complete support for modeling and developing interactive collaborative systems for mobile computing.

This paper continues by briefly explaining some characteristics of CIAM methodology and highlighting the necessity of extending it in order to design and to evaluate mobile applications. Then, our evaluation framework is described, and panoramic view of how it is used in the CIAM context is given.

2   Previous and Related Work

With the aim of facilitating the development of groupware systems, we have proposed CIAM (Collaborative Interactive Applications Methodology). CIAM is a methodological approach for the modeling and development of groupware applications that takes into account the modeling of work in-group and interaction issues [3]. Thus, the objective of CIAM is to serve as a guide for the engineers when creating a conceptual specification of the main aspects that characterize the groupware systems and lead to the design of the interactions that these systems support. CIAM is technologically supported by the CIAT [10] and CIAT-GUI tools [6]. With these tools, a final graphical user interface is semi-automatically obtained.

CIAM includes a notation called CIAN (Collaborative Interactive Application Notation), which allows for modeling of group and human-computer interaction issues [2]. CIAN can be used for collaborative learning modeling systems, adding higher levels of abstraction in the development of educational applications in specified standards, such as IMS-LD [11, 12]. It has been shown that this language can be used to specify CSCL activities and systems, even in mobile contexts [13].

However, CIAN considers device independence as a fundamental principle. Therefore, it is not primarily focused on this paradigm and the effective utilization of CIAM for development of applications to support m-Learning or collaborative m-Learning activities is difficult, since in these cases it is necessary to consider specific aspects of mobile computing as well as the evaluation of artifacts produced, especially when these artifacts contain pedagogical issues.

There are other authors that have addressed this problem by focusing on different aspects. For example, en [14] a model-based tasks and dialectic is described. In [15] a software engineering and learning tasks based approach is presented. Others [16] use ontologies and its main objective is the modeling of learning context and not so much support collaboration. However, CIAM is and approach focused on interaction and collaboration aspects that are necessary for groupware and collaborative learning.

In the following section, we describe how CIAM has been improved by means of a framework to design and evaluate mobile applications, considering aspects of mobile usability and pedagogic usability.

3   Supporting Design and Evaluation of Collaborative m-Learning Applications with CIAM

In order to reach our objective, we have developed a framework of design and evaluation of collaborative m-Learning applications. Then, the application of this framework has been included in the process model of CIAM because our aim is to improve CIAM. However, it could be used in an independent way. Therefore, we provide some guidelines on how it could be applied in a methodological process for modeling of interactive and collaborative applications on the mobile computing paradigm.

3.1   Framework for Design and Evaluation

A framework to design and evaluate mobile applications has been developed. It considers aspects of mobile usability and pedagogic usability [9]. Thus, it is divided in the first level into two categories: *Pedagogical Usability* and *User Interface Usability*. Each category is organized into several dimensions and criteria that must be taken into account. For example, *Pedagogical Usability* is organized into *Content, Multimedia, Activities, Social Interaction*, and *Personalization* dimensions; and *User Interface Usability* is organized into *Operability, User Error Protection, Aesthetics, Feedback, Accessibility*, and *Motivation* dimensions.

Regarding *Social Interaction*, it is considered that socialization is fundamental for the learning process, and an m-Learning application must promote it among students. For the socialization dimension, five criteria are considered: *Dialogue, Collaboration, Cooperation, Discussion*, and *Sharing*. These criteria are defined according to the conceptual framework in which CIAM is based [6].

Figures 1 and 2 show all dimensions considered in the second level of subdivisions. These dimensions and their criteria (or factors) are described in depth in [9].

This framework serves as basis for an evaluation tool that allows for the analyzation of m-Learning applications characteristics and representing results into several types of charts (especially, radar chart). In addition, mechanisms and tools to highlight strengths and weaknesses are incorporated. Figure 3 shows a partial view of the user interface of this tool. It shows a view of the *Usability Pedagogical* dimension. In the middle there is a questionnaire to gather information about *Content* dimension. The items of the questionnaire are related to the criteria of each dimension. On the bottom side, the results

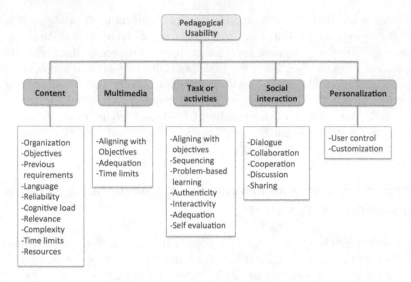

Fig. 1. Factors in Pedagogical Usability

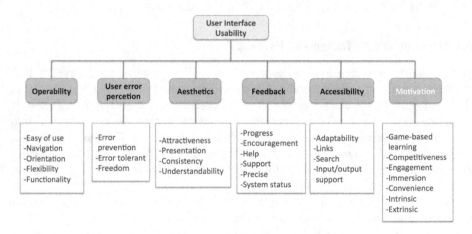

Fig. 2. Factors in User Interface Usability

obtained related to this dimension are shown by mean bar and radar chart. Moreover, some indicators of the reliability of the tests (or measurements) are calculated. For example, in this case it is shown that the *Cronbach's alpha* is calculated (see frame above the questionnaire).

However, our aim in this paper is also focused on the description of how this framework is integrated with CIAM, especially with its process model. Therefore, in the next section this approach is described.

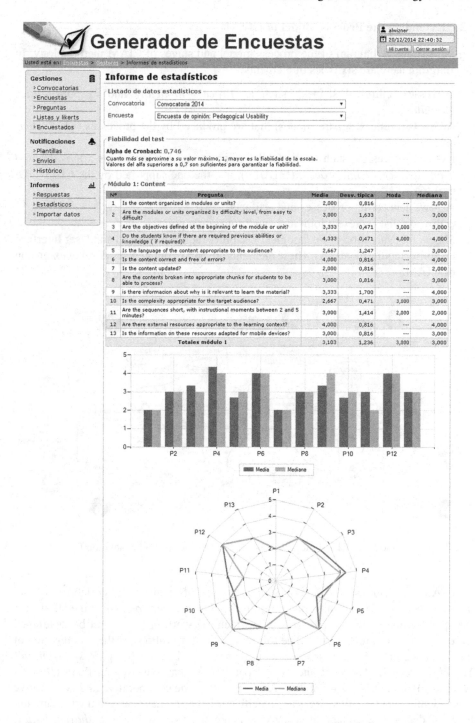

Fig. 3. Partial screenshot of the user interface of the tool for applying the proposed design and evaluation framework (some texts are in Spanish)

3.2 Extending the Process Model of CIAM

Figure 4 shows a diagram of the process model and stages of CIAM methodology. In this diagram there are six types of elements:

1. Processes (elliptical shapes), such as *Process Modeling* and *Responsibilities Modeling*.
2. Artifacts (rounded square shapes) that are produced by the processes (i.e. *Participation Table*).
3. External processes, such as the GUI Design stage, that represents a *model-based user interface design process* (MBUID), like the one supported by the CIAT-GUI tool [6].
4. Arrows connecting processes and artifacts.
5. Gateways that represent joint and synchronization points.
6. Sheets for evaluation of Pedagogical Usability requirements (B) and User Interface Usability requirements (A). These elements are part of our new proposal of extension of CIAM.

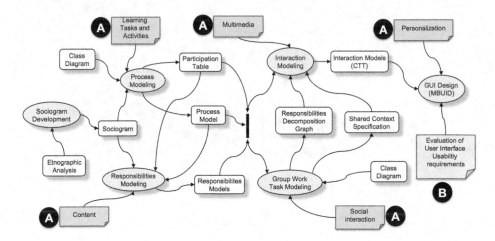

Fig. 4. Process model of CIAM including elements of the design and evaluation framework for m-Learning

CIAM is organized into several stages. In each of them several collaborative and interactive systems issues are specified. The *Sociogram Development* stage allows for the specification of the social context in which the work in-group will be developed (roles, actors, work teams, etc.). The following two stages allow for the specification of the tasks of greater level of abstraction to be performed by the group (*Responsibilities Modeling*) and the temporal and data dependencies that exist among them (*Process Modeling*). In the *Group Work Task Modeling* stage the collaborative and cooperative tasks identified in previous stages are specified in a differentiated way and with a greater level of detail. The collaborative tasks specification is based on the *shared context* definition [17]. In the *Interaction Modeling* stage the interactive tasks to be supported by the application user interface to develop are specified. For this, the CTT [18] notation is used. An interactive task tree will be created for each individual task or individual responsibility and for each work in-group task. In the case of collaborative tasks the interaction model is obtained from the shared context definition.

Regarding the framework of design of evaluation of m-Learning, the dimensions of *Pedagogical Usability* are spread across the most of stages of CIAM. However, the dimensions of *User Interface Usability* are focused on the *GUI Design* stage because it is applied to the artifacts managed by the process of model-based user interface design (MBUID) that is developed in this stage.

We think the main improvement obtained by integrating our proposed framework within CIAM is that pedagogical aspects can be considered during the modeling process. This feature is not taken into account by other proposals for collaborative systems design, especially in m-Learning contexts.

4   Concluding Remarks and Future Work

In this paper, we address the problem of improving CIAM methodology in order to support design, modeling and evaluation of interactive and collaborative mobile applications, especially for m-Learning.

The applying of a framework for design and evaluation of m-Learning applications with has been proposed with special attention to collaborative activities. As a consequence, the dimensions and criteria of this framework that can be incorporated into the process model of CIAM have been described.

Currently, there are tools that support the CIAM processes and the final semi-automatic obtaining of the user interface of a modeled application. Furthermore, there is a tool to apply the design and evaluation framework for assessing of *Pedagogical Usability* and *User Interface Usability* dimensions in m-Learning applications. In future work, we plan to integrate these tools in a single platform supporting the whole of the extended version of CIAM.

Finally, we plan to apply our approach to previous designs of m-Learning applications developed with the initial version of CIAM. Thus, the advantages that this approach provides will be highlighted.

Acknowledgments.   This work has been partially supported by Project EDUCA-Prog of the Ministry of Science and Innovation (TIN2011-29542-C02-01 and TIN2011-29542-C02-02), and the InteGROUP Project (PEII-2014-021-P) of the Government of Castilla-La Mancha (JCCM).

References

1. Grudin, J.: Why CSCW applications fail: problems in the design and evaluation of organizational interfaces. In: Proceedings of the 1988 ACM Conference on Computer-Supported Cooperative Work, pp. 85–93. ACM, Portland, Oregon, USA (1988)

2. Molina, A.I., Redondo, M.A., Ortega, M.: A methodological approach for user interface development of collaborative applications: a case study. Sci. Comput. Program. **74**(9), 754–776 (2009)
3. Molina, A.I., et al.: CIAM: a methodology for the development of groupware user interfaces. J. Univ. Comput. Sci. **14**(9), 1434–1446 (2008)
4. Dix, A.: Human Computer Interaction. Prentice-Hall, New York (1993)
5. Paternò, F.: Model-Based Design and Evaluation on Interactive Applications. Springer, London (1999)
6. Molina, A.I., et al.: CIAT-GUI: a MDE-compliant environment for developing graphical user interfaces of information systems. J. Adv. Eng. Softw. **52**, 10–29 (2012)
7. Crompton, H.: A historical overview of mobile learning: toward learner-centered education. In: Berge, Z.L., Muilenburg, L.Y. (eds.) Handbook of Mobile Learning, pp. 3–14. Rouledge, Florence (2013)
8. Navarro, C.X., Molina, A.I., Redondo, M.A.: Evaluation framework for m-learning systems: current situation and proposal. In: XV International Conference on Human Computer Interaction 2014, pp. 1–3. ACM, Puerto de la Cruz, Tenerife, Spain (2014)
9. Navarro, C.X., Molina, A.I., Redondo, M.Á.: Developing a framework to evaluate usability in m-Learning systems: mapping study and proposal. In: TEEM14, pp. 357–364, Univ. Salamanca, Salamanca, Spain (2014)
10. Giraldo, W.J., et al.: CIAT, a model-based tool for designing groupware user interfaces using CIAM. In: CADUI 2008, Albacete (2008)
11. Molina, A.I., et al.: Specifying scripts and collaborative tasks in CSCL environment using IMS-LD and CIAN. In: ICALT 2008, IEEE Computer Society, Santander (2008)
12. Jurado, F., Molina, A.I., Giraldo, W.J., Redondo, M.A., Ortega, M.: Using CIAN for specifying collaborative scripts in learning design. In: Luo, Y. (ed.) CDVE 2008. LNCS, vol. 5220, pp. 204–211. Springer, Heidelberg (2008)
13. Paredes, M., et al.: Designing collaborative user interfaces for ubiquitous applications using CIAM: the AULA case study. JUCS **14**(16), 2680–2698 (2009)
14. Taylor, J., et al.: Towards a task model for mobile learning: a dialectical approach. Int. J. Learn. Technol. **2**(2/3), 138–158 (2006)
15. Fetaji, B., Fetaji, M.: Software engineering mobile learning software solution using task based learning approach. Eng. Technol. **30**, 395–399 (2009)
16. Berri, J., Benlamri, R., Atif, Y.: Ontology-based framework for context-aware mobile learning. In: IWCMC, pp. 1307–1310. ACM, Vancouver, Canada (2006)
17. Ellis, C.A., Gibbs, S.J., Rein, G.: Groupware: some issues and experiences. Commun. ACM **34**(1), 39–58 (1991)
18. Paternò, F.: ConcurTaskTrees: an engineered notation for task models. In: Diaper, D., Stanton, N. (eds.) The Handbook of Task Analysis for Human-Computer Interaction, pp. 483–501. Lawrence Erlbaum Associates Inc., Mahwah (2004)

SCPL: A Social Cooperative Programming Language to Automate Cooperative Processes

José María Conejero[✉], Fernando Sánchez-Figueroa, Luis-María García-Rodríguez, Roberto Rodríguez-Echeverría, and Juan Carlos Preciado

Quercus Software Engineering Group, University of Extremadura, Avda. de la Universidad, s/n, 10003 Cáceres, Spain
{chemacm,fernando,luismaex,rre,jcpreciado}@unex.es

Abstract. In the last years, the increasing use of social networks and applications has significantly changed the business processes in many organizations. These applications provide new cooperative ways of performing these processes by taking advantages of the interactions among users. However, the high number of these applications has lead to a lack of automation in their interactions and, thus, the need of manually connecting to these networks to perform recurrent and repetitive tasks. In order to automate these operations, this paper presents SCPL, a Domain Specific Language (DSL) that enables the connectivity among different social networks and applications and provides a way to automate their management. The main contribution of this paper is showing how SCPL can be used to specify collaborative tasks using social networks in a transparent way.

Keywords: Cooperative processes · Social networks · Domain specific languages

1 Introduction

Today, the increasing use of social networks and applications has significantly changed the business processes in many organizations. These applications include traditional social networks (e.g. Facebook, Twitter,...) but also social applications (e.g. Google Drive, Dropbox, Doodle, ...). Although these applications have been traditionally used in the domestic domain, they are being more and more used in the industry (e.g. the health domain [1]). Currently the business processes are being enriched from a more social than technical point of view of the end-users involved. Among the benefits provided by these tools, it is worth mentioning the new cooperative ways of performing business processes that they have introduced, e.g. offering support, answering questions, voting on the quality of a service, commenting, following the progress of a service request, networking with other colleagues to share experiences and so on. The appearance of techniques such as Cloud Computing that simplifies data storage, processing and security, is accelerating its broad adoption.

Partially supported by MEC project TIN2011-27340 and Gobierno de Extremadura.

Y. Luo (Ed.): CDVE 2015, LNCS 9320, pp. 19–27, 2015.
DOI: 10.1007/978-3-319-24132-6_3

However, the high number of these applications has caused a great dispersion that makes the user to publish the same content in all the different applications that she uses (redundancy). Similarly, the user may not reuse the tasks that she has performed once (lack of reutilization). Moreover, whenever the user needs to perform an action in a social application different than the one that she is using, a context change is needed with the corresponding waste of time and bad user experience. In other words, the high number of these applications has lead to a lack of automation in their interactions and, thus, the need of manually connecting to these networks to perform recurrent and repetitive tasks.

To solve these problems, the approach presented here comes to the scene. This paper presents SCPL (Social Cooperative Programming Language), a Domain Specific Language (DSL) [5] that enables the connectivity among different social networks and applications and provides a way to automate their management. This DSL relies on the definition of a textual language where these interconnections among the social networks may be defined. Based on this language, the source code of different applications may be generated. These applications integrate the connectivity with the social applications selected, making this connectivity transparent to the user. In that sense, the main contribution of this paper is showing how the company business processes may be improved by integrating cooperative and collaborative tasks provided by social applications in a transparent way.

The rest of paper is as follows: Sect. 2 presents an analysis of similar tools to the presented here. Section 3 introduces a running example used to illustrate the approach. Section 4 presents the social cooperative language. Section 5 provides details on the implementation of the approach and finally Sect. 6 concludes the paper.

2   Related Work

This section shows similar approaches or tools that may be found in the literature or Internet to coordinate several social applications. These tools are compared attending to different wished characteristics. This comparison has a twofold goal, on one hand, compare the tools to classify them in terms of the characteristics supported; on the other hand, to show the suitability of the presented approach, -to the best of our knowledge- the only approach that fulfils all the characteristics considered. As examples, the works in [2, 7] have presented similar approaches to the one described in this paper. Similarly, the European project BPM4People [3, 4] proposed the introduction of social instructions in a BPM notation. However, the utilization of a DSL to coordinate different social applications has not been considered before.

The characteristics that have been selected to compare all the tools are related to the problems mentioned in the previous section so that a tool that fulfils these characteristics may solve the aforementioned problems.

- **The Use of Textual Programming Notation (C1).** Most of existing tools use a graphical notation lacking the flexibility degree provided by textual ones (usually preferred by experienced developers).
- **Simplicity (C2).** This characteristic denotes to how easily a use case may be implemented. Most of the analysed tools are easy to use.
- **Advanced Filters Support (C3).** This characteristic refers to the possibility of limit a problem including conditions and requirements, such as the number of 'I likes'.

- **Advanced Programming Structures Support (C4).** These structures allow the user to define complex actions and conditions. Note that from the computational viewpoint, not all the problems that the user will deal with may be solved by using "If-condition-then-action" structures.
- **Positive User Experience (C5).** Obviously this characteristic is important for the user. Likewise, a **quick learning curve (C6)** and an **intuitive user interface (C7)** are also wished characteristics (authors have measured both characteristics by intensively using the tools).
- **Context Keeping (C8).** This characteristic refers to how the tool allows the user to keep focused on the task without loosing the context.

After analysing the existing tools (see Table 1), we observed: (i) that most of them were based on simple "if-condition-then-action" structures and; (ii) a lack of more powerful tools with complex programming structures. We also observed that the tools that promised these more powerful structures (e.g. itDuzzit) lack of a proper implementation and they were not intuitive enough so that the users often abandoned them.

Table 1. Comparison of functionalities of the analysed tools

Tool	C1	C2	C3	C4	C5	C6	C7	C8
IFTTT[a]		☑			☑	☑	☑	
Zapier[b]		☑			☑	☑	☑	
We Wired Web[c]		☑			☑	☑	☑	
Elastic.io[d]		☑			☑	☑	☑	
Cloud Work[e]		☑			☑	☑	☑	
WappWolf[f]		☑			☑	☑	☑	☑
itDuzzit[g]			☑	☑				
Yahoopipes[h]			☑	☑				
Kissflow[i]			☑		☑			☑
SCPL	☑	☑	☑	☑	☑	☑	☑	☑

[a]https://ifttt.com/
[b]https://zapier.com/
[c]https://wewiredweb.com/
[d]http://www.elastic.io/
[e]https://cloudwork.com/
[f]http://wappwolf.com/
[g]http://cloud.itduzzit.com/
[h]https://pipes.yahoo.com/pipes/
[i]https://kissflow.com/

3 Motivation Example

This section presents a running example that will drive the explanation of the approach. This case study represents an actual situation in the politics domain where decisions must be quickly taken (although the example is also applicable to many other domains).

Let's consider the process to publish a press release by an organization where the cooperation of different groups of people belonging to the organization is required. This process may be composed of the next steps:

1. The press manager of the organization writes the press release and sends it by email to the organization managers in order to be reviewed.
2. The press manager waits for, at least, three confirmation answers from the managers.
3. Then, the press release is published into a LinkedIn group where the organization has a set of affiliated and members. These members belong to a working group that is responsible for identifying possible errors in the organization documents. If the members agree on the press release, they will used the 'I like' option of the social application in order to show their approval.
4. When the press release has 30 'I like', the press manager considers that the press release is accepted to be published.
5. Finally, it is submitted to the media and it is also published through other social networks like Twitter or Facebook.

Note that, to follow this process, the press manager must perform several tasks in different applications such as checking the email, reviewing the publication in LinkedIn waiting for the expected number of 'I like', sending the press release to the media and using the social networks selected to publish the release. This process represents a clear situation where all the problems commented in Sect. 1 may be detected.

4   The Social and Cooperative Programming Language

As aforementioned, SCPL is a language that allows the definition of rules that connect different social applications. This language has been defined as a grammar based on XText [9]. Before showing details of its implementation, the main characteristics of SCPL are described, all of them illustrated by simple examples.

Easy to Use: The language used by the DSL is very close to the natural language so that the definition of rules is really intuitive for the user. In particular, Fig. 1 represents the fragment that solves the problem presented in the motivation example (publishing a cooperative press release).

```
1⊖    send Email(juntadirectiva@googlegroups.com) body "Nota de prensa" = $1
2          wait response('Ok',3) then
3⊖            send Linkedin (group "Afiliados y simpatizantes") body $1
4                wait Ilikes(30) then
5                    send Email(medioA@unex.es & medioB@unex.es) body $1
6                    send Twitter body "Nota de prensa" = $1
```

Fig. 1. Case study

Social Network Configurability: The user may select the social networks that she will use at development time (observe lines 3 and 6 in Fig. 1). However, she also has the chance of deciding the social networks to use at instantiation time (just before the execution of the final application, Fig. 2). That allows also reusing the rule defined for different cases.

```
send SocialNetwork body "Nota de prensa" = $1
```

Fig. 2. Sending to a generic social network

Social APPs: Besides the traditional social networks, other social applications may be used in the language, e.g. Google cloud, Dropbox, Doodle pools and so on (Fig. 3).

```
send Email(hola@sepl.es) body "Mi email \n Estoy seguro que os gustará SEPL"
send GoogleSpreadsheet("/miTabla") body $msg1
```

Fig. 3. Sending to social applications

Global Vars: In order to not repeat the content of the messages in different rules, global vars are used. These vars are defined in the language with the $ symbol (see line 1 in Fig. 1). Global vars also avoid loosing the context and solve the problem of information reusability and repetition.

Sending Public, Private or Group Messages: Obviously, one of the main functionalities of current social networks is to allow the publication of messages in timelines, pages, groups or as private. These functionalities are also contemplated in the proposed language, lines 3 and 6 in Fig. 1. Sending a private message may be done as it is described in Fig. 4.

```
send Twitter(@spel) body "Este es un mensaje privado de prueba"
send Linkedin("David Martín Rodríguez") body "Mensaje privado"
```

Fig. 4. Sending messages

Event Programming: Among the functionalities offered by the language, it is worth mentioning the possibility of programming and, thus, automating events. Based on this functionality, the user does not need to wait for an event end in order to start another one. The language allows the user to define the conditions under an event will be executed.

By using the right expression, the language allows that the execution waits for one or more events before resuming the execution. This is done by using the wait clause, as it is shown in lines 2 and 4 in Fig. 1.

Identifying and Counting 'I like'. One of the main innovations of social networks is the 'I like' concept. This concept is currently used in many other domains and applications as a way to approve or support an idea. Unlike the rest of applications analysed, SCPL supports using, counting and managing the 'I like'. As an example, line 4 in Fig. 1 shows how the number of 'I like' may be counted and used as a condition for a publication.

Reply Identification. The automation of the replying process is also important. Note that any publication or mail is not valid, the reply must avoid loosing the context and must allow working in the same conversation flow. Although a whole analysis of the reply text is out of the scope of this work, a simple analysis of some word in the reply may be performed, as it is represented in line 2 of Fig. 1.

Replying Messages. An automatic reply to the messages received in the social networks may be also specified (similarly to the automatic reply identification). This automatic reply may be applied to both public and private messages or, even, to received emails (see Fig. 5).

```
wait Email('usuario@spel.es') then reply "Gracias por la rápida respuesta"
```

Fig. 5. Replying messages

5 Implementation

Once the language and its main characteristics have been explained, this section presents how it has been implemented. Figure 6 represents the workflow that the process follows to produce the final applications that allow the interaction with the social networks. The process takes as input the source code that a programmer writes in SCPL (according to the grammar). This source code is used by Xtend [8] to be transformed into a simple and serializable structure, based on YAML [10]. The resulting document is then processed by a parser (developed by using Ruby [6]) that interprets and executes the sentences, producing the interaction with the social application APIs or with the users if it is needed (e.g. in order to introduce the authentication data). Next, all these steps are described in more detail.

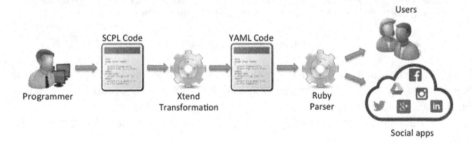

Fig. 6. Tool architecture and execution flow

5.1 Xtend Transformation from SCPL to YAML

Xtend is a programming language that eases the definition of transformations to interpret grammars generating a different output. Xtend uses a syntax similar to the used by Java although improving some of its aspects. In this case, Xtend has been used to generate a YAML representation of the SCPL specification. YAML is a serializable language that allows representing information in a similar format to the used by XML. YAML is used since its representation will be later used by an interpreter to generate the final code of the application.

Xtend allows processing the grammar as a tree so that it defines a DomainModel element that represents the grammar root and this element contains a set of children (they may also have other children) that represent the keywords in the grammar. Each element may contain attributes that represent the values defined in the different keywords (content introduced by the user). Figure 7 shows a class specified in Xtend to define the transformation to YAML of the send structure in the grammar.

```
class YamlModelHelper {
    boolean to=false;
    boolean firstto=false;
    int send=0;

    def dispatch CharSequence toYaml(EObject m)
    '''    «IF m.eCrossReferences.size + m.eContents.size > 0»
            «FOR ref : m.eCrossReferences»
                «ref.eContainingFeature.name» -> «ref.toYamlSig»
            «ENDFOR»
            «FOR child : m.eContents»
                «IF child.eClass.name.equals("Send")»
                    «child.toYamlSend»
                    «child.toYamlSendDisp»
                «ELSE»
                «ENDIF»«restartFirstTo»
«ENDFOR»
«ENDIF»'''
```

Fig. 7. Xtend class for generating the YAML for the send structure

```
 1 -
 2  :type: send
 3  :body: Nota de prensa
 4  :send: Email
 5  :to:
 6    - juntadirectiva@googlegroups.com
 7  :wait: response
 8  :value: (name: [Ok]|
 9  :value: 3
10 -
11  :then: true
12  :type: send
13  :body: $1
14  :send: Linkedin
15  :group: true
16    - Afiliados y simpatizantes
17  :wait: Ilikes
18  :value: 30
19 -
20  :then: true
21  :type: send
22  :body: $1
23  :send: Email
24    - medioA@unex.es
25    - medioB@unex.es
26 -
27  :type: send
28  :body: Nota de prensa
29  :send: Twitter
30 -
```

Fig. 8. YAML output for the send structure

The YAML output generated by the transformation for the send structure may be also observed in Fig. 8.

5.2   Ruby Interpreter Definition

Ruby has been used for the definition of the interpreter of YAML files. Ruby was selected since it provides an important set of gems (like libraries that may be imported to a project) that may be used to easily connect to external APIs like those provided by the social applications.

The interpreter is responsible of analysing the YAML file line by line and executes them. Figure 9 shows an excerpt of the interpreter source code defined to interpret the YAML code generated for the send structure.

```
if ins[:type] == 'send' then
      if ins[:send] == 'Gmail' then
              subjt = ins[:body].split(" %/n ")
              gmail.deliver do
                to ins[:to]
                subject subjt[0]
                text_part do
                  body ins[:body].sub(subjt[0],'').gsub('%twDot%',':').gsub(" %/n ", '

              end
      end
```

Fig. 9.   Excerpt of the source code of the interpreter for the YAML send structure

5.3   Connectivity with Social Networks and User Authentication

As aforementioned, Ruby eases the connections with external applications by means of a wide set of gems. As an example in Fig. 10 a connection with the Twitter API is presented where authentication of the user is performed.

```
get '/twitter/newconnection' do
      user = User.get(session[:userId])

      consumer = OAuth::Consumer.new("", "")
      request_token=consumer.get_request_token(:oauth_callback => "http://#{request.host}:#{request.port}/twitter/callback")
      session[:twrequest_token]=request_token
      twitter = Twitterc.new(:requesttoken => request_token.token, :requestsecret => request_token.secret)
      user.socialnetworks << twitter
      redirect request_token.authorize_url

end
```

Fig. 10.   Connection with Twitter

The connectivity with social networks could imply an important threat to the applicability of the approach, since any change in the networks API could imply a change in the approach. However, this problem is mitigated by the utilization of the Ruby gems that abstract the developer of low level programming details and make the approach independent of the networks API.

The set of social applications being supported by SCPL includes Twitter, Facebook, LinkedIn, GMail, Doodle and Google Drive. However, it is being currently extended to incorporate other applications, such as Instagram or Dropbox.

6   Conclusions and Further Work

This paper has presented a DSL for the definition of social and cooperative applications. Based on this DSL, the user may define rules that connect different social applications without the need of manually interacting with each of them. The DSL is supported by a tool that allows reducing the human intervention to just the definition of the SCPL program (the starting point of the process) and automating the rest of tasks (except the social applications authentication, obviously). The benefits provided by the language include: (i) reusability of the rules so that the user does not need to perform repetitive tasks once and again; (ii) productivity improvement since the user may interact with all these applications without a context change; (iii) user experience improvement, based on the previous benefits commented.

As further work, the approach is being currently extended to provide support for more social applications and a graphical notation is also being implemented in order to provide support to those users that prefer this notation instead of the textual one.

Acknowledgements.   We would like to thank to Róber Morales-Chaparro and Álvaro Gutiérrez-Pérez for their collaboration and advices in the tool implementation.

References

1. Sánchez-Figueroa, F., Preciado, J.C., Conejero, J.M., Rodríguez-Echeverría, R.: Designing cooperative social applications in healthcare by means of SocialBPM. In: Proceedings of 11th International Conference on Cooperative Design, Visualization and Engineering, Seattle, USA (2014)
2. Jara, J., Daniel, F., Casati, F., Marchese, M.: From a simple flow to social applications. In: Sheng, Q.Z., Kjeldskov, J. (eds.) ICWE Workshops 2013. LNCS, vol. 8295, pp. 39–50. Springer, Heidelberg (2013)
3. Brambilla, M., Fraternali, P., Vaca, C.: A notation for supporting social business process modeling. In: Dijkman, R., Hofstetter, J., Koehler, J. (eds.) BPMN 2011. LNBIP, vol. 95, pp. 88–102. Springer, Heidelberg (2011)
4. Brambilla, M., Fraternali, P., Vaca, C., Butti, S.: Combining social web and BPM for improving enterprise performances: the BPM4People approach to social BPM. In: Proceedings of the 21st International Conference Companion on World Wide Web, European-Projects Track, New York, USA (2012)
5. Fowler, M.: Domain-Specific Languages. Pearson Education, Upper Saddle River (2010)
6. Ruby. https://www.ruby-lang.org/
7. Ahmad, S., Battle, A., Malkani, Z., Kamvar, S.: The jabberwocky programming environment for structured social computing. In: Proceedings of the 24th Annual ACM Symposium on User Interface Software and Technology, ACM (2011)
8. Xtend. http://eclipse.org/xtend/documentation/index.html
9. Xtext. https://eclipse.org/Xtext/
10. YAML. http://yaml.org/spec/

Engineering Data Intensive Applications with Cadral

Yoann Didry, Olivier Parisot, and Thomas Tamisier[✉]

Luxembourg Institute of Science and Technology (LIST), 41, Rue du Brill,
4422 Belvaux, Luxembourg
{yoanne.didry,thomas.tamisier}@list.lu

Abstract. Developed through many industrial and research partnerships, the software platform Cadral addresses operational needs of organizations by integrating two complementary modules: a collaborative decision support framework and a visual analytics tool suite for knowledge extraction and data processing. It is used to support the designing of innovative applications, facilitates the comparison and selection of up-to-date technologies and the release of specific pieces of software for operational purposes.

Keywords: Visual analytics · Knowledge extraction · Decision support

1   Introduction

Automated processing of business tasks are increasingly used to cope with the work overload of organizations, and to ensure the rigorous handling of the procedures in an efficient, traceable way. However, modeling the knowledge framework is a painful and time-consuming task, for which business experts must be mobilized. Adequate management and visualization of this knowledge is also necessary to ensure the proper functioning and maintaining an intuitive view of the expected behaviour of the automated systems [1]. Through many years of research and operational partnerships, our aim has been to bring to organizations efficient solutions for automating or helping procedural and decisional tasks. Efforts have been successively carried out in two directions. First, we designed and maintained a modeling module dedicated to business procedural knowledge in order to optimize the editing and updating of procedures used both to perform the tasks and justify the answers returned by the automated system [6]. Then the modeling framework has been used together with historical business data for the automatic extraction of knowledge models. In both cases, the interaction with the user for correcting and updating the knowledge is proposed through visual analysis features. These works have resulted in the implementation of Cadral, a research and application platform mixing visual data processing and decision support. Within Cadral, the knowledge extraction has given birth to a plethora of visual data mining functionalities for interactive analysis of big data sets. Cadral has subsequently evolved to a modular architecture constantly enriched by the integration of up-to-date and original techniques. It is used for new partnerships, allowing the comparing of technologies and methods and deriving tailored pieces of software for solving concrete needs in various domains such as logistics, speech recognition, hydrology and online sales. The rest of the paper is as follows. Section 2 presents the related works.

© Springer International Publishing Switzerland 2015
Y. Luo (Ed.): CDVE 2015, LNCS 9320, pp. 28–35, 2015.
DOI: 10.1007/978-3-319-24132-6_4

Section 3 presents the collaborative knowledge modelling framework and discusses the automatic computation of decisional models. Section 4 explains the advanced visual data mining features of Cadral. Section 5 reviews some practical use cases.

2   Related Works/Existing Tools

Many data mining and visualization tools (commercial and non-commercial) such as R, Orange, Tableau, Weka, Mahout and Matlab are available to the public. On the one hand, most of the available open-source software require a strong machine learning expertise and are not always suitable for data mining-oriented projects [11]. On the other hand, commercial software often needs to be more flexible in order to answer specific business problems. In both cases, there is a gap between business companies' expectations and the available products on offer. The Cadral research and technology platform aims at bridging this gap and has been successfully deployed for collaboration in various domains. It has been designed to be easily fine-tuned and extendable for partnerships. Key accomplishments of Cadral include expanding the end-user interactivity and improving maintainability by providing developers the ability to add new modules based on the recent state of the art. Section 5 reviews the advanced visual data mining techniques that were developed through these partnerships.

3   Interactive Modelling

First of all, Cadral provides a general infrastructure for automatic problem solving, coupled with functionalities for interactive control of the resolution and modelling of domain knowledge. Designed primarily for professional applications in the context of organizations, Cadral eases the work of the user, especially for modelling business expertise. For this purpose, instead of a whole modeling of the domain knowledge, the operating knowledge Cadral concentrates on the explicit drawing of the mental procedures that governs the processing of business procedures, along with the relations between these procedures to the specific administrative, legal, or business background knowledge on which they are drawn. Cadral offers two views on the knowledge model. First, the analytical view, where the knowledge is modelled on elementary rules, with links between the rules and references to the formal domain knowledge. The synthetic view offers a pictorial representation of all the knowledge, and in particular, shows the inter-dependence of the rules and their references (Fig. 1). To avoid over-complicated procedures, modularity is used to restrict the view to sub-models. Rules are processed by a resolution engine (different resolution engines can be selected according to the format of the rule).

Cadral makes sure that the set of rules and the inference mechanism guarantees the exactness of the knowledge and the uniqueness of the returned decision. Moreover, the reasoning process is in every case traceable, and links maintained within the rules to the reference knowledge can be used to exhibit a justification of the resolution. References links within the rules are also used to show the impact of a modification in the reference

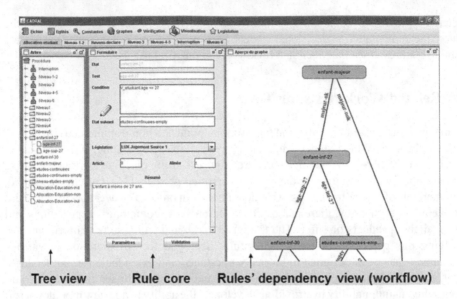

Tree view   Rule core   Rules' dependency view (workflow)

Fig. 1. Editor showing description of a rule (left) and a network of rules (right).

knowledge to the model in order to easily update the rules. Last, Cadral contains semantic and syntactic check functionalities.

Based on the transparency of the knowledge model and the visual interaction features of the editor, allowing the user to understand and update the model, Cadral has been complemented with a module for semi-automatic construction of a knowledge model from historical business. The model is computed in the shape of decision trees by the Cadral knowledge extraction tool. The user has the ability to select an adequate value for the confidence factor [2] to obtain a good comprise between the size of the model and the error rate. The error is defined as the misclassification by the decision tree. The following figure illustrates a given dataset with a high confidence factor and a lower confidence factor. The left decision tree has an error rate of 15 % and contains 121 nodes, while the right decision tree has an error rate of 24 % and contains 13 nodes (Fig. 2).

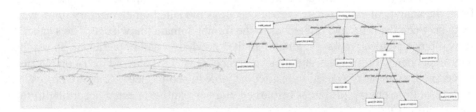

Fig. 2. Model extracted using two different confidence factors.

4   Advanced Visual Data Mining

The knowledge extraction module has given birth to a plethora of functionalities, enabling visual data mining and interactivity. It was then extended to a modular architecture and used in many use-cases involving topics such as logistics, speech recognition, hydrology and online sales. Cadral offers both the pre-processing of data (e.g. by discretization and feature selection), and traceable data transformations. Also, it shows in real time the impact of input data transformation on the output results of processing algorithms. Data analysis is assisted by the visualizations to interactively follow and refine conventional treatments such as cleaning, correction, feature selection, clustering. Various data representation structures are coupled with dimension reduction techniques such as MDS, PCA, SOM [3]. More recent techniques like t-SNE have been integrated and improved using a novel interactive clustering system that allows a user to iteratively update the cluster labels of a data set, and an associated low-dimensional projection [4]. In addition, an experimental framework has been integrated in order to improve the interactivity between the user and the data analysis process [10] (Fig. 3).

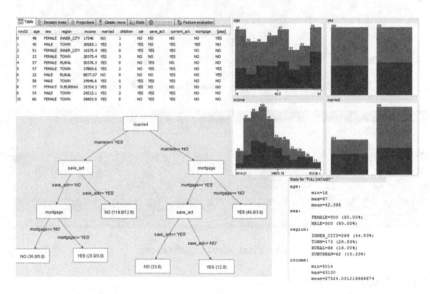

Fig. 3. Interactive pre-processing of the data with statistical overview.

One of the core functionalities of Cadral is decision tree models. Trees are extracted from data using algorithm such as C4.5 [2] and/or collaboratively edited. The readability of such model has been an important focus within Cadral. Visual properties such as the size and depth of the models have been the main focus. To illustrate that, Cadral's original Decision Tree Aware Clustering algorithm (DTA) groups the data in order to optimize their representation, whereas classical clustering is driven by the data and in particular their neighbourhood [5]. This aims at decomposing a knowledge model in a set of modules represented by simple decision trees (Fig. 4).

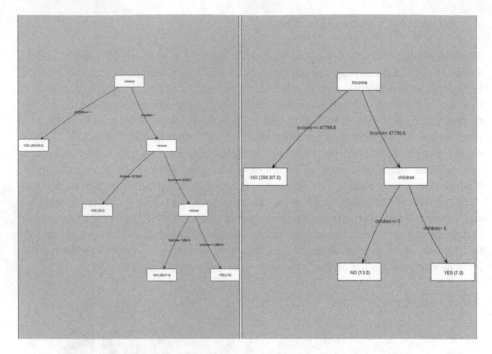

Fig. 4. Simple decision trees obtained using DTA Algorithm.

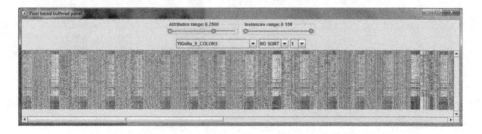

Fig. 5. Pixel based visualization.

5   Use-Cases

Cadral has been enriched and applied through different use-cases.

A partner team of Ozyegin University (Turkey) is specialized in Statistical Speech Synthesis models and their applications (e.g. for mobile phones). More precisely, these models are built using huge data (170 rows/400 000 columns), and data preprocessing is needed in order to improve the results [7]. As a result, Cadral has been used to load, inspect and interpret the results of features selection (Fig. 5). As an example, new pixel based and heat map visualizations have been added for this particular partnership.

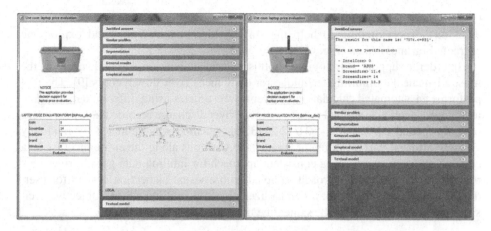

Fig. 6. The OPTOSA user-interface.

Optosa is an ongoing research project with the company InfinAIt Solutions SA (supported by a grant from the Ministry of Economy and External Trade, Grand-Duchy of Luxembourg, under the RDI Law). The goal of the project is to define a Visual Analytics solution for the optimization of sales on online marketplaces (e.g. Amazon or eBay) from the product specification to the price fixing [8]. To this end,

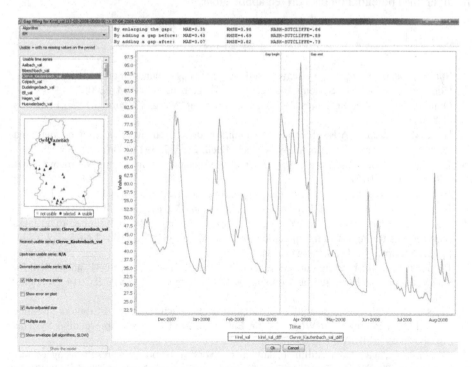

Fig. 7. The gapIt user interface: based on Cadral, the tool provides an interactive method of combining data processing and visualization to deal with missing hydrological data.

Cadral was used to analyze the data, to build predictive models and to provide a decision support module to help the stake-holder to understand and exploit the extracted business rules (Fig. 6).

In order to support hydrologists, gapIt is a visual analytics tool to find and apply the most adequate data-infilling technique for daily mean river flow records [9]. The tool performs an automated calculation of river flow estimates using different data-infilling techniques. gapIt was applied to time series of river discharge recorded in Luxembourg over the period 01/01/2007 – 31/12/2013. The method was validated by randomly creating artificial gaps of different lengths and positions along the entire records. As a conclusion, gapIt represents a consistent approach for infilling data gaps in river flow records. The automated approach, coupled with a visual inspection system for user-defined refinement, allows for a standardized objective infilling, where subjective decisions are allowed but are at the same time traceable (Fig. 7).

6 Conclusion

Cadral offers a unified framework to extract knowledge from data, interactively explore datasets, and uses the resulting knowledge to (semi-)automatically perform business tasks. It deploys the visual analytics paradigm, centering the analysis and calculation on users' needs and control through visual interaction, which allows making the most of the diversified potential on data driven applications.

References

1. Sui, L.: Decision support systems based on knowledge management. In: International Conference on Services Systems and Services Management (ICSSSM) (2005)
2. Quinlan, J.R.: C4.5: Programs for Machine Learning. Morgan Kaufman, San Francisco (1993)
3. Law, M.H.C., Jain, A.K.: Incremental nonlinear dimensionality reduction by manifold learning. IEEE Trans. Pattern Analysis Mach. Intell. **28**, 377–391 (2006)
4. Bruneau, P., et al.: Cluster sculptor, an interactive visual clustering system. Neurocomputing **150**, 627–644 (2015)
5. Parisot, O., et al.: Using clustering to improve decision trees visualization. In: 17th International Conference on Information Visualisation (IV), pp. 186–191 (2013)
6. Tamisier, T., Parisot, O., Didry, Y., Wax, J., Feltz, F.: Adapting decision support to business requirements through data interpretation. In: Luo, Y. (ed.) CDVE 2011. LNCS, vol. 6874, pp. 82–85. Springer, Heidelberg (2011)
7. Bruneau, P., et al.: Finding relevant features for statistical speech synthesis adaptation. In: The 9th Language Resources and Evaluation Conference (LREC), VisLR 2014 Workshop (2014)
8. Parisot, O., et al.: Visual analytics for supporting manufacturers and distributors in online sales. In: 6th International Workshop on Enterprise Modelling and Information Systems Architectures (EMISA 2014) (2014)
9. Giustarini, L., et al.: Data-infilling in daily mean river flow records: first results using a visual analytics tool (gapIt). In: European Geosciences Union General Assembly 2015 (EGU 2015), vol. 17 (2015)

10. Boudjeloud Assala, L., et al.: Interactive and iterative visual clustering. Inf. Vis. 1–7 (2015)
11. Serban, F., et al.: A survey of intelligent assistants for data analysis. ACM Comput. Surv. (CSUR) **45**(3), 31 (2015)

Dynamic Content and User Identification in Social Semantic Tagging Systems

Saman Kamran$^{(\boxtimes)}$ and Mehdi Jazayeri

Faculty of Informatics, Università della Svizzera italian (USI), Lugano, Switzerland
{saman.kamran,mehdi.jazayeri}@usi.ch

Abstract. Collaboration relies on the flow of information among parties. To make informed decisions, shared knowledge should be managed in a way to be accessible for relevant group members to each of the contents. One of the main factors that contribute to the quality of contents recommendations to the relevant users is the quality of the users and contents identification. A variety of automatic and semi-automatic methods exist for extracting or assigning identity to online resources. Although users' perception about contents and also their interests might change over time, most current approaches define a fixed identity for the objects and always recommend them to the users based on their fixed, defined identities because they use a source of knowledge that does not evolve. In our approach, we update identities of the users and Web contents dynamically based on the latest collective opinion of the evolving communities of users related to them in a social semantic tagging system.

Keywords: Collaborative tagging · Dynamic community formation · Semantic tagging · Emergent semantics · Information retrieval · Social semantic tagging systems

1 Introduction

Tagging and bookmarking online resources with related and representative keywords is one of the most popular and practical approaches for giving identity to the objects. Human taggers in social tagging systems give identity to the objects. Tagged objects also represent the perception or identity of their taggers in return. Consequently, identities that are assigned to the objects and taggers have effect on the quality of the recommendation of the related objects to the users's interest. Therefore, social tagging systems have the potential to enable realtime sharing of group perception and to help in making informed group decisions.

Communities formed around the Web are particularly in need of mechanisms to help them share information. Such communities are dynamic with members and their interest and knowledge evolving rapidly. Yet current community and object identification techniques are by and large static.

© Springer International Publishing Switzerland 2015
Y. Luo (Ed.): CDVE 2015, LNCS 9320, pp. 36–47, 2015.
DOI: 10.1007/978-3-319-24132-6_5

Any method that requires its users to enroll in a predefined group or community or search based on fixed terms or tags can certainly not deal with dynamic communities or those that emerge spontaneously.

Today we have huge social involvement and interaction around shared resources on the Web. We can exploit this social involvement to provide services that can dynamically collect the latest collective perception of the majority of the most related users about the defined identities to improve the quality of the recommendations in social systems.

Our work supports collaboration through maintaining an evolving knowledge base on the Web that consists of Web contents (objects), users (taggers), and semantic tags. Semantic tags in social semantic tagging systems have formal definitions because they are mapped to the concepts that are defined in ontologies. Semantic tags are not only able to improve quality of tag assignments by solving some common tags ambiguity problems related to classic folksonomy systems (i.e., in particular polysemy and synonymy), but also to provide some meta data on top of the social relations based on contribution of taggers around semantic tags. Those meta data may be exploited to address the problems of lack of commonly agreed and evolving meaning of tags in social semantic tagging systems [6]. As a proof of concept we have built a prototype called *Collaborative Ontology Development (COD)* which uses the automatic methods to define identity of the objects by assigning semantic tags to them, then it recommends tagged objects to the communities of users who are interested in the topics related to the content of that object based on its initial defined identity. During the lifetime of the objects on the system, users give their feedback on the defined identities by the automatic method and other users. As a result *COD* is able to refine identity of the objects and users based on the latest opinion of the users dynamically.

We have applied *COD* in a case study in the "Entrepreneurship" domain. The entrepreneurship domain is an example of applications that exhibit dynamic and emerging requirements. There are many actors, often not knowing about each other's existence or their common interests. There are different types of investors (business angel, initial stage, venture capital), heterogeneous and overlapping disciplines (ICT, Health Science, High Tech), varying specialties (technical, business, legal, financial), and so on. The goal of *COD*'s dynamic contents and users identification approach is to form evolving communities of related users around the tagged objects and enable them to collaborate to define a commonsense identity for each of the tagged objects. Similar to the "user's interests" that can change during the time on the platform, the assigned identities also will never become fixed in the knowledge base and can always evolve by the dynamic communities of related people which are formed around it according to its latest identity. The goal of a dynamic community formation approach is to enable members of such community to find related contents to their interest on the basis of up to the minute evolving knowledge.

We complete Sect. 1 with introducing the problems that exist in static approaches and the related work. In Sect. 2 we describe all steps of the process and challenges that we addressed in our approach in detail. In Sect. 3 we present preliminary results of our evaluation.

Our approach succeeded in improving identification of contents and users by reducing the sparsity of semantically related tags that are assigned to the Web contents and users through both: (1) initial automatic augmentation of semantically related tags to the assigned tags and (2) after contribution of related human experts to the identity assigned to the Web contents and users. In the final section we offer some conclusions and our plans for improving our method and its thorough evaluation.

1.1   Problem Statement

Several reasons can cause the low quality of identification of the Web contents (i.e., tagged objects) or users (i.e., taggers) in social tagging systems. Those reasons that are related to our approach are the followings: (1) the quality of the meanings of assigned tags to an object, (2) the quality of taggers relatedness to a tagged object and (3) the dynamics of identifications and recommendations.

(1) Using plain words as tags for representing objects in classic bookmarking systems causes ambiguity problems. The sources of such ambiguity include using different plain words as tags for referring to the same concept (synonymy) or referring to different concepts with the same plain word tags (polysemy). For instance, searching for *"Incubator"* on classic tagging systems might show results containing tags related to *"Business incubator"*, for startup businesses, a device used to grow and maintain microbiological cultures or cell cultures, a device for maintaining the eggs of birds or reptiles to allow them to hatch, a device used to care for premature babies in a neonatal intensive-care unit, and so on. One way to narrow results to the *"Business incubator"* would be if people had tagged their objects with a tag such as *#company* and *#startup*. But this has its own problems: not everyone will tag the object with *#company* and others may use other synonym tags such as *#enterprise* even if we assume there is a defined naming convention in the system. Semantic tagging systems have solutions for solving tag ambiguity problems by mapping tags to the concepts that are formally defined in ontologies. If tags have meaning, then the *#business:incubator* would be different from the tag *#device:incubator* and therefore the result of queries on the semantic tags will be more precise.

(2) Often tags represent heterogeneous perceptions of individuals rather than a collective and commonly agreed opinion of a group of users who are knowledgeable about those resources. For instance, the perception about tag *#device:incubator* that is assigned to an object is different for a nurse than a microbiologist. Therefore, the opinion of these two individuals about the correctness of assigning *#device:incubator* to a picture of a device used in a microbiology laboratory will be nearly opposite. This example shows also the advantage of using the opinion of numerous related users over the opinion of individuals on tag assignments. Heterogeneity of users' perception about objects causes higher degree of tags sparsity and as a result low quality of content and user

identification and recommendations. Furthermore, if the system provides collaborative tagging services and improves the initial ontology based on users votes on the assigned tags, the system might achieve a strong agreed upon semantic relation between *"enterprise"* and *"company"* concepts in the ontology behind those tags, and the results of a semantic query on *#business:incubator* which includes *#company* or *#enterprise* will provide the same precise result related to the *"business incubator"*.

(3) While knowledge of people is evolving, their perception of different objects and concepts also evolves over time. Therefore, if bookmarks also represent perception of the taggers on different objects, they should also evolve and update dynamically according to the latest perception of the taggers in order to represent the current state of common knowledge.

COD addresses the above mentioned problems in order to enhance the quality of contents' and users' identification by collaborative semantic annotations, dynamically.

1.2 Related Work

In this Section we discuss the existing tools and methodologies related to COD.

Collaborative Ontology Development Tools such as *Protégé*[1] which has a semi-automatic tool for ontology merging and alignment called *PROMPT* [11]. *SWOOP* [5], *Hozo* [8], *DILIGENT* [15], *ONKI* [16] and *KAON* [2] are also tools for collaborative ontology development by using change logs and version controlling methods. Online platforms enable us to develop ontologies collectively and refine them according to the opinion of the related users. Updating a single agreed ontology can obviate the need for a version control system for different versions of static ontologies.

Community Formation and Detection Methods differ in their purposes and characteristics in the main transactions and in consequence the structure of the social network under study. Papadopoulos et al. [12] categorize community detection and graph clustering methods into five main categories of *Subgraph Discovery, Model-based, Vertex clustering, Quality Optimization* and *Divisive* methods according to the adopted community definition and underlying methodological principles. Every transaction in social systems typically involves different entities. In our system, we consider taggers, tagged objects and semantic tags as the three main entities of the social semantic tagging system under study and represent the transactions among them with a tripartite graph.

Social Semantic Tagging Systems allows for the annotation of resources with tags extended by semantic definitions and descriptions that also evolve collaboratively within the same system [3]. Several reference resources exist that social semantic tagging systems use to extract taxonomy and meaning of words, e.g. *WordNet* [10], *Yago* [14] and *Wikitaxonomy* [13]. Moreover, those references need to cover different topics. *DBpedia*[2] is a project that extracts structured

---

[1] http://protege.stanford.edu/.

[2] http://dbpedia.org/.

information from *Wikipedia* in the form of RDF triples. As *Wikipedia* contains articles about many domains of concepts, *DBpedia* can also be seen as a huge ontology that assigns URIs to a large number of concepts. There exist a few social semantic tagging systems like *Bibsonomy* [4], *Faviki*[3], *GroupMe* [1], *Twine*[4], *Zig-Tag*[5], *ginzr*[6], *Annotea*[7] [7], *Fuzzy*[8] [9] and *SOBOLEO* [18] with different features and purposes. The common feature among them is that all of them allow their users to extend tags used for annotating with additional semantics but only two of them have the community formation feature, (i.e., *Fuzzy* and *SOBOLEO*) [3]. However, the formed communities in those systems are static and built around fixed topics with the categorizing approach of classic folksonomy systems.

2   Proposed Approach

In order to improve representation and in consequence recommendation of contents and users, we proposes the dynamic identification of contents and users in social semantic tagging systems by using recent opinion of most related users in the evolving communities that we form around them. In our previous experiments we have tried to use the already existing bookmarking systems like *Delicious*[9] to form dynamic communities and add the dynamic content and user identification feature to them. We could simulate our approach using the available knowledge on *Delicious* but we couldn't evaluate the quality of our dynamic identifications since we couldn't update the source of knowledge and improve recommendations based on the new defined identities on such systems. Therefore, we have decided to make a new model from scratch that has all the resources, elements and procedure that we designed for such a dynamic system. In this section, we describe all steps of this process and how they are implemented in the first model of *"COD"* on a specific use case related to the *"Entrepreneurship"* topic.

2.1   Initial Knowledge Extraction

Semantic tagging systems need to map tags or plain keywords to the meaningful concepts that are defined in an ontology. In this model of our approach, we extract the required initial knowledge from *Wikipedia*. We assume that each *Wikipedia* article represents a concept and use the articles as the references (or *URIs*) of the concepts in our ontology. We extracted a collection of concepts related to the *"Entrepreneurship"* topic by crawling *Wikipedia*. Five articles were chosen by human experts as the starting nodes of the crawler including: (1) *"Entrepreneurship"*, (2) *"ICT"*, (3) *"Clean-Tech"*, (4) *"High-Tech"* and

---

[3] http://www.faviki.com.
[4] http://twine.com.
[5] http://zigtag.com.
[6] http://code.google.com/p/gnizr/.
[7] http://www.annotea.org/.
[8] http://www.fuzzzy.com.
[9] https://delicious.com/.

(5) *"Bio-Tech"*. Then the crawler collected all concepts that were linked to these initial concepts. Afterward, we measured semantic similarity between each two of the concepts in the collection.

We measured semantic similarity between articles by using *Wikipedia Link-based Measure (WLM)* [17] which measures similarity of articles based on number of common hyperlinks between them. In this model we use existing hyperlinks as well as common links and their occurrence in a collection of *Wikipedia* articles. Similar to classic *Vector Space Model (VSM)*, *WLM* also considers representativeness of each link for each article according to its frequency in the whole collection by measuring *Inverse Link Frequency (ILF)* (i.e., similar to *IDF* measure in *VSM*). The main advantage of using *WLM* instead of other approaches for measuring semantic similarity is its performance. *WLM* is a very light approach that can be executed frequently on large collections as soon as there is any updates on the links of the articles in *Wikipedia* – which is a dynamic source of knowledge by itself.

2.2 Automatic Contents and Users Identification

In the second step of our approach, we automatically parsed unstructured content of some online resources related to "Entrepreneurship" and assigned meaningful tags (i.e., semantic tags) to them in order to define an initial identity for t hem. We use *Wikipedia* articles (i.e., or *DBpedia* concepts) as the reference of the semantic tags assigned to the contents. *"Spotlight"*[10] is also one of the practical *DBpedia* web services that can be used for extracting *DBpedia* concepts from a plain text content. We map extracted keywords from a content to the meaningful concepts in our defined ontology around *"Entrepreneurship"*. We have also defined some *Perl* scripts to automatically extract tags and semantic relations (i.e., object, predicate and subject triples) from some semi-structured resources related to *"Entrepreneurship"*.

In the next step we form communities around each of the tagged objects and recommend extracted semantic tags and relations to the *CODers* (i.e., *COD* users) to verify relatedness of them to the content of the tagged objects.

2.3 Communities Formation Around Each of the Contents

The main contribution of our approach is on this and the next step where results also have recursive effect on the previous steps. As we mentioned in Sect. 1.1, one of the most important factors that affects the quality of tag assignment, and in consequence objects identification, is relatedness of the taggers to the content of an object that is tagged by them. Generalizing contents and users in some predefined and fixed categories is one of the most popular community formation approaches in tagging systems but is not necessarily the most reliable approach and doesn't guarantee a high degree of users and objects relatedness. Content of most of the objects belong to multiple disciplines. Even if all the related disciplines of an

---

[10] https://github.com/dbpedia-spotlight/.

object are identified accurately, most of the tagging systems recommend them to all of users who are grouped in some general categories related to those disciplines. Therefore, we have decided to identify each unique content with as many tags that are assigned to it (automatically or manually) and measure similarity of combination of them with collection of each user's interests.

The main challenge of this step was the high degree of tags sparsity among users and objects in social tagging systems. We model the main entities of social tagging systems with three disjoint sets of U (representing Users or taggers in the system), T (representing semantic tags in semantic tagging systems) and O (representing the tagged Objects or bookmarked Web contents) that are vertices of a hypergraph. We consider each of these entities as a vertex of the graph and connect them through edges if there exist a transaction among them. Edges of this graph have weight based on the number of times that there were interaction between them. We represent three facets of this hypergraph including its entities and interactions between them with three matrices. Matrices TU, TO and OU represent all transactions among tags and users, tags and objects and objects and users respectively. Values of the cells in those matrices represent the frequency of their co-occurrences. Recording these three main transactions in these separate matrices (i.e., sparse matrices) allow us to retrieve and update them with a high performance according to the goal of similarity measures and community formation. After having the proper data structure in our model for high performance retrieval and updates, we need to address the problem of tags sparsity in those matrices. Different approaches exist for addressing this problem. Using Eigen Vectors is one of the most common approaches which removes less significant tags from the collection to achieve higher degree of similarity between objects and users. But this approach is not a promising solution for tagging systems because removing tags only because they are not used frequently in the whole collection doesn't guarantee their low importance and representativeness for an object or a user. In order to address the sparsity problem, we proposed feeding TU and TO matrices with semantic similarity measures from an external source of knowledge. We update TU and TO matrices with initial semantic similarities that are measured in the first step at the beginning and then updating those measures according to the users' opinions (i.e., the next step). The following pseudocode (Algorithm 1) illustrates how we update the TO matrix. We apply the same update on the TU matrix.

2.4   Dynamic Update of the Contents' and Users' Identities

Users of the formed communities around the objects can vote on the correctness of the tags assigned to them. Every time that a new transaction happens in the system, similar to the previous step, in addition to updating the corresponding cells in the TU and TO matrices we also update the semantically related cells according to the recent measured semantic relatedness values in the semantic similarity matrix. Experience showed that considering a threshold on the number of related cells (tags) to the modified cell that are going to be updated can prevent the saturation of the semantic relatedness values for the very general

Algorithm 1. Augmenting Tag-Object (TO) matrix with semantic similarity measures, resulting in AugTO matrix

```
1: procedure TOMATRIXUPDATE
2:     tags ← Number of TO rows(Tags) integer
3:     objects ← Number of TO columns(Objects) integer
4:     TO ← Original Tag-Object Matrix double
5:     Sim ← Tags Semantic Similarity Matrix double
6:     for j = 1, to objects step1 do
7:         for i1 = 1, to tags step 1 do
8:             for i2 = 1, to tags step 1 do
9:                 AugTO(i2,j) = AugTO(i2,j) + (Sim(i1,i2) . TO(i2,j))
                 end for
             end for
         end for
```

semantic tags. We can also modify the value of the threshold according to the number of tags that are semantically related to each tag (i.e., the more the tags are related, the less the threshold value is set for that tag).

3   COD Results on the "Entrepreneurship" Domain

To evaluate our approach, we conducted a case study related to *"Entrepreneurship"*. In the first step, we extracted 844 concepts by crawling *Wikipedia* hyperlinks. As described in Sect. 2.1, human experts defined 5 initial concepts related to "Entrepreneurship" as the starting pages of the crawler program. We have collected 1370 Web contents (objects) from web pages related to Entrepreneurship including startup companies, individual investors, investing foundations and business angels. We parsed those objects and tagged them with the keywords in their content that could be mapped to the concepts in our ontology. Even though the concepts in our ontology are all related to entrepreneurship, not unexpectedly, the Tag-Object (TO) matrix was still very sparse. Only 83 concepts out of 844 concepts in the collection could be assigned automatically more than once to those objects. Then in the next step we added semantic similarity measures to the original TO matrix and generated AugTO matrix with an optimized *Matlab* code of the algorithm explained in Sect. 2.3. This step reduced the sparsity of the TO matrix by 18.52 % after considering similar tags to the assigned tags for each object. In the example from the results of this step that is illustrated in Fig. 1, the tag that was assigned to the Web content for introducing the focus of a startup is *"Diagnostics"* and the tags that were assigned to the Web content for introducing the profile and investment focus of an investor were *"Life Science"* and *"Biotech"*. The similarity between these two objects was measured 11.79 % considering only the assigned tags. In the same figure augmented semantically similar tags to the assigned tags to that startup and investor based on AugTo matrix are illustrated as well with colored lines. After augmenting similar tags to the assigned tags in the AugTO the similarity between those two objects was

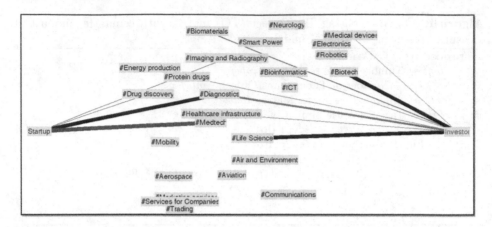

Fig. 1. An instance from the results of the AugTO matrix. The initial tagged that were assigned to a startup and an investor illustrated with black lines and augmented semantically similar tags to the assigned tags to this startup are illustrated with blue lines and to the investor are illustrated with red lines. The thickness of the lines are set based on the weight of the tags for each object (Color figure online).

increased to 35.22 % and in some cases even from 0 % to 95.30 %. This example shows how could we improve the recommendation of this startup to a related investor by augmenting semantically similar tags to the assigned tags to their initial identity. In the final step, we asked human experts to confirm and assign the highly related tags to the tags assigned to each object as well.

After updating again the TO matrix with new assigned tags (ExpAugTO matrix) by the expert to the objects and running the procedure that is explained in Sect. 2.4, we were able to reduce the sparsity of the TO matrix by 25.76 %. This improvement can be viewed as the result of collaboration among the human experts in pooling their common knowledge. Reduction of the tags sparsity in the TO matrix resulted in better matching of similar objects. Three matrices in Fig. 2 illustrate how similarity between startups (in the rows of the matrices) and investors (in the columns of the matrices) were evolved after augmenting the semantically similar tags to the assigned tags and also after applying the confirmation of the experts on the similar tags assignments in the next step. The measured similarities for the two instances of Fig. 1 are illustrated with the red empty squares at the bottom-left of the Fig. 2 matrices as well.

Human experts involvement can have different effects on the results of contents and users identification and in consequence their recommendations. Identification of the objects should be according to the goal of tag assignment. For instance, in this use case, tagging startups with more general tags could match them with higher number of investors but not most related ones.

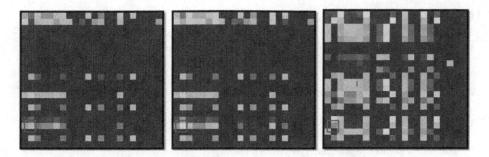

Fig. 2. Evolution of the measured similarities for recommendation of the related startups to the investors' interests. The left matrix illustrates the measured similarities based on original TO matrix, the middle matrix based the AugTO matrix and the right matrix based on the ExpAugTO matrix. The colors are ranging form blue (which represents low similarity) to red (which represents high similarity) (Color figure online).

4   Conclusions and Future Work

In this paper we have discussed the problems that exist with static contents and users identification that can cause poor recommendation of the contents to the users and hamper up to the minute sharing of information and knowledge. Since people's perception in each specific area of knowledge is evolving over time, the goal of our approach is to also evolve the represented knowledge in semantic tagging systems dynamically according to the latest perception of the related taggers. We proposed dynamic users and contents identification through evolving communities of most related users around the objects. We developed *COD*, a social semantic tagging system as a model of our proposed approach and ran some experiments with a specific use case. We described all steps of this dynamic process and also the challenges we had for developing those parts. The preliminary results of our evaluation show that our approach was able to improve the identification of contents and users by reducing the sparsity of semantically related tags that are assigned to the objects. This reduction is achieved through both automatic augmentation of semantics to the assigned tags and also after contribution of related human experts to the assigned identity to the objects. At the moment we are in the test phase of *COD* with a few test users. We have plans to test our model with more users in the following months and evaluate it with more users interactions and on different use cases. We would also like to optimize the influence of the most related users to the latest defined identity of the objects by adding a new feature to our platform. *COD* development is an ongoing activity, and we are enhancing it in different aspects, ranging from the recommendation engine to user-interaction to visualization.

References

1. Abel, F., Henze, F., Krause, D., Plappert, D., Siehndel, P.: Group me! where semantic web meets web 2.0. In: Proceedings of the 6th International Semantic Web Conference (2007)
2. Bozsak, E., Ehrig, M., Handschuh, S., Hotho, A., Maedche, A., Motik, B., Oberle, D., Schmitz, C., Staab, S., Stojanovic, L., Stojanovic, N., Studer, R., Stumme, G., Sure, Y., Tane, J., Volz, R., Zacharias, V.: KAON - Towards a large scale semantic web. In: Bauknecht, K., Tjoa, A.M., Quirchmayr, G. (eds.) EC-Web 2002. LNCS, vol. 2455, p. 304. Springer, Heidelberg (2002)
3. Braun, S., Schora, C., Zacharias, V.: Semantics to the bookmarks: a review of social semantic bookmarking systems. In: Proceedings of I-KNOW (2009)
4. Hotho, A., Jaschke, R., Schmitz, C., Stumme, G.: Bibsonomy: a social bookmark and publication sharing system. In: CS-TIW06. Aalborg University Press, Aalborg (2006)
5. Kalayanpour, A., Parsia, B., Sirin, E., Grau, B.C., Hendler, J.: Swoop: a web ontology editing browser. Web Semant. Sci. Serv. Agents World Wide Web 4(2), 144–153 (2006). Elsevier
6. Kamran, S.: Dynamic communities formation through semantic tags. In: Proceedings of the Companion Publication of the 23rd International Conference on World Wide Web Companion, pp. 45–50 (2014)
7. Koivunen, M.: Semantic authoring by tagging with annotea social bookmarks and topics. In: Proceedings of the Semantic Authoring and Annotation Workshop at the International Semantic Web Conference, ISWC 2006 (2006)
8. Kozaki, K., Sunagawa, E., Kitamura, Y., Mizoguchi, R.: A framework for cooperative ontology construction based on dependency management of modules. In: ESOE, pp. 33–44 (2007)
9. Lachica, R., Karabeg, D.: Quality, relevance and importance in information retrieval with fuzzy semantic networks. In: Proceedings of TMRA 2008, University of Leipzig LIV (2008). Series Post-Proceeding Paper
10. Miller, G.A.: Wordnet: A lexical database for english. Commun. ACM 38(1), 39–41 (1995)
11. Noy, N., Musen, M.: The PROMPT suite: interactive tools for ontology merging and mapping. Int. J. Hum Comput Stud. 59(6), 983–1024 (2003)
12. Papadopoulos, S., Kompatsiaris, Y., Vakali, A., Spyridonos, P.: Community detection in social media performance and application considerations. Data. Min. Knowl. Disc. 24, 515–554 (2012)
13. Ponzetto, S., Strube, M.: Deriving a large-scale taxonomy from wikipedia. In: AAAI, pp. 1440–1445. AAAI Press, Menlo Park (2007)
14. Suchanek, F.M., Kasneci, G., Weikum, G.: Yago: a core of semantic knowledge. In: 16th International World Wide Web Conference (WWW 2007). ACM Press, New York (2007)
15. Tempich, C., Pinto, H.S., Sure, Y., Staab, S.: An argumentation ontology for distributed, loosely-controlled and evolving engineering processes of ontologies (DILIGENT). In: Gómez-Pérez, A., Euzenat, J. (eds.) ESWC 2005. LNCS, vol. 3532, pp. 241–256. Springer, Heidelberg (2005)
16. Valo, A., Hyvonen, E., Komurainen, V.: A tool for collaborative ontology development for the semantic web. In: Proceedings of DC (2005)

17. Witten, I., Milne, D.: An effective, low-cost measure of semantic relatedness obtained from wikipedia links. In: Proceeding of AAAI Workshop on Wikipedia Links and Artificial Intelligence: An Evolving Synergy, pp. 25–30. AAAI Press, Chicago (2008)
18. Zacharias, V., Braun, S.: Soboleo: social bookmarking and lightweight ontology engineering. In: Proceedings of the Workshop on Social and Collaborative Construction of Structured Knowledge at WWW07, vol. 273 (2007). CEUR Workshop Prodeedings

Challenges of Big Data in the Age of Building Information Modeling: A High-Level Conceptual Pipeline

Conrad Boton[1,2(✉)], Gilles Halin[2], Sylvain Kubicki[3], and Daniel Forgues[1]

[1] École de Technologie Supérieure, 1100, rue Notre-Dame Ouest, Montreal, QC, Canada
`conrad.boton.1@ens.etsmtl.ca, daniel.forgues@etsmtl.ca`
[2] Research Centre in Architecture and Engineering, 2, rue Bastien Lepage, Nancy, France
`gilles.halin@crai.archi.fr`
[3] Luxembourg Institute of Science and Technology, 5, av. Hauts-Fourneaux,
Sanem, Luxembourg
`sylvain.kubicki@list.lu`

Abstract. N-dimensional BIM models integrate many aspects of Architecture, Engineering and Construction (AEC) projects information. These models are well structured and allow users to practically query them, however they are more and more combined with other data sources, provided e.g. by Geographic Information Systems (GIS), Building Automation Systems (BAS) or Facility Management (FM) systems. Construction project managers are facing an important challenge related to making meaningful deduction from these heterogeneous data sets. In this context the current data mining approaches are showing their limitations. Big Data is then gradually getting a reality in the construction industry. This paper characterizes AEC project management data following the conceptual definition of Big Data and proposes a high-level conceptual pipeline aiming at bridging the gap between BIM-based related visualization works and information visualization domain.

Keywords: BIM · Big data · Information visualization · Information pipeline · Architecture, engineering and construction

1 Introduction

With the advent of Building Information Modeling (BIM) in the construction industry, the approaches to "information management" are rapidly changing. Reddy compared the transformative aspect of BIM to the Internet and stated that it is becoming necessary to manage building data on projects of any size [1]. According to him, "the most interesting aspect of BIM in the long term is the application of data mining and analyzing" [1]. Moreover, building information models are increasingly associated with other sources, including urban cartographies, Geographic Information Systems (GIS) [2, 3], Building Automation Systems (BAS), Facility Management Systems (FM) [4, 5], Electronic Document Management Systems (EDMS) [6] and Computerized Maintenance Management Systems (CMMS) [7]. Beyond the interoperability issues well addressed in literature, combining such

© Springer International Publishing Switzerland 2015
Y. Luo (Ed.): CDVE 2015, LNCS 9320, pp. 48–56, 2015.
DOI: 10.1007/978-3-319-24132-6_6

different sources in order to extend the BIM-based decision-support can quickly become very complex for current data mining tools due to the variety and the amount of the information.

Thus, Big Data has the potential to become a common reality in the industry. In 2011, the McKinsley Global Institute proposed a map showing the value potential capture of Big Data cross sectors. On a scale of five, construction sector is positioned on the third quintile for IT intensity, for data-driven mind-set, and for data availability, as well as for the overall ease of capture index [8].

Because of the peculiarity of the industry, data integration and management is a challenging issue in the development of Architecture, Engineering and Construction (AEC) projects. It is worth to remind that fragmentation, non-standardized collaboration and heterogeneity of actors and skills characterize collaborative processes in AEC projects management [9, 10]. Furthermore it is not trivial to give a precise definition of what Big Data currently means in construction projects. Moreover, with the growing development of Building Information Modeling approach, one can state that information-related issues are only treated from data interoperability and exchange processes viewpoints. The management of raw data (e.g. from BIM as well as from other sources) is not really conceptually formalized so far. This paper proposes to explore the literature in order to define what Big Data really means in construction industry. It then proposes a conceptual pipeline model of Big Data based on previous seminal frameworks and information visualization theories.

2   Big Data in BIM-Based Construction Management: What Does It Mean?

Provost and Fawcett defined Big Data as "datasets that are too large for traditional data-processing systems and that therefore require new technologies" [11]. According to the McKinsley Global Institute, it "refers to datasets whose size is beyond the ability of typical database software tools to capture, store, manage, and analyze" [8]. McAfee and Brynjolfsson (2012) identified three key differences between Big Data and data processing used before. These differences are related to the variety, the volume, and the velocity of the data [12].

2.1   As Regards the Variety

A large variety of information is produced, managed and used during construction projects. It generally encompasses functional brief requirements, feasibility studies, architectural drawings, engineering drawings, technical specifications, tender documents, bills of quantities, cost estimations, invoices, reports, lifecycle information, technical data sheets, as-built records. This list is far to be exhaustive and one can add design know-how, building regulations, construction know-how, client brief, schematic drawings, observations, measurements, etc. [13].

Jiao et al. (2013) distinguishes project engineering data (PED) from project management data (PMD). According to them, PED refers to "geometric presentation, parametric descriptions and legal regulations associated with the construction of a building" [14]. PMD are "control and communication information that are generated in and closely related to management activities throughout the construction lifecycle". Björk showed that information is required to control the material activities, to specify the building requirements (design information) and the activities to be performed (management information) [13]. Moreover the construction projects' information is also presented in Table 36 of the OmniClass[1] classification. Its three broad categories (general references, office resources, project information) and their content well illustrate the variety of information related to construction projects.

With the worldwide development of the BIM approach, both PMD and PED are integrated and coordinated with the aim of managing information in the form of "nD models". nD modeling can be defined as the addition of supplementary information to tridimensional model(s) for analyses and simulation purposes. Thus, it is commonly agreed that a 4D model links scheduling information to 3D model's objects in order to simulate construction process over time. The fifth dimension is related to costs information. It is more and more accepted that the sixth dimension is related to assets information useful for facility management processes but it is important to note that beyond the fifth dimension (i.e. cost), there is no consensus in the literature about what each dimension represents. Lee et al. identify eight possible dimensions which notably show how nD modelling can increase the variety of information to be managed around BIM. These dimensions are: maintenance needs, acoustics, process, cost, energy requirements, crime deterrent features, sustainability, people's accessibility [15].

This variety of model-related dimensions of information is highly structured and relies on object-based conceptual modeling techniques, such as BuildingSmart's IFC schema. However, design and construction processes also rely on huge raw datasets, such as the 3D point clouds delivered in the surveying tasks using laser scanning techniques. Moreover, as mentioned in the introduction many research works have reported other information sources which can be integrated with BIM. Such integration approaches of course dramatically increase the variety of information to be managed, but also the volume.

The variety is also related to the variety of practitioners involved in a project. Due to the fragmentation in the industry, construction projects teams are very heterogeneous, with practitioners coming from collaborative organizations and continually changing. Management information systems (MIS) should take into account these peculiarities. According to Jiao et al., "most current systems (MIS) are unable to handle the complicated multi-organizational relationship of AEC/FM sector due to their top-down, predefined (hetero-organization) approach" [12].

2.2 As Regards the Volume

As regards the volume, it is hard to say beyond which size data can be called Big Data because it depends on the sector, the advances of the technology over time and the complexity of data [8]. In the AEC industry, "construction projects are associated with

---

[1] http://omniclass.org.

voluminous and often unstructured data sets" [16]. According to Jiao et al., "individual file sizes currently range from Megabytes to Gigabytes, however there is an apparent trend of increasing file size" [14]. These authors mention a huge volume of data representing "tens of thousands of files" at a project level. The McKinsey Global Institute (2011) estimated the data storage for the USA construction industry in 2009 at 51 petabytes, with 231 terabytes for each of the 222 firms with more than 1000 employees [8]. Obviously these data volumes are not too high to be managed by traditional data processing tools but the main difficulty lies in the heterogeneity of data formats and putting together a variety of data sources for analysis and decision-support purposes.

Traditionally, the stored data is in the form of images and text/numbers but with BIM and nD modeling, other forms of data are now stored. For example, 4D models are commonly exported and stored as video animations. In the frame of nD modeling, the size of the handled data can grow very rapidly due to the multiple dimensions conveyed, their size, their variety and their complexity. Joyce recently published in a professional journal a very interesting case related to 4D modelling. He stated that when managers associate costs information to "the three-day schedule of a crane, the five-day schedule of its crew, the seven-day schedule of the materials and the cost of the crew's labor" the size of the data to manage can rapidly get out of control [17]. According to him, with the growth of 4D BIM in the construction sector, "Big Data arrives each day with an ever-louder thud" [17].

2.3 As Regards the Velocity

Thanks to new delivery methods including Integrated Project Delivery (IPD), BIM level 3 (i.e. collaborative model server) has already been adopted in a few construction projects. A survey conducted in 2010 by Kent and Becerik-Gerber showed that the adoption of IPD by construction professionals in the United States was still not very significant, but noted a huge interest in the principle and some good perspectives [18]. Both experienced professionals (66.7 %) and informed ones (58.3 %) see the IPD becoming one day a widely adopted method for project delivery. BIM level 3 is defined as network-based integration, a collaborative use of an integrated object-oriented model, shared over a network in which users can connect to feed and use the model, within their respective areas of responsibility [19–21]. Beyond "building-related" data, recent policies plan to integrate "infrastructure-related" data to the models required for public tendering in UK.

Two main methods are currently used for models integration in the BIM approach. The first method use object-oriented database named "BIM servers" to manage IFC objects with their versions, their variants, their business views and the associated notifications. The interface with the BIM server is enabled via BIM authoring software systems or intermediary viewers coupled to the server with APIs. The second method consists in the use of Project Lifecycle Management (PLM) collaborative platforms to establish and maintain the link between IFC objects collections corresponding to the responsibility and the production of the different stakeholders within the same construction phase or among different phases of the project. This requires the use of new technologies such as "cloud computing" [22].

Whether for PLM or BIM server, the velocity of data will be an important challenge in the next years. Indeed, the bandwidth needed for data input/output is getting increasingly higher because data must be processed quickly despite its big volume. In fact, the volume of data and the diversity of transactions coming from multiple sources considerably increase the flow of information. Jiao et al. (2013) have notably well illustrated these challenges through the *LubanWay* project, where among other things they worked on the integration of 3 *as-built* BIM models (from tools dedicated to construction in China) with as-planned BIM models from Revit™ and business social network services.

3   A Big Data Conceptual Pipeline for Construction Industry

3.1   Background

The proposition described below relies on important previous works dedicated to both (1) the information technology and flow in construction and (2) the (Big) data flow proposed by Information Visualization scientific fields.

In 1999, Björk established a definition and the main research issues associated with the emerging domain of Information Technology in construction. The paper proposed a global model of construction process relying on two interacting sub-processes: the material process and the information process [13]. It then used the IDEF0 formalism to model the interactions of the four generic information process activities: person-to-person communication, creation of new information, information search and retrieval, making information available. Due to the complexity of processes in construction and their interrelations, Turk proposed to distinguish the glue processes (or integration processes) from the base processes [23]. According to Turk, while base processes are the core processes (including information creation processes and information utilization processes), glue processes "make sure that material items or information flow from creation process to utilization process and that the utilization process can use them" [23]. Information creation includes four steps: create, edit, record, and distribute [23]. The glue process includes five steps: find, retrieve, store, convert, and store (the converted version). According to Turk, information processes have five main features: input, output, performer, customer, method, and time frame.

As developed in previous sections, BIM can generate voluminous and various data sets to support the management functions in construction projects. For Russell et al. (2009), making meaningful deduction from this data is one important challenge construction project managers are facing. He also remarked that information processing and visualization can be very helpful, a statement that can be generalized in the Big Data research. Mazza defined visualization as a "cognitive activity, facilitated by external visual representations from which people build an internal mental representation of the world" [24]. Geovisualization (about geospatial data), Scientific Visualization (about physical "things") and Information Visualization (about abstract data) are the three main research fields that provide scientific body of knowledge on information processing and visualization. With the advances in IT, many tools are now available to assist users in creating visual representations of abstract data. Although these tools are very different from each other, they all follow the same steps and process for generating visual representations. Mazza (2009) presented a conceptual model inspired from the pipeline proposed by Haber and McNabb [25]. Three main steps are identified: pre-processing, visual mapping, and view creation. The reference model provided by Wood et al. [26] in collaborative visualization is also based on this pipeline.

Russell et al. identified four main steps required for an efficient information processing activity in construction industry: identifying the purpose, selecting the data representations and transformations, choosing the visual representation and the interaction technology, as well as presenting and disseminating [16]. More recently, assuming that 4D/nD simulation works are largely collaborative, Boton et al. proposed a method to design adapted visualization in collaborative 4D applications [27, 28]. The method includes four main steps: characterizing collaborative situation, identifying visualization needs, selecting adapted views, composing coordinated multiple views.

The amount of data in every sectors and function of the global economy has been exploding and the current models and applications seem inappropriate to manage the volume, the variety and the velocity of data in a near future. New conceptual models are then appearing. In 2012, Fisher et al. proposed a conceptual Big Data pipeline, based on interviews with experienced practitioners [29]. Five main steps appeared in the proposed pipeline: acquiring data, choosing architecture, shaping data into architecture, coding/debugging, and reflecting.

3.2   A New (Big) Data Pipeline Dedicated to Construction Industry

In this section, and based on the previous approaches, the authors propose a conceptual data pipeline for construction industry. The IDEF0 formalism is used, which is well known by the Information Technology in Construction scientific community. IDEF0 is used for the enterprise activities and information flows modeling [30].

The proposed pipeline relies both on the pipeline proposed by Fisher et al. (2012) and the literature in the construction IT community, including the 4 main steps identified by Russell et al. (2009) and the method proposed by Boton et al. (2013). It identifies four main steps: acquiring data, choosing architecture, Shaping and coding data, reflecting and interacting.

The first challenge in the implementation of a Big Data pipeline is related to *acquiring data*. Data can come from BIM models but also from other sources including GIS, FM systems, CMMS, BAS and EDMS. In such an approach, the structured BIM data would have to be deconstructed in order to be processed, restructured and analyzed. Data would be provided from owners, contractors and other experts. BIM charters and data improvement standards should be nevertheless used to control the way data are acquired. The second challenge in the Big Data pipeline is related to *choosing the IT architecture*. This activity would mainly be devoted to developers and data mining experts. The formats and the volume of the data from the previous step would highly determine the choice. The cost, the velocity and other performance criterion should be used for comparison of potential architectures in order to choose the most appropriate one. The third challenge in the Big Data pipeline is related to *shaping and coding data*. Raw data acquired at the first step is shaped and coded in the frame of the chosen architecture. It is important here to understand users' visualization and interaction needs.

It is also interesting to take into account the cloud computing requirements. This activity should also devoted to data mining experts. The fourth challenge in the Big Data pipeline is related to *reflecting information* and *interacting* with it. The aim is to provide users, policy makers and other practitioners with decision support dashboards which present meaningful information through coordinated multiple views. Users' visualization goals are important input in the achievement of this step. Interactions principles related to visualization tasks and views coordination mechanism are also to be considered (Fig. 1).

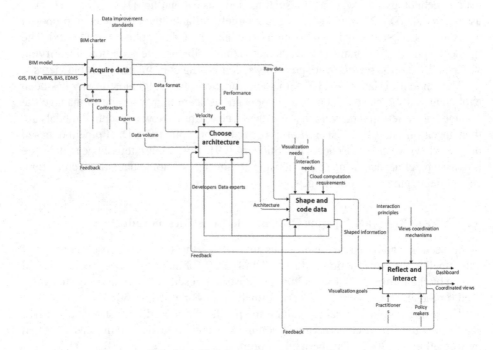

Fig. 1. A high-level conceptual pipeline

4   Conclusion

This paper explored the literature in order to define what Big Data can mean for the construction industry, especially when considering the increasing use of modern information systems like Building Information Modeling, GIS and others. It also proposed a high-level conceptual model dedicated to the construction projects management based on previous seminal frameworks identified both in construction IT research and data processing field. This framework moreover integrates theories and methods for the information visualization domain.

This is a first step of a larger research which aim at bridging the gap between BIM-based related visualization works and information visualization domain, usually applied to unstructured data. Future works will apply the proposed pipeline to real construction organization in order to evaluate it.

References

1. Reddy, K.P.: BIM for Building Owners and Developers: Making a Business Case for Using BIM on Projects. Wiley, Hoboken (2012)
2. DeLaat, R., VanBerlo, L.: Integration of BIM and GIS: the development of the CityGML GeoBIM extension. In: Lecture Notes in Geoinformation and Cartography, pp. 211–225 (2011)
3. Irizarry, J., Karan, E.P., Jalaei, F.: Integrating BIM and GIS to improve the visual monitoring of construction supply chain management. Autom. Constr. **31**, 241–254 (2013)
4. Forns-Samso, F., Laine, T., Hensel, B.: Building information modeling supporting facilities management. In: Proceedings ECPPM Ework and Ebusiness in Architecture, Engineering and Construction, pp. 51–57 (2012)
5. Becerik-Gerber, B., Jazizadeh, F., Li, N., Calis, G.: Application areas and data requirements for BIM-Enabled facilities management. J. Constr. Eng. Manag. **138**, 431–442 (2012)
6. Goedert, J.D., Meadati, P.: Integration of construction process documentation into building information modeling. J. Constr. Eng. Manag. **134**, 509–516 (2008)
7. Motawa, I., Almarshad, A.: A knowledge-based BIM system for building maintenance. Autom. Constr. **29**, 173–182 (2013)
8. Manyika, J., Chui, M.: Big Data: The Next Frontier for Innovation, Competition, and Productivity. McKinsey Global Institute, Washington (2011)
9. Howard, H., Levitt, R., Paulson, B.C., Pohl, J.G., Tatum, C.B.: Computer integration: reducing fragmentation in AEC industry. J. Comput. Civ. Eng. **3**, 18–32 (1989)
10. Kubicki, S., Bignon, J.C., Halin, G., Humbert, P.: Assistance to building construction coordination – towards a multi-view cooperative platform. ITcon **11**, 565–586 (2006)
11. Provost, F., Fawcett, T.: Data science and its relationship to big data and data-driven decision making. Big Data. **1**, 51–59 (2013)
12. McAfee, A., Brynjolfsson, E.: Big data: the management revolution. Harv. Bus. Rev. **90**, 60–68 (2012)
13. Björk, B.C.: Information technology in construction–domain definition and research issues. Int. J. Comput. Integr. Des. Constr. **1**, 1–16 (1999)
14. Jiao, Y., Wang, Y., Zhang, S., Li, Y., Yang, B., Yuan, L.: A cloud approach to unified lifecycle data management in architecture, engineering, construction and facilities management: integrating BIMs and SNS. Adv. Eng. Inf. **27**, 173–188 (2013)
15. Lee, A., Aouad, G., Cooper, R., Fu, C., Marshall-Ponting, A., Tah, J., Wu, S.: nD modelling-a driver or enabler for construction improvement? RICS Res Pap Ser RICS **5**, 1–16 (2005). London
16. Russell, A.D., Chiu, C.-Y., Korde, T.: Visual representation of construction management data. Autom. Constr. **18**, 1045–1062 (2009)
17. Joyce, E.: What You Don't Know About Your (Big) Data Can Hurt You. http://enr.construction.com/technology/construction_technology/2012/1203-big-data-little-data-and-aec.asp
18. Kent, D.C., Becerik-gerber, B.: Understanding construction industry experience and attitudes toward integrated project delivery. J. Constr. Eng. Manag. **136**, 815–825 (2010)
19. Succar, B.: Building information modelling framework: a research and delivery foundation for industry stakeholders. Autom. Constr. **18**, 357–375 (2009)
20. Boton, C., Kubicki, S.: Maturité des pratiques BIM: Dimensions de modélisation, pratiques collaboratives et technologies. In: Interaction des Maquettes Numériques, Actes du 6ème Séminaire de Conception Architecturale Numérique (SCAN2014) (2014)

21. Bew, M., Underwood, J.: Delivering BIM to the UK market. In: Handbook of research on building information modeling and construction informatics: concepts and technologies, pp. 30–64 (2010)
22. Chong, H.-Y., Wong, J.S., Wang, X.: An explanatory case study on cloud computing applications in the built environment. Autom. Constr. **44**, 152–162 (2014)
23. Turk, Z.: Construction IT: definition, framework and research issues. In: Faculty of Civil and Geodetic Engineering on the Doorstep of the Millennium : on the Occasion of Its 80th Anniversary, pp. 17–32 (2000)
24. Mazza, R.: Introduction to Information Visualization. Springer, London (2009)
25. Haber, R.B., McNabb, D.A.: Visualization Idioms: A Conceptual Model for Scientific Visualization. Visualization in Scientific Computing. pp. 74–93. IEEE (1990)
26. Wood, J., Wright, H., Brodlie, K.: CSCV - Computer supported collaborative visualization. In: International Conference on Visualization and Modelling, Leeds (1995)
27. Boton, C., Kubicki, S., Halin, G.: Designing adapted visualization for collaborative 4D applications. Autom. Constr. **36**, 152–167 (2013)
28. Halin, G., Kubicki, S., Boton, C., Zignale, D.: From collaborative business practices to user's adapted visualization services: towards a usage-centered method dedicated to the AEC sector. In: Luo, Y. (ed.) CDVE 2011. LNCS, vol. 6874, pp. 145–153. Springer, Heidelberg (2011)
29. Fisher, D., DeLine, R., Czerwinski, M., Drucker, S.: Interactions with big data analytics population by running controlled. Interactions **19**(3), 50–59 (2012)
30. Dorador, J.M., Young, R.I.M.: Application of IDEF0, IDEF3 and UML methodologies in the creation of information models. Int. J. Comput. Integr. Manuf. **13**, 430–445 (2000)

SMART: Design and Evaluation of a Collaborative Museum Visiting Application

Weidong Huang[1], Bridgette Kaminski[1], Jing Luo[2(✉)], Xiaodi Huang[3], Jingwei Li[1], Aaron Ross[1], Jason Wright[1], and Dohyung An[1]

[1] University of Tasmania, Launceston, Australia
{tony.huang,bvek,jli20,rossam,jwright9,andh}@utas.edu.au
[2] Chongqing Jiaotong University, Chongqing, China
luojing0923@sina.com
[3] Charles Sturt University, Albury, Australia
xhuang@csu.edu.au

Abstract. Many systems and applications have been developed to help visitors get around the museum and interact with the items on exhibition. However, most of the existing systems are developed to serve as a virtual tour guide and/or provide additional digital information using Augmented Reality techniques. Little attention has been paid to enabling visitors to interact with each other and share their experience with outsiders. In this paper, we describe the design and evaluation of a prototype of a museum touring application called SMART. This system was designed to explore how mobile devices can be used to connect museum visitors and their friends. It is intended to be a smart and novel mobile application that enables groups of museum visitors to select tours by their preferences, display relevant information about their tour and objects, provide interactive activities for tourists and let them mark their favourite exhibits. It also aims to streamline traditional museum tours by providing more interesting, more meaningful and more interactive parts to the tour.

Keywords: Museum · Collaborative design · Evaluation · User experience · Mobile collaboration · Online interaction

1 Introduction

Recently, mobile and wearable devices have become more affordable and popular and have been used as part of our daily activities. As the same time, people are enabled to be more socially interactive due to the wide use of mobile devices and social media such as Facebook and Twitter. One of the many applications of these new social tools is to provide quality services and information to museum visitors.

A large body of research has been done to facilitate tourists visiting museums including navigation, guidance, and information retrieval. Kenteris and Gavalas [1] divided in a survey the literature of mobile tourist guide into two categories: application-led research mainly conducted by usability designers and technology-led research mainly conducted by technology designers. It was found that most systems provide

© Springer International Publishing Switzerland 2015
Y. Luo (Ed.): CDVE 2015, LNCS 9320, pp. 57–64, 2015.
DOI: 10.1007/978-3-319-24132-6_7

information in a decentralized web-based fashion, while others offer personalized information to visitors via traditional hierarchy based menus.

In order to avoid the limitation of pre-installation of tools on user's personal devices and use of dedicated devices, Takrouri et al. [2] introduced a mobile multimedia application called HolstenTour that offers context-based and location-aware services without pre-installation. This application enables visitors to focus on intended exhibition objects with the flexibility of browsing the museum in a personalized sequence of rooms and exhibits. Going beyond identifying objects and presenting information, Gao et al. [5] developed W2Go, a travel guidance system that can automatically recognize and rank touring sites. The ranking feature was realized via their proposed ALP method that makes use of information from online sources for ranking. Further, to support shared group experience, a mobile phone based guidance system built by Suh et al. [4] allows group users to eavesdrop on each other's audio with a synchronized audio control. This system provides not only information for linear touring exploration, but also GPS based group awareness.

Augmented Reality [7] based applications are also common in this area. Chen et al. [3] introduced an AR based system museum guidance. This system uses computer vision to identify locations/items of interest through marked symbols, retrieve corresponding information and augment the target with the retrieved digital data. This approach has the advantage of not requiring common tactile peripheral devices such as keyboard, thus making the system more usable in a public environment. Huang and Alem [8] developed a system in which remote digital information is augmented with the local workspace to build a shared visual space. In addition to visual augmentation, Langlotz et al. [6] presented an approach that can spatially align audio annotations to the outdoor space. This approach also has application in museum visit to enhance user experience.

However, despite the much effort in developing a wide range of museum and culture visit related applications, little attention has been paid to enabling visitors to interact with each other and share their experience with outsiders. In this paper, we present an ongoing project that aims to explore how mobile devices can be used to connect museum visitors and their friends. More specifically, we describe the design and evaluation of a prototype of a museum touring application called SMART, with a focus on the method in the next sections.

2   System Design

We took the approach of participatory design for user requirements understanding and interface design of SMART. Participatory design is a design method that brings end users into the design process [9]. It helps designers discover what users know, how they feel and what they expect. At the same time, it helps users understand how and to what extent their expectations can be realized. We describe our approach in the next subsections.

2.1   User Requirements

To validate our assumption for the need of facilitating interactions between users on social media and solicit user requirements for our museum application, we conducted an online survey on a random selection of potential users. We had 87 people participate in our survey aged between 14–59 with the average age of 23, 48.24 % being female and 51.76 % being male. User responses to some of our questions are summarised in Fig. 1.

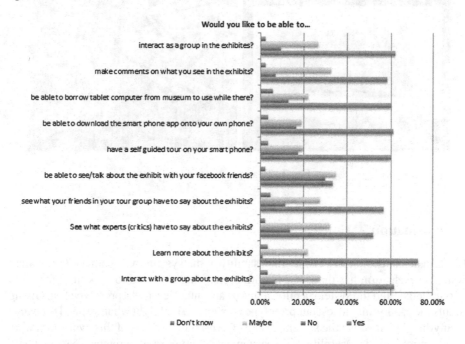

Fig. 1. User responses to some questions of the survey.

We also asked questions including: how often do they visit a museum? Who do they go with? What is purpose of the visit? What activities do they usually do before, during and after the visit? What makes the visit interesting? These questions would help us define our application to meet their needs.

2.2   Paper Based Prototyping

After completing our survey and follow up questions we looked to see what most possible clients were looking for in the way of a museum application. We took this into consideration and came to the idea of having an application that would allow people to learn, as this was a key thing people were looking to do at a museum as shown in Fig. 1 by more than 70 % of the respondents. We felt that augmented reality and location tracking would be good features as well. The application should allow for group collaboration so that people can talk in small groups or over social networking, discuss the works on the show and have friends who are not present being able to see their comments on the works.

We took the approach of paper based prototyping for the system design to avoid costly rework later during the implementation process [10, 11]. We worked with a few users during the process to ensure that user requirements were properly addressed. Figure 2 shows interface examples of our paper prototyping.

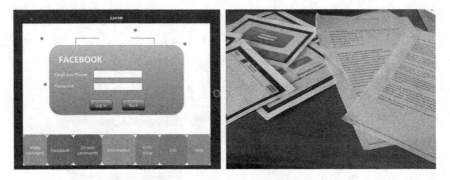

Fig. 2. Exampes of interfaces

3   Evaluation

To validate our design and ensure the usability of the system, we conducted an evaluation. The evaluation has three stages with users being involved to seek their feedback on our method and the system: a pilot, a survey and interview and a prototype test. Giving clients the opportunity to test our prototype allows us to highlight what we need to change (if anything) to improve the system design. The primary focuses of this evaluation were to determine both the usability of the system and the type of experience a person would get when interacting with the system. The pilot was conducted to validate our survey questions and the testing protocol. The survey and the prototype test were designed to complement each other with each having a different focus: the survey was more focused on the overall look and informativeness of the interface, while the test was more on functionality. We give more details of the survey and the testing in what follows.

3.1   Survey

The survey was ran through SurveyMonkey. Except those seeking demographic information, questions in the survey each include an image of a typical interface we designed for the application. Participants were asked to respond to the questions in relation to the interfaces shown. Five representative interfaces were chosen for the survey and Fig. 3 shows an example of them and its associated questions. Seventeen people participated in the study.

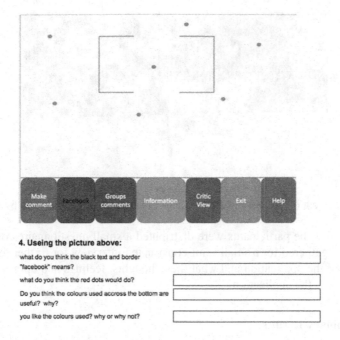

Fig. 3. A user interface and its associated questions (Color figure online).

The questions we asked are all open questions to avoid any possible bias caused by the revealing of designers personal preferences. These questions can be divided into three categories: "look of feel" of the interfaces, including color, layout, shape etc.; purposes of the interface elements; relationships between the elements.

3.2 Prototype Test

This was done based on a paper based prototype we developed [10]. It was run in a spare quiet room/office space with five different participants on a volunteer basis. Before the test, the participants were briefed about the purposes of the system and the procedure of the test. We did each test of our participants separately, giving them a small scenario that was read out. That was followed by having them carry out a set of tasks that were pre-defined so that everyone did the same tasks.

Since the test was paper based, the participants were asked to speak out their thoughts and actions during the process and a facilitator was sitting with the participant taking out the old interface and putting in the resulting interface in response to the action taken by the participant (Fig. 4). The participants were required to go through five tasks in total which cover all user interfaces and typical task scenarios. The test sessions were video recorded. By taking a video of the participants completing the tasks we could see how long each task took them and how any errors were made so that we could then go back and compare with others' test results to see where common errors lie.

Fig. 4. A participant (left) is performing a task with the paper prototype assisted by a facilitator.

After the test the participants were distributed a small questionnaires on usability and were also gathered for a small semi-constructed interview for further feedback on how they used the application and what their thoughts, feelings and opinions were on different areas of the application.

3.3 Preliminary Results

Overall, the feedback we received from the participants was generally positive, which was also supported by our observations of user behaviors. At the same time, a number of issues, such as highlighting the button of the focus, were also raised which are to be addressed in the next round of the design and evaluation process.

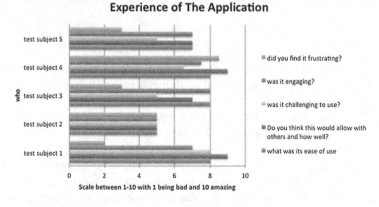

Fig. 5. User feedback of experience based on a scale of 0 to 10.

Experience: In the questionnaire questions were asked to solicit user feedback on their experience using the prototype. As can be seen from Fig. 5, participants had positive experience. Note that the questions were mixed with positive and negative statements that was to make sure that they were paying attention to the questions.

Usability: We wanted to get their first impression of the application and we received a few different comments such as "what is group log in", "it's straightforward and basically easy to use", "quite clean, consistent", "very consistent" and "simple but not too simple". All of these answers are fairly positive and show that we are creating a good first impression of the application. When asked about the purpose of the application we got a mix of answers, these being "to give information", "engaging and getting interactive information", "to provide an interactive way to visit museums", "guide of a museum" and "to help group users to visit museum". All of these are good answers and it is interesting for us to see how different people each interpreted the application in different ways. Everyone could find what they were looking for "for the most part" and discovered that most pages could be found from the homepage and main page. The only missing button, as pointed out by Test Subject 4, was a "home button so as to not be in any group view". Again everyone thought the application could be helpful as "it's easy to navigate and find information". This is something that people thought could be helpful and that it was very easy to use and navigate through, which showed that we had a decent design.

4   Concluding Remarks and Future Work

Our literature review and user survey indicated that relatively less attention had been paid to developing systems and tools for users to interact with each other and share their museums experience with their social connections. As an effort towards this direction, we proposed a museum visiting application SMART. This paper presented the design and evaluation of it with a focus on the process of paper prototyping. Potential end users were made involved in the whole process and the user feedback received indicated that the proposed application could be usable and useful if fully implemented. We are currently conducting in-depth analysis of the data. The next step after that is to refine and implement the interfaces into a working system.

References

1. Kenteris, M., Gavalas, D., Economou, D.: Electronic mobile guides: a survey. Pers. Ubiquit. Comput. **15**(1), 97–111 (2011)
2. Al Takrouri, B., Detken, K., Martinez, C., Oja, M.K., Stein, S., Zhu, L., Schrader, A.: Mobile HolstenTour: contextualized multimedia museum guide. In: Proceedings of the 6th International Conference on Advances in Mobile Computing and Multimedia (MoMM 2008), pp. 460–463 (2008)
3. Chen, C.-Y., Chang, B.R., Huang, P.-S.: Multimedia augmented reality information system for museum guidance. Pers. Ubiquit. Comput. **18**(2), 315–322 (2014)
4. Suh, Y., Shin, C., Woo, W., Dow, S., Macintyre, B.: Enhancing and evaluating users' social experience with a mobile phone guide applied to cultural heritage. Pers. Ubiquit. Comput. **15**(6), 649–665 (2011)
5. Gao, Y., Tang, J., Hong, R., Dai, Q., Chua, T.-S., Jain, R.: W2Go: a travel guidance system by automatic landmark ranking. In: Proceedings of the International Conference on Multimedia (MM 2010), pp. 123–132 (2010)

6. Langlotz, T., Regenbrecht, H., Zollmann, S., Schmalstieg, D.: Audio stickies visually-guided spatial audio annotations on a mobile augmented reality platform. In: Proceedings of the 25th Australian Computer-Human Interaction Conference: Augmentation, Application, Innovation, Collaboration (OzCHI 2013), pp. 545–554 (2013)
7. Alem, L., Huang, W.: Recent trends of mobile collaborative augmented reality systems. Springer-Verlag, New York (2011)
8. Huang, W., Alem, L.: HandsinAir: a wearable system for remote collaboration on physical tasks. In: Proceedings of the 2013 Conference on Computer Supported Cooperative Work Companion (CSCW 2013), pp. 153–156 (2013)
9. Snyder, C.: Paper Prototyping: The Fast and Easy Way to Design and Refine User Interfaces. Morgan Kaufmann, Massachusetts (2003)
10. Spinuzzi, C.: The Methodology of Participatory Design. Tech. Commun. 52(2), 163–174(12) (2005)
11. Mifsud, J.: Paper Prototyping as a Usability Testing Technique 2012. http://usabilitygeek.com/paper-prototyping-as-a-usability-testing-technique/. Accessed April 2015

The Design of Wall Pictures to Relieve Driving Fatigue in the Long Tunnel

Meng-Cong Zheng[✉]

National Taipei University of Technology, 1, Sec. 3, Chung-hsiao E. Rd.,
Taipei 10608, Taiwan, R.O.C
zmcdesign@gmail.com

Abstract. The purpose of this study was to use specially-designed of wall pictures in tunnels to reduce drivers' negative emotions and enhance positive ones. The three experiments were: investigation of the current driving experience in Hsuehshan Tunnel, the selection of wall pictures, and simulated driving with the designated pictures. The results showed that drivers had more positive emotions and less negative responses in the tunnel with pictures than in the one without pictures. When the pictures changed between each stage, more positive emotions occurred. Pictures with brightness and color changes showed better effects. The length and brightness of the pictures affected drivers' visual and spatial feelings. Drivers had different speed feelings in stages with different pictures. The rules of pictures' changes should be able to be recognized by drivers. Pictures lacking a good order will cause negative responses. Brightness changes resemble the change of lightness in the environment. Proper use the design of wall pictures helps ease drivers' negative emotions and enhance positive ones.

Keywords: Cooperative design · Driving fatigue · Design of wall picture · Long tunnel

1 Introduction

In the long and narrow Taiwan island, the central Range and Hsuehshan Range forms a barrier affecting the transportation between the east and the west side. To promote the development of the east area, the government constructed the Hsuehsan Tunnel, which shortens the car ride from two hours to forty minutes. However, it is uncomfortable for drivers to drive through an almost 12.9-kilometer long tunnel. Besides, the confined and dull tunnel environment may make drivers feel tired and directly affect driving safety. Monotony reduces brain activities. When there's a lack of stimuli, the flow coming from the central nerve decreases, and under the interaction with the cerebral cortex, it decreases the layer of activities of the cerebral cortex. This leads to fatigue and driving errors.

This study proposes using wall design to affect the perception and judgments of drivers. Shinar (2002) pointed out that the reaction process of drivers includes attention, visual research, perception and perceptual judgments, judgments and time of judgments, and also the reflexes [1]. Visual perception is the primary way for drivers to gain

© Springer International Publishing Switzerland 2015
Y. Luo (Ed.): CDVE 2015, LNCS 9320, pp. 65–71, 2015.
DOI: 10.1007/978-3-319-24132-6_8

information, with about 90 % of the information relying on visual research and perception; second are the sense of hearing and sensation [2]. When people are driving, their brain and the visual stimuli they receive produce a corresponding relationship. Once the environmental stimuli work, they react to roads, cars, signs, and pedestrians. While people are driving, the sensation of speed is also monitored; they predict how fast they are driving and the degree of the movement of external fixtures. The road landscape refers to the sequential landscape dynamics around us when we drive along the roads. Road landscape is divided into the external and the internal one. It is composed of the central driving area and the natural and artificial landscape beside the road, including the types of roads, structures, signs, close shot and long shot etc. The design of tunnels has become the commonest way to enrich the road landscape. The purpose of this study is to discuss how to make the design of wall pictures efficiently relieve drivers' passive emotions and enhance the positive ones.

The present design of Taiwanese tunnels' walls are signs or pictures in a fixed frequency (like milestones and aboriginal totems) or changes in the pictures on entrances and exits. However, the content and colors of the pictures are not proven to be helpful to road safety. A design for improving drivers' concentration when driving in long tunnels will definitely contribute to road safety. Taiwan's Hsuehshan Tunnel is a representative tunnel in Asia. The purpose of this study is to figure out what kind of design can efficiently reduce drivers' tiredness when driving in a 13-kilometer-long road with an enclosed landscape. This study will be bring in more humanity into Taiwan's road planning and help strike the balance between aesthetics and functions.

2   Method

Three experiments were implemented in this study. The purpose of the first experiment was to understand the emotional changes in drivers when they drive in Hsuehshan Tunnel and evaluate how the current facilities and road types influence the drivers. Ten males and ten females were invited to join the first experiment. They were requested to fill out a checklist of individual strength to evaluate how tired they felt when they were doing the experiment. When the real scene of driving in Hsuehshan Tunnel was being played, participants pressed the counter on the steering wheel according to their anxiety level. The emotional changes were recorded following the time frames and different sections in the tunnel.

In the second experiment, participants with a design background were asked to select several combinations of wall pictures which they considered appropriate for use in the tunnel. The design of tunnel wall pictures showed the tunnel could be divided into four stages: Beginning, Relaying, Transferring, and Concluding (Table 1). Fifteen males and fifteen females who had received professional training in design for more than two years were invited to choose the most appropriate wall pictures for each stage. A hundred kinds of wall picture design were derived from different changes in basic shapes like lines, rectangles, circles, arrows, printed in A1 and A4.

In the third Experiment, the pictures that have been chosen for the most times for each stage from the second experiment were installed into the 3D simulated driving

Table 1. The journey in the tunnel can be divided into four stages [3]

Stage	Distance	Description
Beginning (I)	0 ~ 3 KM	Drivers just enter the tunnel. Their sight transfers from a bright space to a dark space.
Relaying(II)	3 ~ 5 KM	Drivers enter the tunnel for a certain distance and their eyes become accustomed to the tunnel.
Transferring(III)	5 ~ 8 KM	Drivers start to feel bored and annoyed with the tunnel environment. Traffic accidents tend to occur in this stage. It is important to enhance drivers' attention here.
Concluding(IV)	8 ~ 12.9 KM	Drivers look forward to exiting the tunnel.

environment. In total, fourteen males and fourteen females were asked to conduct simulated driving in two tunnel environments; one was the tunnel without any wall pictures, and the other was the tunnel installed with pictures chosen in the second experiment. Participants were asked to describe the pictures, the tunnel environment, and their emotional feelings in full sentences.

3   Results

Results of the First Experiment.   The results showed that over 50 % of the participants noticed there were white wall pictures. A total of 70 % of them noticed color pictures with great contrast on the left wall. Participants felt bored and annoyed when driving straight. The counter was pressed the most often after having travelled for eight kilometers. This was the longest curve in the tunnel. Totally, 25 % of the participants thought they would arrive at the exit after the long curve.

Results of the Second Experiment.   In the beginning stage, most participants chose the picture with brightness change (Fig. 1, stage I). Participants considered brightness change to be identical to the environmental change in this stage. Most participants suggested wall pictures with less provocative changes, that is, linear graphs should be utilized in the beginning stage because drivers jave just entered the tunnel and needed time to become accustomed to the light and spatial pressure of the tunnel. Most participants selected circles with vibration change for the second stage, relaying. Circles placed in different vertical positions created a vibrating rhythm. Drivers felt the balls were jumping up and down in the wall pictures (Fig. 1). In the third stage, transferring, drivers will feel the most annoyed. When the vibration feeling in the second stage gradually faded away, the tiredness of drivers will simultaneously increased. When they found they hadn't arrived at the exit, their disappointment enhanced their felling of irritation. Most participants chose the picture with rectangles and vibration changes (Fig. 1). Rectangles can give drivers feeling of greater steadiness when driving through curves. This visual graph brings audio association to drivers' feelings, simultaneously creating a steady sensation. In the concluding stage (stage IV), participants considered pictures with brightness change to be more suitable. Most of them chose pictures with more brightness changes and with different sized rectangles (Fig. 1). Besides, the pictures in this stage echoed the one in the first stage. This gave drivers a signal that the exit was near, reducing their anxiety and allowing them to prepare for a change in the road landscape in advance.

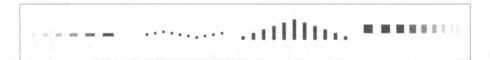

Fig. 1. The Stages I, II, III and IV

Results of the Third Experiment. Each participant experienced two simulated drives: one without wall pictures and the other with the chosen pictures. During the entire process, participants' reports were recorded as follows: reports on environmental changes including pictures' changing and the road environment; reports on participants' emotions including positive emotions, negative emotions, and the sense of speed; reports on easing emotional tension (to ease their mind or change their current behavior). At the end of the experiment, participants estimated the traveling time.

Positive reports occurred only 37 times in the simulated tunnel without pictures. The number of reports climbed up to 88 times in the simulated tunnel with pictures, especially in the beginning stage and the concluding stage. There were 107 negative reports from participants in the tunnel without pictures, whereas there were only 79 times when in the tunnel with pictures. Besides, negative reports were less common at every stage of the journey in the tunnel with pictures than in the one without pictures. Participants' negative emotional reaction began to increase from the second stage (relaying stage) in both two types of simulated driving. They reported the most negative emotional reports in the concluding stage. In addition, there were clearly more reports of an easing of emotional tension in the tunnel with pictures than in the one without pictures. This phenomenon could be seen clearly in the third (transferring) and the fourth (concluding) stage.

All of the participants considered they had travelled for longer time in the tunnel without pictures than in the tunnel with pictures (12.3 min > 8 min on average). It can be concluded that the tunnel with pictures made drivers feel the traveling time was shorter, enhanced positive emotions, and reduced negative emotions.

In the experiment of the tunnel with pictures, it was found reports on environmental changes mostly focused on pictures' changing (76.7 %). The results showed these kinds of reports would occur in ones about emotions. At most stages of the journey, positive reports were greater than negative ones (Fig. 2). The highest number of reports on pictures' changing was for the change of different patterns (27 %). 91.7 % of them were accompanied by positive emotional reports. We could conclude that changing pictures enhanced drivers' positive emotions. Only 28.6 % of all the pattern changes were noticed by the participants. The second highest number of reports on pictures' changing was the change of different colors (23.6 %). In the beginning stage, only a quarter of the participants noticed the change. However, almost half of the participants notice the change in the concluding stage. Thinner lines with brightness change might not be easily noticed when driving.

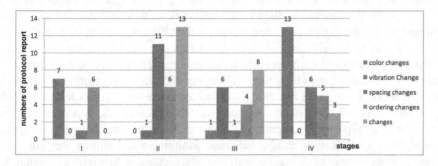

Fig. 2. Drivers' Reports about the Changes of Pictures (Color figure online)

In the relaying stage, participants reported unstructured reports. A quarter of them thought the size of the pictures changed (actually there were no such changes in this stage). We could conclude that most participants did not recognize the picture was "a vibrating wave with circles." They could only know there were dots irregularly drawn on the wall. When the pictures are displayed in a messy way, drivers will have difficulty understanding the order of the pictures. This could explain why, of the four stages, negative reports were greater than positive ones only in the relaying stage.

In the transferring stage, the vibration changes were the most noticeable. A quarter of the participants noted there were vibration changes in the pictures. Besides, in all stages of the experiment, there were one-fifth of participants considered the pictures were changed in a regular frequency. This showed that these participants noticed there were basic graphs appearing repeatedly and they recognized the basic rule of the pictures' changing. Participants found that the changing rules for the pictures were not easily recognized only in the second (relaying) stage, thus causing many negative emotions. When being asked about the sense of speed, 40 % of participants felt the speed was higher in the second (relaying) stage. This is the only stage where the circles and vibration changes were used as the wall pictures. The rhythm created from the graphs' jumping up and down indeed made drivers feel their speed had increased.

4 Discussion

In the first experiment, most participants noticed white blocks on the left wall, but almost none of them noticed the mileposts of the tunnel on the right side. Obviously the vision of drivers will be distracted by the graphs on the left hand side. It was found that drivers feel bored and annoyed when driving straight. A common driving experience the participants shared was changes in road characteristics will foretell a new environment. Although Hsuehshan Tunnel will not end directly after the curve, some changes in the environment within the tunnel may help to reduce negative emotions. The second

Experiment showed that when the participants with the expertise in design training chose suitable graphs, they considered how the graphs would fit with the changes in the environment in the tunnel. They choose pictures with brightness changes for the first stage (beginning) and the fourth stage (concluding). This kind of pictures informs drivers the environment is going to change from bright to dark (in the beginning stage) and from dark to bright (in the concluding stage). They will indicate that the environment is going to change, so drivers can prepare themselves for the changes, such as turning on headlights. In the third experiment, each participant experienced driving simulations: one without wall pictures and the other with chosen pictures. The results clearly showed the tunnel environment with wall pictures effectively enhanced the positive emotions of drivers, reduced the negative emotions, and shortened the time drivers felt they would spend in the tunnel. When the pictures changed, drivers noticed the appearance of new pictures and they reported many positive comments. Changing the pictures at an appropriate frequency needs to be considered when arranging wall pictures. Regarding the effects of different types of changes in wall pictures, pictures with brightness change are the most easily noticed. Although this kind of change was used in the first stage (beginning) and the last stage (concluding), drivers didn't notice the brightness change in the first stage where the pictures were drawn in thinner lines. In the concluding stage, graphs like blocks were used and added with brightness change, making the pictures more noticeable. Vibrating waves with circles will make drivers feel they are moving at a higher speed, whereas pictures with vertical lines make them feel they are slowing down. The change in pictures' length (from long to short and pictures turning from a dark into light color) will have a visual effect where the space is compressed, making drivers have felling of greater speed (Fig. 3). The results pointed out that drivers reported more negative responses than positive ones toward picture's changing only in the second stage (relaying). Drivers understood the rules of wall pictures in the beginning, transferring, and concluding stages. They pointed out that wall pictures in the beginning and concluding stages were changing in colors, while it was vibration changes that were used in the transferring stage. In the relaying stage, most drivers could not understand the underlying principle of the changes.

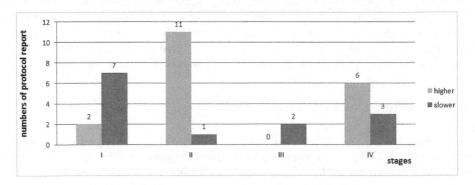

Fig. 3. The Sense of Speed in Four Stages (Color figure online)

5   Conclusions

Wall pictures and mileposts should be on the same side, so they can be seen by drivers at the same time. When there will be significant changes in the road environment, especially lasting for a long time, changing pictures or emphasizing mileposts are suggested to be used to fit the environmental changes. In addition to environmental changes and drivers' emotions, how pictures will change when moving and drivers' perspectives should both be taken into considered when choosing wall pictures. Changes in wall pictures should be appropriately utilized to enhance drivers' positive emotions. Pictures with brightness change have better effects. Larger color blocks to present brightness and color changes are suggested. Using the visual effect created by changing pictures is a good way to alter drivers' subjective feelings of speed. The rules of pictures' changes should be able to be recognized by drivers. Pictures lacking a good order will result in negative responses.

References

1. Ben-Yaacov, A., Maltz, M., Shinar, D.: Effects of an in-vehicle collision, avoidance warning system on short and long-time driving performance. Hum. Fact. **44**, 335–342 (2002)
2. Hills, B.L.: Vision, visibility, and perception in driving. Perception **9**, 183–216 (1980)
3. Nagami, Y., Nagata, Y.: A study on applying repetition effect to motorway scenery: pattern design on tunnel wall not to let drivers get tired. In: The 56th Annual Conference of JSSD, Session: P16 (2009)

Towards an Implementable Aesthetic Measure for Collaborative Architecture Design

Agnieszka Mars[(⊠)] and Ewa Grabska

Faculty of Physics, Astronomy and Applied Computer Science,
Jagiellonian University, Kraków, Poland
{agnieszka.mars,ewa.grabska}@uj.edu.pl

Abstract. This paper aims to present how hitherto existing aesthetic measure approaches could be enriched by contemporary perception models, which would be useful in computer aided design of architecture. Proposed measure allows designers for collaborative decision making to find an average aesthetic value.

Keywords: Aesthetic measure · Computer aided design · Collaborative design

1 Introduction

Although aesthetics in architecture design has been discussed since ancient times, nowadays it confronts a relatively new challenge – computational design. This paper aims to present how hitherto existing aesthetic measure approaches could be enriched by contemporary perception models, which would be useful in computer aided design of architecture. Birkhoff aesthetic measure adapted for 3D objects is confronted with Biederman's structural object representation and complexity perception theories. In result, modification in computing aesthetic value of architecture is proposed. The measure's components are defined in order to improve collaborative design and find a compromise between different approaches to aesthetic evaluation.

2 Birkhoff Aesthetic Measure

George D. Birkhoff was the first who defined measure of aesthetic experiences in a formal way [1]. He proposed the following formula: M (measure) = O (order)/C (complexity), and precisely developed it for different kinds of aesthetic experiences, among others human perception of polygonal forms. The aesthetic measure for polygons describes order as a composition of the following elements: vertical symmetry, equilibrium, rotational symmetry, relation to a horizontal-vertical network, and unsatisfactory form, whereas complexity is determined by a number of straight lines containing polygon's edges.

This measure extended to 3D objects – polyhedrons can be useful for architecture [2]. It is worth noticing that Birkhoff measure doesn't pay attention to the length of planes or lines, so directions of the main component are treated equally to directions of minor components. Moreover, limitation to polygonal or polyhedronal forms excludes more complex objects, which have a significant role in architecture design, and

© Springer International Publishing Switzerland 2015
Y. Luo (Ed.): CDVE 2015, LNCS 9320, pp. 72–75, 2015.
DOI: 10.1007/978-3-319-24132-6_9

complexity of Birkhoff's measure always decreases the result of formula when order is greater than 0. This may be a too radical approach, because complexity brings information important for viewer's cognitive satisfaction. According to Biederman's and Vessel's research [3], a human brain is provided with a mechanism that rewards us for gathering information about the environment. Although complex objects are often regarded as discouraging, it is comprehension that is crucial in stimuli preference, and when an object is possible to understand, its novelty transforms from a disadvantage into positive quality [4].

3 Modifications According to Biederman's RBC Theory

Considering described remarks about Birkhoff's definition of complexity, its modification in order to improve adequacy of solids' assessment seems necessary. Because aesthetic measure by definition must indicate human preferences, it is obvious that it is the human visual system and its way of data processing that should be taken into account when thinking of visual complexity.

In 1987 Biederman proposed a model of visual perception [5] based on Marr's view-independent theory. According to Biederman's concept, images processed by a human brain consist of basic elements in a similar way to speech consist of phonemes. Such primitive components – geons (for "geometrical icons") and a set of relations between them constitute an alphabet for more complex objects.

Dividing a solid into Biederman's geons may be a good idea for representing aesthetic language of architecture, because not only does it make possible to determine the number of components, which is crucial for complexity assessment, but it also enables investigation of relations between them. This approach can be combined with Birkhoff's measure adapted to 3D-objects, which appears as a proper basic formula due to its definition, concerning aspects coherent with a common idea of harmony and beauty in architecture (like symmetry or equilibrium). In order to make this measure more adequate to human preferences according to contemporary concepts of cognition the following modifications are proposed:

1. Basic components extraction – as mentioned, the process of perception may require division of an object's form into elementary shapes.
2. Considering geons' size – ornaments composed of significantly smaller geons have less influence of observer's impression.
3. Considering a positive side of complexity – Birkhoff's measure defines aesthetic value as a ratio of the pleasure gained from perceiving a piece of art to the cost of data processing. Dividing the idea of complexity into two aspects – a positive and a negative one – will reduce the problem of unwanted decrease of complex objects' measure. The positive complexity should be defined by the number of ordered geons, whereas the negative one should include a total number of geons, as well as their complexity and number of geon types. This approach will value complex, well ordered forms, but also won't neglect the cost of perception.
4. Order as a set of relations between components – basing on the Birkhoff's definition of order, we can determine the following relations: partial, composed by subsets of

geons - vertical symmetry, rotational symmetry and relation to a h-v network, as well as equilibrium and satisfactory form, which must refer to the whole object. Birkhoff considered number of directions as an indicator of complexity – the smaller this number, the greater the final aesthetic value of an object. Instead, we propose a new type of relation, alignment, and count geons aligned to the common plane. This solution will work for all types of geons, like sphere or cone, not only for polyhedrons as it currently is. From two objects of the same ratio of ordered to unordered geons, the one with a greater total number of geons should be valued more (greater amount of information is preferred). Relations of order should be defined as functions of geons number, where the following dependency occurs: f(a) + f(b) < f(a + b), where f is a relation, and a, b numbers of its elements. This will prevent a situation like when a symmetrical object is valued less than an asymmetrical one composed of several symmetrical parts.

Regarding the described requirements, we propose a formula M of aesthetic measure, in which importance of particular components depends on relevant ratios c that should be determined as an average of the constants ranging from 0 to 1. These constants should proposed by designers involved in collaborative work, who may value each of the components differently. The definition of the formula is as follows:

$$M = \frac{A + V + R + H + E + F}{T + X + G}, \text{ where:}$$

- alignment $A = c_A \sum_{i=1}^{n_A} k_i^2$, $2 \leq i \leq n_A$, where k_i is a number of geons aligned to one plane or line, and n_A is a number of relations of alignment between object's geons (i.e., a number of different planes and lines geons are aligned to);

- vertical symmetry $V = c_V \sum_{i=1}^{n_V} k_i^2$, and k_i, $1 \leq i \leq n_V$ is a number of geons composing one vertically symmetrical part of an object, where n_V is a number of relations of vertical symmetry between object's geons (i.e., a number of different vertical axes of symmetry in an object);

- rotational symmetry $R = c_R \sum_{i=1}^{n_R} k_i^2$, and k_i, $1 \leq i \leq n_R$ is a number of geons composing one rotationally symmetrical part of an object, where n_R is a number of relations of rotational symmetry between object's geons (i.e., a number of different axes of rotational symmetry in an object);

- relation to the horizontal-vertical network $H = c_H\, l$, and l is a number of geons that can fitted to the horizontal-vertical network;

- equilibrium E, a constant value indicating whether an object's equilibrium fulfills Birkhoff's conditions;

- satisfactory form F, a constant value indicating whether object's form fulfills Birkhoff's conditions of unsatisfactory form. Contrary to Birkhoff's definition, this value should be positive if the condition of Birkhoff's unsatisfactory form isn't fulfilled. This will prevent a situation, when an order value is negative and the complexity level increases it instead of decreasing;

- number of geon types $T = c_T m$, and m is a number of different geon types an object is built of;
- complexity of geons $X = c_x z$, and z is a sum a sum of each geon's complexity, regarding that geon's complexity is a constant value dependent of its type;
- number of geons $G = c_G n$, and n is a number of geons an object is built of.

We assume that in each case where geons number is considered, significantly smaller geons (ornaments) are counted as 0.1.

4 Conclusions

Biederman's visual perception theory can positively influence computer aided design of architecture, especially when combined with other cognitive models of complexity and order. Computational aesthetic measure should regard contemporary approach to the perception of art, although former achievements in this area are still worth consideration. Birkhoff's measure adapted for 3D objects would perform more accurately after extracting object's basic elements (geons) in order to assess its complexity and investigate relations between components.

References

1. Birkhoff, G.D.: Aesthetic Measure. Harvard University Press, Cambridge (1933)
2. Tarko, J., Grabska, E.: Aesthetic measure for three-dimensional objects. Mach. Graph. Vision **20**(4), 439–454 (2011)
3. Biederman, I., Vessel, E.A.: Perceptual pleasure and the brain. Am. Sci. **94**, 249–255 (2006)
4. Wallendorf, M., Zinkhan, G., Zinkhan, L.S.: Cognitive complexity and aesthetic preference. In: Hirschman, E.C., Holbrook, M.B. (eds.) SV - Symbolic Consumer Behavior, pp. 52–59. Association for Consumer Research, New York (1981)
5. Biederman, I.: Recognition-by-components: a theory of human image understanding. Psychol. Rev. **94**, 115–147 (1987)

Cooperative Monitoring of the Delivery of Fresh Products

Sandra Sendra[1(✉)], Jaime Lloret[1], Raquel Lacuesta[2], and Jose Miguel Jimenez[1]

[1] Universitat Politècnica de Valencia, Valencia, Spain
sansenco@posgrado.upv.es,
{jlloret,jojiher}@dcom.upv.es
[2] Escuela Politécnica Superior de Teruel, Universidad de Zaragoza,
Saragossa, Spain
lacuesta@unizar.es

Abstract. The proper transport of hit sensitive products, such as fish and fruit, is very important because their deterioration may cause the value lost and even the product rejection by the buyer. For this reason, in this paper we present a cooperative monitoring system for the delivery of fresh products. The system consists of fixed wireless nodes and a mobile wireless node that is installed in the packet. This mobile node is able to take data of the internal temperature, external temperature and the 3 axis movement. With the information stored in the network, a vendor can know the optimal conditions of the transport. Finally, we test the maximum distance to the fixed nodes, as well as the data collected by the sensor.

Keywords: Cooperative monitoring · WSN · Delivery · Fresh products

1 Introduction

Our current consumer society works in a global environment. Companies and individuals acquire more and more products anywhere in the world. There are multiple patents and proposals about systems for tracking and delivering packets. For example, Michigan Versus Technology, Inc. [1] proposed a real-time method for locating a mobile object or person in a tracking environment and R. Witmond et al. presented a method for tracking a mail piece [2] which introduced a system and process for verifying the status of a mail piece in an email stream. For this reason, currently, there are lots of systems and technologies used to locate a packet. Among them, we can find active and passive RFID systems, WiFi, Global Position Systems (GPS), Infrared, and Bluetooth, although, the most commonly used technology for locating objects is RFID. This kind of technology is being widely investigated, mainly in security [3] and protocol performance [4]. Scanning an object equipped with an RFID target can provide a variety of data including the manufacturer, item information, its path to get to the store, and almost any other relevant data. However, this information is not currently being used for any other purpose. GPS also assists in determining the location. However, the detail of the movement is still not generally monitored. Sometimes, the object

© Springer International Publishing Switzerland 2015
Y. Luo (Ed.): CDVE 2015, LNCS 9320, pp. 76–86, 2015.
DOI: 10.1007/978-3-319-24132-6_10

contained inside a packet is broken. This indicates that it has suffered a hit or an incorrect handling. However, it is not possible to know when and where the hit happened. Finally, the conditions in which a packet, with a special transport conditions, should be prepared is also a problem. Normally, when a packed of fresh products like fruits or fish is transported, the product must be refrigerated or covered with ice. Wireless sensor networks (WSN) can help to solve this problem. It is widely known the wide range of applications where a WSN can be applied [5–7]. Moreover, if we were capable of relating the environmental conditions with the transportation features, we would be able to use the resources more efficiently. But this kind of decisions can only be made if we have lot of information from systems with similar characteristics. It is known as collaborative decisions [8, 9].

In this paper, we propose a WSN composed by both mobile and fixed nodes that tracks the position and monitors the packet status. In addition, the system has been developed to fuse the information provided by professionals and business owners who work with fresh products such as fruit and fish. The system uses Zigbee technology, which network nodes are distributed over a city, allowing end users and vendors controlling the progress of the package as well as the conditions of internal and external temperature and if it has had any hit. Initially, the company sending the product adds some data about the product (size, level of fragility, etc.), then the sensors include the information provided by the transported packets.

The rest of this paper is structured as follows. Section 2 shows some systems developed to track packets. The description of the system and the used hardware arc shown in Sect. 3. Section 4 shows real measurements of maximum distances from the fixed nodes to the mobile node in real environments and how nodes collect data form the sensors. The collaborative algorithm for combining the data of nodes is shown in Sect. 5. Finally, conclusion and future work are shown in Sect. 6.

2 Related Work

This section presents some interesting works related to prototypes and platforms for tracking packets [10].

C.A. Vock, presented in [7] a system aimed to sense and report events associated with the movement, environmental factors such as temperature, health functions, fitness effects, and changing conditions. They developed a movement monitor device (MMD) including an adhesive strip, a processor, a detector, and a communication port. The detector was an accelerometer. The MMD included a battery and a real-time clock so that the MMD tags the events with time and date information. MMD could practically be attached to almost any object to obtain movement information and monitoring among other aspects: impacts, accelerations, rotations, altitude variation, etc.

R. Jedermann et al. [8] presented a reduced scale prototype of an autonomous transport monitoring system. Authors tested the application of KQ-Models for quality supervision of tomatoes. The reduced scale prototype demonstrated that it is feasible to integrate a real-time supervision system into standard reefer trucks or containers. The information to select the appropriate model was stored in a standard RFID tag that was attached to the freight item. A software agent provided the freight operator with an estimation of the keeping quality and updated the estimation only to prevent data transmission costs.

D. Ko et al. [9] presented an architecture to monitor and track the yields and distribution of agricultural products with WSN techniques. The work explained the sensor nodes, communication hubs, the communication protocol, and an event detection engine. The event detection engine detected events by using the location of each sensor node, previous events and registered places. Authors concluded that adding other sensors such as temperature, humidity, the area of application could be extended.

In [10], authors explored the potential of wireless sensor technology for monitoring fruit storage and transport conditions. They studied the feasibility of using two types of wireless nodes (Xbee and Xbow). They stated that the performance of this kind of systems could be improved by the implementation of advanced network topologies, such as point-to-multipoint, peer-to-peer and mesh, improving the reliability and robustness of the system.

A. Shamsuzzoha et al. [11] presented an overall approach to track in real-time the delivery shipment from the starting point to the end customer. The paper discussed and analyzed the outcomes from the case project to be useful for tracking needs. They considered the operational ways of the tracking devices in respect to frequency of data transfer, interpretation of the data in a usable format, specification of the tracking devices (battery life, power consumption, data roaming, etc.), essential programming for the devices, etc., with the view to implement the tracking technology on delivery networks.

All these systems are focused on the tagging or tracking of packets, which can be useful even in emergency and rescue scenarios [12], but none of them try to know the packet status. In addition, they do not take into account the data gathered from the network to improve conditions for subsequent shipments and to make a more efficient use of the available resources.

3   System Description and Used Hardware

This section presents our systems and the hardware used to implement it. The system is based on a wireless network using IEEE 802.15.4 standard, which is able to transmit the information about the packet status and how the distributors and vendors can cooperatively contribute to update the information of the ambient temperature for preparing their orders of fresh products.

3.1   System Description

The main aim of this system is the cooperative monitoring of fresh products such as fish, shellfish or fresh fruit to be transported carefully in order to avoid damaging the product by hits or temperature changes and keep well conserved for its consumption. We propose a communication architecture based on a wireless ad hoc network to extend the communication along the city. Devices of the network are deployed using a Waspmote node and a wireless XBee Pro module [13]. The packet of fresh products is equipped with the Waspmote node and a temperature sensor. This node communicates with fixed nodes that are scattered around the city. While the packet is transported, the node sends the packet status information (packet movement and inner temperature) and the environmental temperature to the fixed nodes. At the same time, vendors, distributors and even end buyers can check the package status and include any external parameter such as the delivery time, or any type of threshold in the temperature or the movement. This information can be accessed at any time by distributors and vendors of fresh products when they are sending them to the restaurants and shops. Using this information, they can prepare the packets in the right way to make an efficient use of the resources, such as the amount of ice used to keep fish cold and properly program the temperature of the refrigerated vehicles. In this way, users update the information available in the network and they can use this useful information to prepare their own orders (See Fig. 1). End buyers can track and monitor the packet only accessing through Internet and check at any time if the packet has suffered a hit or the content has experienced excessive temperature change.

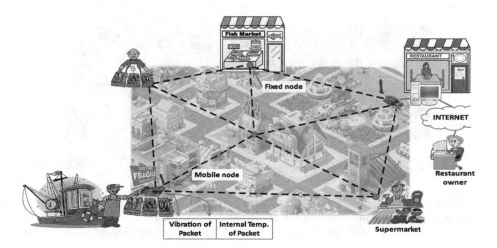

Fig. 1. Network architecture in a real application

3.2   Used Hardware

Libelium Waspmote with the Xbee-pro Module [13] (Fig. 2a) is a device designed to create wireless sensor networks with some quite specific requirements and intended to be deployed in a real scenario. Libelium Waspmote can be seen as an evolution of other devices such as Arduino, which is usually used in school settings. It has a consumption of 0.7 μA in sleep mode and seven different models of radios that can be chosen according to the frequency and the transmission power. According to its specifications, Waspmote should reach up to one mile working at 2.4 GHz and 63 mW of transmission power. In addition, Waspmote module has an integrated 3-axis accelerometer which allows real-time monitoring of the Waspmote movements or vibration. Finally, the module is powered with a lithium battery that can be recharged via a connector prepared for solar panel. This option is especially interesting for deployments in natural and rural environments such as forests and crop fields.

3.3 Sensor of the Internal Temperature of the Packet

In order to detect the internal temperature of the packet, we will use a small NTC (Negative Temperature Coefficient) thermistor (See Fig. 2b). A thermistor is a resistive temperature sensor. Its operation is based on the variation of the semiconductor having a resistive value as a function of the temperature. The operation is based on the variation of the semiconductor resistance due to the change of the ambient temperature, creating a variation in the carrier concentration. In NTC thermistors, when temperature increases, the carrier concentration also increases, so that resistance is lower. Hence the coefficient is negative. Resistance variation is not linear with the temperature. A NTC thermistor presents a hyperbolic behavior, i.e., for small temperature rise, a large resistance rise is obtained.

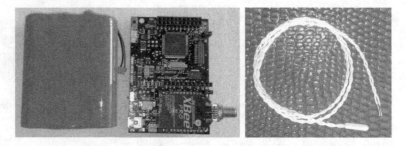

Fig. 2. (a) Zigbee module, (b) sensor of internal temperature

To acquire the temperature value, we only need to read the value from an analog input with the command "*int VAL1 = analogRead(ANALOG1);*". With this command, the Waspmote reads the input identified as ANALOG1 and stores its value in the variable VAL1.

3.4 Algorithm for Collaborative Monitoring

Finally, the system needs an algorithm to exchange data between fixed nodes and network users [14] in order to combine them and estimate the transport parameters.

As Fig. 3 shows, the system takes data from a database (DB) that stores the data provided by the fixed nodes and the users of the network, i.e., vendors, distributors and end users. The wireless sensor node gathers the transport parameters, such as transport temperature threshold, maximum delivery time, maximum movement of the packet, etc., and monitors them during the delivery time. Sensor node installed in the packet periodically saves data. If parameters are stable, the system will wait till the packet reaches its destination to send the collected data to the DB. If a sensor detects a sudden change, the system sends an alarm message to the vendor and the buyer with information about the event happened and the position where it occurred.

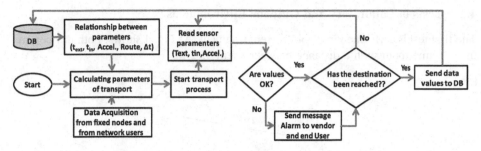

Fig. 3. Smart algorithm for collaborative monitoring.

4 Distances in Real Scenarios

To determine the number of devices needed to cover a particular area, the actual device performance and its maximum radio coverage must be measured. In order to perform, these tests we selected two scenarios. The first test is performed in a laboratory environment. For the second tests, we selected several locations in an urban environment. On the one hand, we have selected 2 cases where there are objects like buildings and vegetation where there are objects that interfere with the line of sight between the transmitter and receiver. On the other hand, we have also checked a case where transmitter and receiver are in the line of sight without objects that interference the transmission. All tests are performed in real scenarios.. This section shows the theoretical values and the scenario where tests are performed. Finally, the results of these tests are shown.

4.1 Theoretical Values of XBee-PRO

Waspmote official specification details that the coverage range of XBee-Pro IEEE 802.15.4 is about 1,600 m when the transmitter and receiver are in the line of sight. Table 1 shows the theoretical values.

Normally, in indoors the main problems of signal losses are generated by walls and the signal reflections on them. In outdoors, the presence of buildings, vegetation and adverse weather conditions are the main causes that generates losses in signal.

Table 1. Summary of results

Parameter	Value
Antenna	5 dBi
Power output	10 mW
Indoor/Urban range	Up to 300 ft (90 m)
Outdoor/RF line-of-sight range	Up to 1 mile (1.6 km) RF LOS
RF data rate	250 Kbps

4.2   Tests in Laboratory and Outdoor Environments

The first test is performed in laboratory environment. As Fig. 4 shows, both devices are in the same room with a distance between them of 2 m.

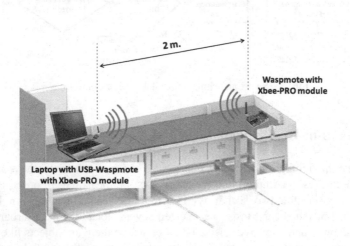

Fig. 4. Scenario of tests in indoors.

We also tested 2 different scenarios in outdoors. Tests were conducted in open field in the city Teruel, Spain. Figure 5 shows the 3 tests performed in an area where builds and vegetation can interference the signal. Figure 6 shows a scenario where the sight between both transmitter and receiver is not interfered by any object.

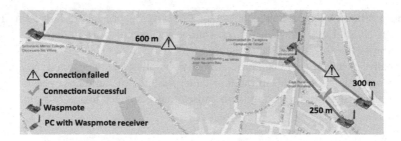

Fig. 5. First test of maximum distances

To perform these tests, we have used 3 different Waspmotes transmitting messages of 8 and 32 characters, during 5 min.

After completing different communication tests at different distances and conditions, we can conclude that the theoretical maximum distances of the Waspmote is not accurate. Moreover, as Fig. 6 shows, we can get maximum distances of 450 m when there is a free line of sight between the transmitter and the receiver. However, in an

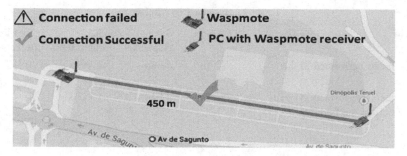

Fig. 6. Second test of maximum distances

environment where there are obstacles and buildings, we have not reached distances larger than 250 m (See Fig. 5).

Finally, we performed various tests related to the transmission time between the sender and the receiver. The first scenario is a laboratory where the distance between transmitter and receiver is 2 m. Second test was performed in an open air having a distance of 250 m between the transmitter and the receiver. We also use 2 types of messages, i.e., 8-characters and 32-characters packets. Figure 7 shows the transmission time for both scenarios.

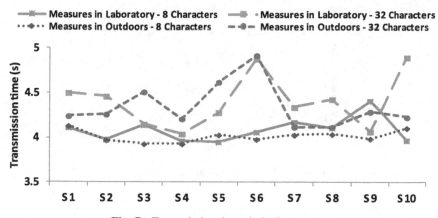

Fig. 7. Transmission times in both scenarios

As we can see, in both cases the transmission time is around 4 s. When transmission is performed with a 32-characters message, the transmission time is slightly higher than the transmission time of an 8-characters message. Table 2 shows the average time values for both scenarios and the number of lost packets. As we can see, the transmission time is not proportional to the distance between transmitter and receiver. However, the number of lost packets when transmitting at 250 m is 90 %.

Table 2. Summary of results

Scenario	Distance	8 characters	32 characters	% of lost packets
Measurements performed in the laboratory	2 m	4.086 s	4.405 s	0 %
Measurements performed in open space outside the building	250 m	4.014 s	4.352 s	90 %

5   Data Sensor Measurements

This section shows the measures gathered by a Waspmote placed inside a packet. To perform this test, we have prepared a packet with the Zigbee module and the temperature sensor. The packet has been monitored during 2 min and a half.

Figures 8, 9 and 10 show the data recorded by the accelerometer on its X-axis, Y-axis, and Z-axis respectively. One of the most important parameters to be controlled in our system is the internal temperature of the packet. Figure 11 shows the outside temperature (taken by the node board) and the internal temperature of the packet (taken with the NTC). The value of the NTC is collected through one of the analog inputs. As we can see, in both cases the temperature remains virtually constant at 25 °C (outside temperature) and 8.1 °C (internal temperature).

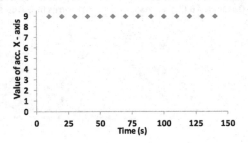

Fig. 8. X-Axis values of the accelerometer

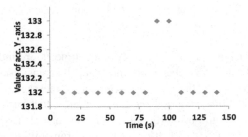

Fig. 9. Y-Axis values of the accelerometer

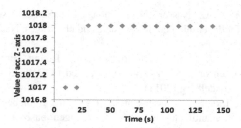

Fig. 10. Z-Axis values of the accelerometer

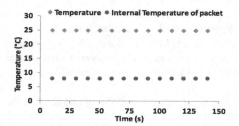

Fig. 11. Values of temperature.

6 Conclusion and Future Work

In this paper, we have presented a cooperative monitoring system for fresh products. Mobile and fixed nodes use Zigbee technology. The paper has presented the architecture design, as well as the different test bench performed in real scenarios. In addition, we have explained the smart algorithm where thanks to the data stored in the network and data provided by users, we can make more efficient decisions.

As future work, we would like to integrate secure mechanisms to make our infrastructure more reliable and secure, as well as add an energy harvesting system [15]. Moreover, we are going to extend it using group-based topologies [16].

References

1. Derks, H.G., Buehler, W.S., Hall, M.B.: Real-time method and system for locating a mobile object or person in a tracking environment. US Patent 8514071 B2, 20 August 2013
2. Witmond, R., Dutta, R., Charroppin, P.: Method for tracking a mail piece. US Patent 7003376 B2, 21 February 2006
3. Lu, L., Liu, Y., Han, J.: ACTION: breaking the privacy barrier for RFID systems. Ad Hoc Sens. Wirel. Netw. 24(1–2), 135–159 (2015)
4. Dhakal, S., Shin, S.: Precise time system efficiency of a frame slotted aloha based anti-collision algorithm in a RFID system. Netw. Protoc. Algorithms 5(2), 16–27 (2013)
5. Garcia, M., Bri, D., Sendra, S., Lloret, J.: Practical deployments of wireless sensor networks: a survey. Int. J. Adv. Netw. Serv. 3(1&2), 163–178 (2010)
6. Bri, D., Garcia, M., Lloret, J., Dini, P.: Real deployments of wireless sensor networks. In: Third International Conference on Sensor Technologies and Applications (SENSORCOMM 2009), Athens, Greece, 18–23 June 2009, pp. 415–423

7. Karim, L., Anpalagan, A., Nasser, N., Almhana, J.: Sensor-based M2M agriculture monitoring systems for developing countries: state and challenges. Netw. Protoc. Algorithms **5**(3), 68–86 (2013)
8. Garcia, M., Lloret, J., Sendra, S., Rodrigues, J.J.: Taking cooperative decisions in group-based wireless sensor networks. In: Luo, Y. (ed.) CDVE 2011. LNCS, vol. 6874, pp. 61–65. Springer, Heidelberg (2011)
9. Garcia-Sabater, J.P., Lloret, J., Marin-Garcia, J.A., Puig-Bernabeu, X.: Coordinating a cooperative automotive manufacturing network – an agent-based model. In: Luo, Y. (ed.) CDVE 2010. LNCS, vol. 6240, pp. 231–238. Springer, Heidelberg (2010)
10. Li, J., Cao, J.: Survey of object tracking in wireless sensor networks. Netw. Protoc. Algorithms **25**(1–2), 89–120 (2015)
11. Vock, C.A., Larkin, A.F., Amsbury, B.W., Youngs, P.: Device for monitoring movement of shipped goods. U.S. Patent 8,280,682, 2 October 2012
12. Jedermann, R., Schouten, R., Sklorz, A., Lang, W., Van Kooten, O.: Linking keeping quality models and sensor systems to an autonomous transport supervision system. In: The 2nd International Workshop Cold Chain Management, Bonn, Germany, 8–9 May 2006, pp. 3–18
13. Ko, D., Kwak, Y., Song, S.: Real time traceability and monitoring system for agricultural products based on wireless sensor network. Int. J. Distrib. Sens. Netw. **2014**, 1–7 (2014). Article ID 832510
14. Ruiz-Garcia, L., Barreiro, P., Robla, J.I.: Performance of ZigBee-based wireless sensor nodes for real-time monitoring of fruit logistics. J. Food Eng. **87**(3), 405–415 (2008)
15. Shamsuzzoha, A., Addo-Tenkorang, R., Phuong, D., Helo, P.: Logistics tracking: an implementation issue for delivery network. In: PICMET 2011Conference Technology Management in the Energy Smart World, Portland, Oregon, USA, July 31–August 4 2011, pp. 1–10
16. Torres, R.V., Sanchez, J.C., Galan, L.M.: Unmarked point and adjacency vertex, mobility models for the generation of emergency and rescue scenarios in urban areas. Ad Hoc Sens. Wirel. Netw. **23**(3–4), 211–233 (2014)
17. Waspmote features. In Digi Web Site. http://www.digi.com/products/wireless-wired-embedded-solutions/zigbee-rf-modules/point-multipoint-rfmodules/xbee-series1-module#specs. Accessed 18 April 2015
18. Meghanathan, N., Mumford, P.: Centralized and distributed algorithms for stability-based data gathering in mobile sensor networks. Netw. Protoc. Algorithms **5**(4), 84–116 (2013)
19. Alrajeh, N.A., Khan, S., Lloret, J., Loo, J.: Artificial neural network based detection of energy exhaustion attacks in wireless sensor networks capable of energy harvesting. Ad Hoc Sens. Wirel. Netw. **22**(3–4), 109–133 (2014)
20. Garcia, M., Sendra, S., Lloret, J., Canovas, A.: Saving energy and improving communications using cooperative group-based wireless sensor networks. Telecommun. Syst. **52**(4), 2489–2502 (2013)

Evaluating a Micro-payment System
for Mobile Electronic Commence

Xiaodi Huang[1], Xiaoling Dai[1], Edwin Singh[2], and Weidong Huang[3(✉)]

[1] Charles Sturt University, Albury, Australia
{xhuang,sdai}@csu.edu.au
[2] University of the South Pacific, Suva, Fiji
singh_edwin@yahoo.com
[3] University of Tasmania, Hobart, Australia
tony.huang@utas.edu.au

Abstract. As an increasing number of people use wireless communication to purchase goods and services, we have developed a new micropayment system called M&E-NetPay for mobile electronic commerce. This system has open interoperability and mobility, uses Web services to inter-connect brokers and vendors, and provides secure, flexible, usable, and reliable credit services over the Internet. M&E-NetPay makes use of a secure, cheap, available, and debit-based off-line protocol that allows vendors to interact only with customers after an initial validation of coins. To validate the system, we have conducted an evaluation of the system performance. The results demonstrate that by using fast hashing functions that validate e-coin unspent indexes, M&E-NetPay achieves secure transactions with a high volume per item. It was also confirmed that the .Net framework architecture 4.0 with Web Services used in M&E-NetPay improves client-to-server communications, leading to high system performance. We report on this evaluation in this paper.

Keywords: Mobile and electronic commerce · Micro-payment · Web services · Electronic wallet · Mobile networks

1 Introduction

Due to the exponential growth of the number of Internet users, and repaid advancement of wireless communication technologies, mobile commerce has quickly become a hot topic in the research community [1]. It enables high-volume, low-cost-per-item transactions. As a result, a number of micro-payment systems have been developed supporting vendors and customers to conduct business activities over the Internet [7, 8]. In these systems, customers are engaged in the formal banking sector. Banks are able to provide services to customers. Vendors make great sales of goods and services without extra costs. On behalf of banks, micro-finance institutions (i.e. broker) provide services to customers such as managing their bank accounts and facilitating micro-payments across multiple vendors.

© Springer International Publishing Switzerland 2015
Y. Luo (Ed.): CDVE 2015, LNCS 9320, pp. 87–92, 2015.
DOI: 10.1007/978-3-319-24132-6_11

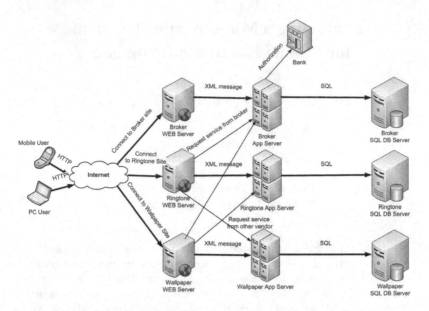

Fig. 1. Basic M&E-NetPay deployment architecture

One of big challenges for micro-payment systems is that e-coins should be allowed to spend at a wide range of vendors. Micro-payment systems should enable mobile users to leverage buy-once-spend-(almost) anywhere behaviour. Another challenge is the minimization of overheads on the servers of the sites of the brokers and vendors.

To address these challenges, we have developed M&E-NetPay. Figure 1 shows the basic M&E-NetPay deployment architecture of the system. It has following features:

1. M&E-NetPay uses Web Service interfaces as a middleware for interconnecting the sites of brokers and vendors. Web Service interfaces simplify the transferring e-coins among vendors. E-coins in M&E-NetPay are easily transferred between multiple vendors so that M&E users can make multiple purchases.
2. M&E-NetPay is a fully distributed multi-tier system deployed over several servers. It is able to achieve minimal downtime and maximal competence. The .Net framework architecture 4.0 with Web Services in M&E-NetPay improves client-to-server communications, greatly improving the system performance.
3. The architecture with Web services provides a fast, secure, and cheap communications amongst mobile users and vendor systems. In addition, the M&E-NetPay architecture also supports servers running on different platforms and vendor applications developed using different programming languages. This allows an M&E-NetPay-enabled vendor to act as a purchasing portal for existing non-M&E-NetPay supporting vendors.

M&E-NetPay evolves from NetPay [2], which is an off-line micro-payment system using a secure, cheap, and debit-based protocol. M&E-NetPay replaces the CORBA middleware of NetPay with Web Services, which provide the interoperability (i.e. platform-independent and language-independent). The web services is an emerging distributed middleware technique that uses a simple XML based protocol and SOAP, and allows applications to exchange data over the Web [3]. This new technique manoeuvres openness of specific Internet technologies to address many interoperability issues of CORBA.

In this paper, we report on an evaluation of M&E-NetPay. The purpose of the evaluation was to examine whether the system had achieved our design goals, particularly on system performance. In what follows, we describe the evaluation design in Sect. 2, followed by the results presented in Sect. 3. In Sect. 4, we briefly discuss the findings with future work.

2   Experimental Design

Rowley [4] and Sumak et al. [5] conducted comprehensive reviews of e-service evaluation frameworks. Based on their work, we compare the performance of the M&E-NetPay prototype against that of the CORBA-based NetPay system in terms of user response time. This evaluation aims to compare how long it takes to download wallpapers in the two different payment systems.

System Setup: M&E-NetPay was deployed over three servers:

- Web Server hosts the presentation layer
- Application Server hosts Web Services, business logic components and data adapter layer
- Database Server hosts the relational database

And the CORBA-based NetPay system was deployed over three servers:

- Web Server hosts JSP pages as the presentation layer
- CORBA application server hosts business logic components
- Database Server hosts the relational database

A number of PCs connected to the network is used by the participants. Both prototypes are deployed over multiple machines connected via a high speed LAN.

Subjects: Ten users were recruited on a volunteer basis. These users represented a mixture of non-IT specialists, graduate students, and college students.

Experimental Tasks: the users are required to download the same file from both M&E-NetPay and CORBA-based NetPay systems.

Data Collection: The response times of searching for wallpapers, buying e-coins, and redeeming e-coins were recorded. These data gave an indication of the likely scalability of the prototype systems under heavy loading conditions.

3   Results

As shown in Table 1 and Fig. 2, we compared the performance of both M&E-NetPay and CORBA-based NetPay systems on their response time of downloading wallpapers.

The response time delay was the time taken for a wallpaper to be downloaded. All ten users downloaded the same wallpaper with the size of 38.4 KB.

Table 1. Times for downloading wallpapers

Test	Response delay time with M&E-NetPay (ms)	Response delay time with CORBA-based NetPay (ms)
1	2149	2410
2	2390	2509
3	1734	2294
4	3065	2354
5	2012	2432
6	1976	2091
7	2190	2256
8	1734	2168
9	1637	2005
10	1815	2344
Average	**1976**	**2286**

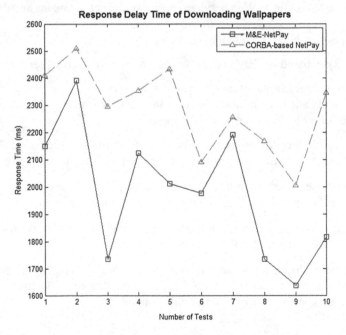

Fig. 2. Response delay time of downloading wallpaper

The result of the t test on data in the two columns of Table 1 rejected the null hypothesis that there was no significant differences in time between the two systems at the default 5 % significance level. In other words, the two response delay times of downloading the wallpaper from the two systems had a statistically significant difference. The test parameters are given below: The p-value: 0.0033; confidence interval for the difference in population means of the response time in M&E-NetPay and CORBA-based NetPay: -502.5709 and -117.8291; the test statistic: -3.3878; degrees of freedom (df): 18; and estimation of the population standard deviation: 204.7455.

It is obvious that the above statistical test result was limited by the small size of sample tests. Despite this, the average response delay time for downloading a wallpaper from CORBA-based NetPay was slightly higher than that from M&E-NetPay. On average, the clients took 1976 ms from M&E-NetPay and 2286 ms from CORBA-based NetPay to download the same wallpaper. The time difference is 310 ms. Except for downloading time, we also compared the two systems against the response times of the respective operations of searching for wallpapers, buying and redeeming e-coins. The results are shown in Table 2.

Table 2. Results of searching wallpapers, buying, and redeeming e-coins

	Average response delay time with M&E-NetPay (ms)	Average response delay time CORBA-based NetPay (ms)
Search wallpapers	1501	1703
Buy e-coins	895	920
Redeem e-coins	1990	2110

As shown in Table 2, the time spend for searching for wallpapers in M&E-NetPay was 202 ms, which was faster than that in CORBA based NetPay. Buying and redeeming e-coins also took less time in M&E-NetPay.

Despite that there may be other factors that affected the response time of the systems, the experiment results still indicated that M&E-NetPay responded to user interactions faster than NetPay. This observation resulted from CORBA's limitation in client-to-server communications. In contrast, .Net framework architecture 4.0 with Web Services in M&E-NetPay improved client-to-server communications. It provided a relatively fast communications amongst the vendor and broker. In addition, M&E-NetPay, built on a stable, secure, and simple architecture, was deployed over multiple servers to share workload among them.

4   Discussion and Future Work

We have described an evaluation on the M&E-NetPay prototype to assess the performance impact of the system. The performance evaluation was done on two prototypes of CORBA-based NetPay and M&E-NetPay. The results demonstrate that by using fast hashing functions that validate e-coin unspent indexes, M&E-NetPay achieves secure transactions with a high volume per item. It was also confirmed that the .Net framework architecture 4.0 with Web Services in M&E-NetPay improves client-to-server communications, leading to high system performance. For future work, we will conduct another two types of evaluations: usability and heuristic evaluations in order to fully understand the pros and cons of the system [6].

References

1. Huang, X., Dai, X., Liang, W.: BulaPay: a novel web service based third-party payment system for e-commerce. Electro. Comm. Res. **14**(14), 611–633 (2014)
2. Dai, X., Grundy, J.: Net pay: an off-line, decentralized micro-payment system for thin-client applications. Electron. Comm. Res. Appl. **6**(1), 91–101 (2007)
3. Dai, X., Grundy, J.: Architecture of a micro-payment system for thin-client web applications. In: Proceedings of the 2002 International Conference on Internet Computing, pp. 444–450. CSREA Press, Las Vegas, 24–27 June 2002
4. Rowley, J.: An analysis of the e-service literature: towards a research agenda. Internet Res. **16**(3), 339–359 (2006)
5. Sumak, B., Polancic, G., Hericko, M.: Towards an e-service knowledge system for improving the quality and adoption of e-services. In: Proceedings of the 22nd Bled 'eEnablement: Facilitating an Open, Effective and Representative Society', Bled, Slovenia, 14–17 June 2009
6. Williams, L., Smith, C.: Performance evaluation of software architectures. In: Proceedings of the 1st International Workshop on Software and Performance, pp. 164–177. ACM (1998)
7. Monteiro, D.M., Rodrigues, J.J.P.C., Lloret, J., Sendra, S.: A hybrid NFC–bluetooth secure protocol for credit transfer among mobile phones. Secur. Commun. Netw. **7**, 325–337 (2014)
8. Monteiro, D.M., Rodrigues, J.J.P.C., Lloret, J.: A secure NFC application for credit transfer among mobile phones. In: Proceeding of 2012 International Conference on Computer, Information and Telecommunication Systems (CITS 2012), Amman, Jordan, 14–16 May 2012

A Cloud Model for Internet of Things on Logistic Supply Chain

Guofeng Qin[✉], Lisheng Wang, and Qiyan Li

The Computer Science and Technology Department, Tongji University,
Shanghai 201804, China
gfqing@yahoo.com.cn, qylcad@sina.com

Abstract. In this paper we propose a cloud model of internet of things for logistic supply chains. In the cloud model, the cloud terminals can collect, receive and deliver information by integration of mobile networks, wireless networks, networks of sensors, including data, video and audio information. The data and information are classified and dealt with in the cloud service platform where the communication cluster servers, application servers, middleware servers and database servers are located. In this model the cluster service, resource dispatch and load balance are cooperative for every application group in the cloud in order to serve for the management and monitoring during the logistic supply chain lifecycle. In order to support high performance of cloud service, NIO (Non-blocking Input/Output) and RMI (Remote Method Invocation) are applied for the resource cooperative dispatch.

Keywords: Internet of things model · Network integration · Cloud service · Real time systems · Supply chain lifecycle

1 Background

The Internet of things is more and more popular because of its intelligence, integration and automation with Internet, Intranet, WAN, LAN, CANBUS, 3&4G, and other sensor network such as Radio-frequency Identification networks (RFID), Bluetooth, CANBUS, Video collection networks and so on. A Hybrid Cluster-based (HC) WSN model was proposed by Huang et al. [6], which provided a feasible cluster-based WSN architecture. It can save the energy of the sensor node when things are normal, while transmits emergency data packets in an efficient manner to the sink node during an emergency. An insect organize model was setup in sensor networks by Ma and Krings [5], which proposed potential new research problems inspired by insect sensory system with focusing on unexplored fields. They justified how and why insect sensory systems might inspire novel computing and communications paradigms. The distributed detection on a binary target is considered with wireless sensors sending local decisions to a fusion center by Kim et al. [4]. There are two new concepts called detection outage and detection diversity in the long-term system performance. The detection outage

© Springer International Publishing Switzerland 2015
Y. Luo (Ed.): CDVE 2015, LNCS 9320, pp. 93–104, 2015.
DOI: 10.1007/978-3-319-24132-6_12

probability is defined as the probability that the instantaneous J-divergence is smaller than a certain threshold. Detection diversity order is defined as the slope of the outage probability curve (versus system power consumption) when things are plotted in logarithm domain.

Saaty and Shih [3] considered a network structure must satisfy two requirements, which are logical in identifying and grouping similar things together, and keep relationship among them accurately according to the flow of influence. A new algorithm was studied in the ABC networks based on the QoS needs of the user in order to consider a better traffic distribution between the various networks of the same operator by Haydar et al. [2]. Many experimentations verified that the lightweight and scalability can be inferred, and easy to implement requiring only minor modifications to the core diameter protocol by Tsakountakis et al., 2009 [1]. A cooperative information integration platform was studied by Qin and Li [7] and Qin et al. [8–10], which consists of the intelligent mobile terminals, software systems, integrated 3&4G, including GPS, GPRS (CDMA), Internet (Intranet), remote video monitor and M-DMB (mobile digital media broadcast) networks. In this structure, high performance cluster computing and load balancing for cloud services just in time play a very important role for internet of things.

In this paper, a cloud model on internet of things for logistic supply chains is studied. An integration system structure is proposed, in which the cluster computing method and load balancing method are applied. At last, an application case using a prototype system for the cloud model will be reported.

2 The Level Structure of the Cloud Model

Our cloud service platform for the internet of things consists of a large set of intelligent mobile cloud terminals with software systems, integrated 3&4G units, remote video monitors, and different kinds of communication networks such as GPS, GPRS (CDMA), Internet (Intranet), RFID, CANBUS, wireless network, Blue-teeth and so on.

During the service process, the vehicles' GPS information, driver request messages, sensor information (for example RFID, temperature, pressure, stress, angle), and application tasks in all the terminals are sent to the cloud platform; On the other hand, the control center commands are sent to application terminals by the integrated WAN on 3&4G and Internet (Intranet). Different types of information, including messages, data files, stream media, etc. can be sent and received freely and safely via internet.

In the business layered structure, the users can do anything with client personal computers or cloud terminals, including mobile phone and PAD. The users are from all kinds of groups. They are vehicle drivers, operators and managers from group organizers, manufactures, factories, branch companies, procurement buyers, suppliers, banks, steel factories, management department, warehouse centers etc. The users can dispatch vehicles to transport the goods, monitor and manage status of the goods, and finish the financial settlement among the different organizers in the product life cycle at any-time and any-where by all available networks in the system. Our method for cloud service has been greatly promoting business to business, business to development and speeding up the integration for multi-network communication.

2.1 Core Unit on the Cloud Model

In the cloud platform, there are management, operation and device execution three layers in the application layer as Fig. 1. There are the mobile cloud terminals, B/S (Browser/Server structure) clients, C/S (Client/Server structure) clients in the application layer. B/S client software is in charge of dynamic dispatch, alarm monitor, service, map browsing, query, table and data back-up. C/S client software is in charge of map browsing, database management, table printing, and so on. The network layer comprises wireless communication network, Internet, Intranet, and wireless sensor network. The mobile cloud terminals and executive devices are connected to the cloud service platform with 3G or 4G and internet. The B/S clients are connected the cloud platform through Internet and Intranet, also the C/S clients are connected the cloud platform with the Intranet. The logical layer includes the platform group tool-wares and middle wares to deal with parallel application cases among servers. There are software tools for communication, application, GIS, Web Server and the interface in the cloud platform. The middleware tools are composed of XML data protocol transfer ware, JDBC, NIO (Non-blocking Input/Output), RMI (Remote Method Invocation), Load balancer, and so on. The data layer includes all the databases which contain data, video and audio. The detail can be seen in Fig. 2.

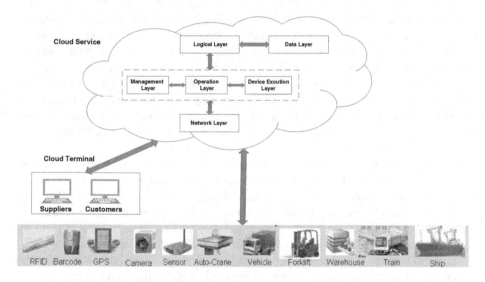

Fig. 1. Level structure of the cloud service platform

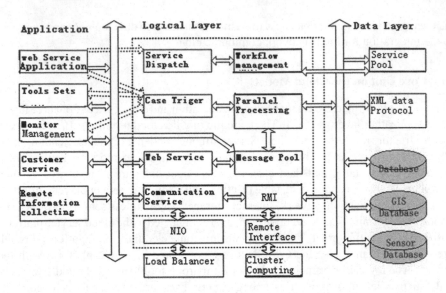

Fig. 2. Software tools for cloud service

3 Multi-core Load Balancing for Cloud Service

More and more servers have used the multi-core architecture. But there exists some problems in utilizing the multi-core processors. First, it is known to us that I/O operation is much slower than the CPU processing speed, thus the traditional blocking I/O keeps CPU waiting simultaneously instead of doing any practical jobs [12]. Second, tasks are distributed unevenly to threads which lead to workloads unbalancing among cores [13]. These problems affect the overall utilization and performance of parallel processors.

In order to solve these problems, this paper proposes a multi-core load balancing model based on the Java NIO (Java New I/O) framework. The model utilizes both the high-performance non-blocking I/O in Java NIO framework and parallel processing ability of multi-core processors. Besides, load balancing is achieved.

To keep CPU from waiting I/O simultaneously, the model uses Java NIO Framework which was included in JDK1.4 API. Java NIO was designed to provide access to the low-level operations of modern operating systems and the intent is to facilitate an implementation that can directly use the most efficient operations of the underlying platform [14]. It makes up for the traditional way of I/O, namely blocking I/O by providing buffer-based multi-channel non-blocking I/O methods in Java language.

Java NIO makes use of the Reactor design pattern and events are selected by the selector at set intervals. When a non-blocking method is dealing with I/O operations it might return without waiting for the I/O to finish, thus achieving higher performance and greater parallel processing capacity. The details of work mechanize on NIO can be seen in Fig. 3. A ServerSocketChannel is first registered to the selector as an acceptor or a request handler. Then the acceptor handles the client requests passed from the selector and spawns SocketChannels to receive or send data. The Selector polls all channels and dispatches client requests or I/O operations at set intervals. Of course, under multi-core architecture, thread pool is often used to contain many threads.

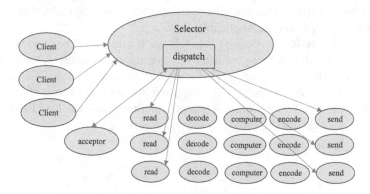

Fig. 3. Work mechanize on NIO

3.1   Load Balancing Among Multi-cores

In this section, we will discuss multi-core load balancing in a user-level way rather than a kernel way, including the type of load balancing involved, Java Fork/Join framework which is the basis of the model proposed later, a multi-core load balancing model and an overall framework combing Java NIO and the model.

There is the problem of multi-core load unbalancing because tasks distributed unevenly to multi-threads.

First, from the version of JDK1.2 Java thread is implemented by native thread which means how operating system supports native thread decides the implementation of JVM threads. Both the Windows version and the Linux version of Sun JDK use the 1:1 mapping to implement Java thread which means a Java thread is mapped to a LWP (light-weight process) and could be regarded as a native thread. This paper bases on Linux and can be extends to other operating systems.

Second, after comparing different combination of CPU workload factors Kunz pointed out that the number of tasks in running queue is the best factor for evaluating the CPU workload in Linux [16], and the Linux kernel actually put it in utilize. In Linux, a task is a thread. As it is mentioned, a Java thread is a native thread or a kernel thread, therefore, a 1-slice Java thread and a 10-slices Java thread are equivalent when scheduled to cores by the Linux kernel. Thus multi-core load unbalancing emerges.

When developing an application under multi-core architecture, distributing tasks evenly to cores by using multi-threading techniques is an effective way to enhance system performance [17]. This paper proposes a task scheduling model to solve the problem.

3.2 Fork/Join Framework on NIO

The proposed model is based on the Java Fork/Join framework introduced in JDK1.7. Fork/Join framework is a classic way of dealing with parallel programming. Though it could not solve all the problems, it is able to utilize multi-cores and make them cooperate to finish heavy tasks within its Applicable scope.

The theory of Fork/Join framework is as follows. If a task could be divided into some subtasks and the result could be obtained by combining these subtasks, then the task is fit to be solved by Fork/Join framework. Figure 4 shows how it works. The task above is dependent on the subtasks below. The request will not get the result of Task 0 until all the subtasks return. Other problems relating parallelism such as load balancing and synchronization could also be solved by the framework.

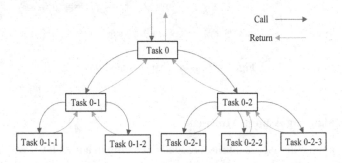

Fig. 4. Fork/Join framework on NIO

3.3 Task Scheduling Model

3.3.1 Task Parallelization and Serialization

When dealing client requests server applications are likely to handle both heavy tasks and lightweight tasks. If one heavy task is distributed to one thread, it would cause load unbalancing. Analogously, too many lightweight tasks that each occupies a thread would lead to high system cost [13]. Thus tasks executed in threads should be controlled in a suitable size. Figure 5 shows a way of task size controlling by parallelizing heavy tasks and serializing light-weight (LW) tasks.

3.3.2 Task Scheduling Algorithm

As lightweight task Serialization is relatively easy to attain, it just waits for enough tasks to arrive and fetches a thread from the thread pool to execute the tasks. Thus we mainly discuss the heavy task parallelization here. The task scheduling algorithm is based on Java Fork/Join framework and makes an improvement of classic task scheduling algorithm.

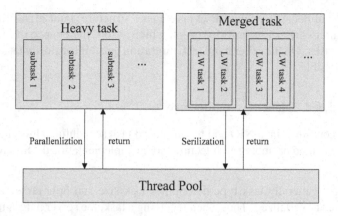

Fig. 5. Task parallelization and serialization

The task scheduling algorithm in Fig. 6 is described as follow.

(1) The server has n processors $P_1, P_2, ..., P_n$, and each processor P_i has a running task queue Q_i which the subtasks run on. (2) There are also n worker threads $W_1, W_2, ..., W_n$ and W_i executes the tasks on Q_i. (3) There are k tasks $T_1, T_2, ..., T_k$ whose priority ranges strictly from high to low. T_j could be divided into m parallel subtasks $t_{j,1}, t_{j,2} ..., t_{j,m}$ (m may differ for different tasks) which inherit the priority from their parent task by fork operation.

The steps of the algorithm are the following:

I.   For task T_j, the parallel subtasks $t_{j,1}, t_{j,2}, ..., t_{j,m}$ are distributed evenly to all task queues, so each queue has m/n parallel tasks. Tasks with higher priorities are queued earlier than other tasks. Thus the distribution of parallel tasks is obtained and is presented in Fig. 6.

II.   If Q_i is not empty, W_i dequeues a task from it to execute; else go to Step III.

III. W_i searches the system for the processor which has the longest task queue, locates the task that has the highest priority and migrates it to Q_i. Go back to Step II.

IV.   If the migration in Step III is failed, W_i tries to migrate lower-priority tasks or search for other processors to repeat the migration. If all these failures and Q_i is still empty, W_i blocks and waits for new task to awake.

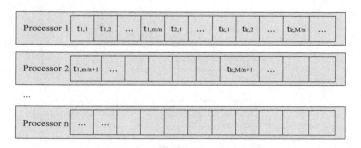

Fig. 6. Dispatch of subtasks on multi-cores

On one hand because of the FIFO task queue structure, later high-priority tasks are queued after earlier low-priority tasks, which assure the chance of execution of low-priority tasks. On the other hand task migration gets high-priority tasks executed as soon as possible.

3.4   Server Load Balancing Architecture

This section combines Java NIO and the proposed task scheduling algorithm to obtain an overall server load balancing architecture. Some implementation details are presented as follows:

a. Task Type: generally task type determines task size and how tasks are handled-parallelized or serialized. Thus when receiving a task, the server judges its task type first to decide what to do next. For example, a file access task or a mathematical calculation task has more work to do than a form submitting task and had better to be parallelized.
b. Message Priority Queue: in order to handle messages with different priorities, a data structure of message priority queue is introduced to classify the messages. When these queues are polled, more messages in high-priority queues would be chosen and forked.
c. I/O: in the architecture Java NIO is used in both network I/O and native I/O to minimize the time of waiting for processors.
d. CPU Affinity: as a worker thread takes charge of a processor's queue tasks, it is likely to be bound to the processor. But Java language does not provide CPU affinity, thus we use JNI (Java Native Interface) and set CPU affinity of worker thread by invocating a low-level C language dynamic library.

The architecture is presented in Fig. 7. The load balancing module implements the proposed task scheduling algorithm and is the key to multi-core load balancing and system performance.

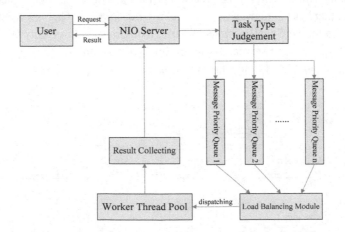

Fig. 7. Server load balancing architecture

4 Experiment and Analysis

In this section, an experiment is done to test the task scheduling algorithm in load balancing and utilizing multi-core processors. It compares the results of task execution with one core, two cores and four cores. We adopt three types of classic tasks for test, they are the Fibonnaci program with argument 40(Fib), quick sorting of 20,000 integers (Sort) and multiplication of 512-bit and 512-bit integer (Mul). All three types have the same priority. For each type of task, number of subtasks executed on cores and the total execution time was gathered. The tasks are executed 10 times and the results are averaged. The results are presented in Tables 1, 2 and Fig. 8.

Table 1. Number of subtasks on cores

	1 Core	2 Cores		4 Cores			
	CPU0	CPU0	CPU1	CPU0	CPU1	CPU2	CPU3
Fib	35421	17635	17806	8868	8990	8820	8742
Sort	66670	33020	33754	16253	17120	16879	16445
Mul	87381	43912	43469	21769	21773	21964	21874

Table 2. Execution time of tasks (unit: milliseconds)

	1 Core	2 Cores	4 Cores
Fib	6300	5895	4496
Sort	9788	8772	6857
Mul	11302	10129	7994

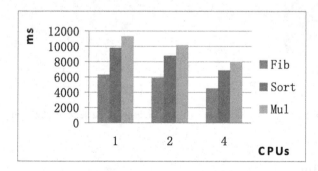

Fig. 8. Execution time of tasks

Experiment environment: Intel Core i7 Q720 1.6 GHz, Linux 2.6.32, JDK 1.7. We use VMware Workstation 8.0 as the running environment to configure the number of cores.

Table 1 shows that subtasks are evenly distributed and executed on cores. From Table 2 we can see that with the number of cores increasing time cost of each type of task decreases, but it does not have a strictly inverse relationship with number of cores. According to Fig. 8, if the task size is larger, the utilization of multi-core processors can be higher.

5   Application Case

In the cloud platform on internet of things for logistic supply chain, many cameras are integrated to a mobile cloud vehicle terminal with CANBUS or USB interface, which can provide service for about millions mobile cloud terminals and two thousands thousand pc clients according to its designed parameter, currently there are three hundred mobile cloud terminals and forty PC clients in the platform. The video stream data with JPG image format is collected and sent to the cooperative information platform. In the platform, the continue JPG frames are transferred to a video file, the recognition software deals with the images, and a security emulation software analyze status of the vehicle and alarm according to deviation index of lane line. The day reports of the vehicles will be output in the platform.

The case details of the algorithm application can be seen as Fig. 9.

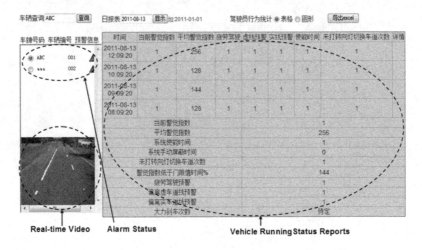

Fig. 9. Status and security for vehicle in cloud service platform

6   Conclusion

In cloud model of networks of things, many flexible methods should be supported to obtain data and information from sensors and terminals, in order to resolve information collection and cooperation of group wares in software layer and communication cluster service. The cloud model is applied to collect and delivery the structure and bio-structure data with the NIO (non-block input and output) and load balancer technologies. A multi-core load balancing algorithm based on Java NIO framework for cloud service was studied. By experiment, the cloud model and the algorithm were tested and proved to be feasible and efficient. An application verified the implementation results are satisfied according to designed parameters of the platform. In future, the necessary works are to improve the system dependability, scalability, and other Quality of Service.

Acknowledgments. The researcher is supported by the national 863 program in Ministry of Science and Technology of the People's Republic of China. Project number: 2013AA040302.

References

1. Tsakountakis, A., Kambourakis, G., Gritzalis, S.: A generic accounting scheme for next generation networks. Comput. Netw. **53**(14), 2408–2426 (2009)
2. Haydar, J., Ibrahim, A., Pujolle, G.: A new access selection strategy in heterogeneous wireless networks based on traffic distribution. In: 1ST IFIP Wireless Days Conference, Dubai, United Arab Emirates, pp. 295–299. IEEE, 24–27 November 2008
3. Saaty, T.L., Shih, H.-S.: Structures in decision making: on the subjective geometry of hierarchies and networks. Eur. J. Oper. Res. **199**(3), 867–872 (2009)
4. Kim, H.-S., Wang, J., Cai, P., Cui, S.: Detection outage and detection diversity in a homogeneous distributed sensor network. IEEE Trans. Sig. Process. **57**(7), 2875–2881 (2009)
5. Ma, Z.S., Krings, A.W.: Insect sensory systems inspired computing and communications. Ad Hoc Netw. **7**(4), 742–755 (2009)
6. Huang, M.W., Liu, H.J., Hsieh, W.S.: A hybrid protocol for cluster-based wireless sensor networks. In: 13th Asia-Pacific Computer Systems Architecture Conference, Hsinchu, Taiwan, pp. 16–20. IEEE, 04–06 August 2008
7. Qin, G., Li, Q.: An information integration platform for mobile computing. In: Luo, Y. (ed.) CDVE 2006. LNCS, vol. 4101, pp. 123–131. Springer, Heidelberg (2006)
8. Qin, Guofeng, Li, Qiyan, Deng, Xiuying: Resource sharing and remote utilization in communication servers. In: Luo, Y. (ed.) CDVE 2007. LNCS, vol. 4674, pp. 331–339. Springer, Heidelberg (2007)
9. Qin, G., Li, Q.: Dynamic resource dispatch strategy for WebGIS cluster services. In: Luo, Y. (ed.) CDVE 2007. LNCS, vol. 4674, pp. 349–352. Springer, Heidelberg (2007)
10. Qin, G., Wang, X., Wang, L., Li, Y., Li, Qiyan: Remote video monitor of vehicles in cooperative information platform. In: Luo, Y. (ed.) CDVE 2009. LNCS, vol. 5738, pp. 208–215. Springer, Heidelberg (2009)
11. Wikipedia: Asynchronous i/o. http://en.wikipedia.org/wiki/Asynchronous_I/O
12. Li, S., Liu, N., Guo, J.: Multi-threading workload balance under multi-core architecture. Comput. Appl. **28**(z2), 138–140 (2008)
13. Wikipedia: New i/o. http://en.wikipedia.org/wiki/New_I/O
14. Zhou, Z.: Understanding the JVM Advanced Features and Best Practices, pp. 336–337. China Machine Press, Beijing (2011)
15. Kunz, T.: The influence of different workload description on a heuristic load balance scheme. IEEE Trans. Softw. Eng. **17**(7), 725–730 (1991)
16. Akhter, S., Roberts, J.: Multi-core Programming: Increasing Performance Through Software Multi-threading, pp. 12–13. China Machine Press, Beijing (2007)

17. Gun, Z., Dai, X.: The fork/join framework in JDK 7. http://www.ibm.com/developerworks/cn/java/j-lo-forkjoin/. Accessed 23 August 2007
18. Lea, D.: A java fork/join framework. In: Proceedings of the ACM 2000 Conference on Java Grande, JAVA 2000, pp. 36–43 (2000)
19. Hofmeyr, S., Iancu, C., Blagojevic, F.: Load balancing on speed. In: Proceedings of the ACM SIGPLAN Symposium on Principles and Practice of Parallel Programming, PPOPP, pp. 124–157 (2010)
20. Kale, V., Gropp, W.: Load balancing for regular meshes on SMPs with MPI. In: Keller, R., Gabriel, E., Resch, M., Dongarra, J. (eds.) EuroMPI 2010. LNCS, vol. 6305, pp. 229–238. Springer, Heidelberg (2010)

A Collaborative Requirement Mining Framework to Support OEMs

Romain Pinquié[1]([✉]), Philippe Véron[1], Frédéric Segonds[2], and Nicolas Croué[3]

[1] Arts et Métiers ParisTech, LSIS, UMR CNRS 7296, Aix-en-Provence, France
{romain.pinquie,philippe.veron}@ensam.eu
[2] Arts et Métiers ParisTech, LCPI, Paris, France
frederic.segonds@ensam.eu
[3] Keonys, Toulouse, France
nicolas.croue@keonys.com

Abstract. With the fastidiously ever-increasing complexity of systems, the relentless, massive customisation of products and the mushrooming accumulation of legal documents (standards, policies and laws), we can observe a significant increase in requirements. We consider the tremendous volume of requirements as big data with which companies struggle to make strategic decisions early on. This paper proposes a collaborative requirement mining framework to enable the decision-makers of an Original Equipment Manufacturer (OEM) to gain insight and discover opportunities in a massive set of requirements so as to make early effective strategic decisions. The framework supports OEMs willing to uncover a subset of key requirements by distilling large unstructured and semi-structured specifications.

Keywords: Requirements · Exploration · Cooperative engineering · Collaborative decision making · Visual analytics · Framework

1 Introduction

The development of complex systems prompts organisations to build partnerships to pool knowledge and resources and to share risks.

Within the supply chain, a stakeholder is either a system integrator[1] or an Original Equipment Manufacturer (OEM)[2]. Nonetheless, any stakeholder at tier N can, in turn, be an integrator of OEMs' subsystems developed at tier $N - 1$, and an OEM that provides a subsystem to an integrator at tier $N + 1$.

The development of a system-of-interest starts with the requirements development phase from the point of view of the integrator. Requirements analysts elicit hundreds or thousands of requirements to specify the design, manufacturing, use, maintenance and disposal of a complex system-of-interest. For instance,

---

[1] An integrator is sometimes known as an acquirer, a customer, a contractor or a contracting authority.

[2] An OEM is sometimes known as a subsystem provider, a subsystem supplier or a subcontractor.

© Springer International Publishing Switzerland 2015
Y. Luo (Ed.): CDVE 2015, LNCS 9320, pp. 105–114, 2015.
DOI: 10.1007/978-3-319-24132-6_13

at Mercedes-Benz, the size of a system-of-interest specification varies from 60 to 2000 pages and prescribes between 1000 and 50 000 requirements [1]. Once the system-of-interest is fully specified, systems architects develop functional and physical architectural alternatives. As soon as architects have committed themselves to one preferred architecture, requirements analysts apportion the performance requirements of the current hierarchical level to the functions of the next lower level. This recursive decomposition process, which aims at simplifying the problem to be solved, results in various Stakeholder Requirements Specifications (StRSs)[3] whose implementations require domain-specific knowledge from various OEMs. Therefore, an OEM is the one that takes over all the requirements of a given subsystem.

In its Chaos Manifesto report [2], the Standish Group points out that there is never enough time or money to do everything. Thus, the report argues that focusing on the 20 % of the features and functions that give organisations 80 % of the value will maximise the investment and improve overall user satisfaction. It is therefore strongly recommended to reduce the scope and spend more time focusing on high-value requirements rather than completing 100 % of them. Such a strategy is currently fashionable since the report indicates that the features and functions developed went down, with 74 % of the specified requirements completed in 2010, dropping to 69 % in 2012. However, as Sawyer et al. (2002) [3] state, there is no tool that supports the OEMs willing to adopt such a strategy. Hence, so far, when an OEM collects the StRS and the applicable documents to which the StRS refers to, it has no other alternative than go through the documents to identify and prioritise a subset of key requirements.

2   Literature Review and Proposition

2.1   Related Work

An up-to-date literature review of the existing visual requirements analytics[4] frameworks can be found in Reddivari et al. [5] and Cooper et al. [6]. Coatanéa et al. [7] and Lash [8] extract requirements and relationships from unstructured specifications. Zeni et al. [9] propose GaiuST, a framework that supports the extraction of legal requirements for regulatory compliance. Few articles broach the topic of contradictions in natural language [7,10]. However, much research attempts to diagnose quality defects by using NLP and text mining techniques [11–17]. Recent work has been done to classify requirements thanks to machine learning [18] or linguistics analysis [16]. Zhang et al. [19] suggest an approach to qualify and quantify customer value for value-based requirements engineering. Numerous requirements prioritisation techniques, which are reviewed in [20], have been developed to rank requirements. Finally, there is an stimulating interest to use recommendation systems in requirements engineering [21].

---

[3] One StRS for each system element.

[4] Reddivari et al. [5] coined the term *visual requirements analytics* that is the use of *visual analytics* applied to requirements engineering. Visual analytics is "the science of analytical reasoning facilitated by interactive visual interfaces" [4].

2.2   Limitations of Existing Solutions

In current commercial requirements engineering software can be divided into four main categories: (1) the everlasting document-based specifications (e.g. Word, Excel, PDF) that are easy to use and cheap; (2) the centralised database-based specifications (e.g. Rational DOORS[5], ENOVIA V6 Requirements Central[6]) that ease collaboration and configuration management; the model-based systems engineering specifications (e.g. SysML) that offer new elements such as relationships between requirements; and (4) the requirements editors and analysers that assist analysts with ensuring the quality of requirements (e.g. The Requirements Quality Suite[7]).

Feedback from industrialists reveals that these technologies benefit the systems integrators whose main tasks are requirements writing and management, but they do not help the OEMs willing to distil a large set of requirements. Moreover, they do not offer any contextual view of the requirements and their interdependencies, but only offer a graphical table that imitates the form of a spreadsheet. We can also notice that requirements analysis tools mainly focus on the processing task, but provide very limited visual analytics capabilities. Conversely, visual analytics solutions concentrate on the depiction of requirements' features without including advanced processing capabilities. Finally, to the best of our knowledge, current solutions do not provide any statistical capabilities that may help uncovering patterns in a set of decision-making attributes associated to requirements.

This literature review prompts us to claim that there is an absolute necessity to imagine a framework that supports OEMs willing to distil a large set of requirements by integrating computational engineering with visual analytics.

2.3   Proposition

We propose a collaborative requirement-mining framework that addresses the **problem** of an OEM receiving a request for proposal consisting in a StRS and the referenced applicable documents, all of them prescribing a massive set of requirements that cannot be implemented within cost and schedule constraints.

The **mission** of the framework is to support the business analysts willing to distil a large set of requirements, that is, to create an optimised Sytem Requirements Specification (SyRS) that is ready to be managed in configuration thanks to requirements management tools. By using the "distil" we mean to get and show only the most important part of a large set of requirements. We qualify the SyRS as optimised because it is the outcome of the distilling process that results in a subset of **key requirements**. The key requirements gather:

- **legal requirements:** non negotiable requirements that are required for regulatory compliance.

---

[5] http://www-03.ibm.com/software/products/fr/ratidoor.

[6] http://www.3ds.com/products-services/enovia/products/v6/portfolio/d/
collaborative-innovation/s/governance-user/p/requirements-central/.

[7] http://www.reusecompany.com/requirements-quality-suite.

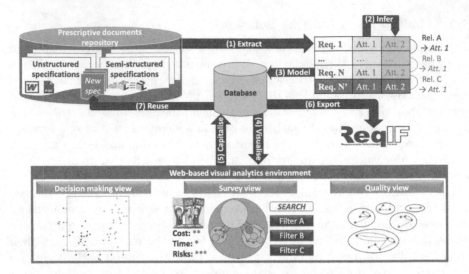

Fig. 1. An over-simplified operational scenario of the collaborative framework.

– **basic requirements:** non negotiable requirements without which no one would buy the product.
– **added-value requirements:** negotiable requirements corresponding to key product differentiators.

Figure 1 illustrates the **operational scenario** that we propose to answer the question "What is the subset of key requirements?". To begin, for a given project, the project manager collects the unstructured and semi-structured documents corresponding to the StRS and the applicable documents and places them into a common repository. Then, the operational scenario is as follows:

1. **Extract** explicitly stated attributes (e.g. original author, version, statement, original document source title, etc.) that make up each requirement and relationship from unstructured and semi-structured specifications. We use an attribute scheme to structure each requirement as a set of attributes so as to be compliant with the meta-model of the standardised Requirements Interchange Format (ReqIF)[8].
2. **Infer** implicit requirements attributes, such as the business category (e.g. mechanics, electronics, I&T, marketing, safety, etc.), the functional *vs.* non-functional category, the textual cross-references to the referenced applicable prescriptive documents (e.g. The system shall comply with the *CS.25*) standard. Implicit relationships such as the linguistic interdependencies (e.g. synonymy, hypernymy, hyponymy, etc.) among the requirements keywords, the potential redundancies and contradictions, and the occurrence of proscribed terms can also be created.
3. **Model** the requirements and the relationships as a property graph data model into a graph database.

---

[8] http://www.omg.org/spec/ReqIF/.

4. **Visualise** the requirements and the relationships from different perspectives enabling contextual and multidimensional exploration of the attributes through interactive functionalities. Users can interact with visuals, perform the classic CRUD[9] operations, and save changes to the database. When the data set is updated by saving changes in the database, the processing tasks have to be restarted to update the data model and the visuals. So far we have identified five interactive visuals:
   - **Quality view:** highlights the quality defects that are not only inherent to a requirement statement (e.g. ambiguities, incompleteness, etc.), but also among a set of requirements (e.g. redundancies and contradictions).
   - **Cross-references view:** illustrates the interdependencies among the StRS and the referenced applicable documents.
   - **Survey view:** helps the domain-experts to retrieve the requirements that are relevant to their profile so as to estimate various decision-making criteria (e.g. cost, time, risks, quality, etc.).
   - **Decision making view:** supports analysts for uncovering unanticipated patterns in the dataset resulting from a statistical analysis of the decision-making criteria estimated by domain-experts in the *survey view*.
   - **Configuration management view:** depicts the history of changes (created, modified and deleted requirements and relations).
5. **Capitalise** the information and the strategic decisions made by the business analysts by keeping an historical record of subsequent projects.
6. **Export** into a ReqIF compliant XML data file the subset of key requirements that will be managed in configuration throughout the downstream system's life cycle phases thanks to requirements management tools.
7. **Reuse** the capitalised information throughout the entire distilling process whenever a new specification is added in the repository or whenever a new set of specifications corresponding to a new request for proposal is received.

In the next sections we introduce the framework according to two perspectives: *functional* - WHAT functions need to be performed to fulfil the mission? - and *software* - HOW shall the framework accomplish the required functions?

3 The Collaborative Requirement Mining Framework

3.1 Functions of the Framework - "WHAT"

In this section we present a Functional Flow Block Diagram (see Fig. 2) that not only defines the functions that the framework must perform to fulfil its mission, but also depicts their logical, sequential relationship, as well as what flow goes in and out of each function. It is the definition of "what" the framework must do without guessing a particular answer to "how" the functions will be performed.

The first step consists in extracting the explicit attributes that make up each requirement (F1 and F2). For unstructured specifications (F1), attributes

---

[9] Create, Read, Update and Delete.

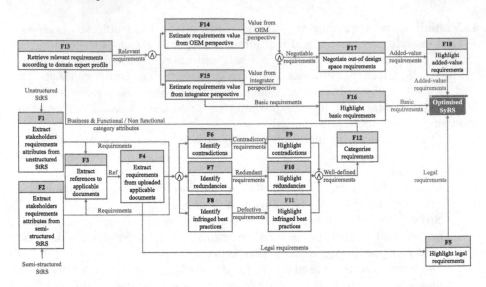

Fig. 2. A FFBD depicting the lowest abstraction level of the functional architecture.

include a unique identifier for each requirement, the metadata corresponding to the author and version of each specification, as well as the statement of each requirement. For semi-structured specifications (F2) such as SysML requirements diagrams saved as an XML file, we only extract the statement attribute and the "derive" relationship elements. Then, the requirement statements are processed to extract the textual cross-references that refer to applicable documents (F3) from which the software extracts additional requirements. Legal requirements have to be highlighted (F5) in a visuals because they are non-negotiable key requirements. It is therefore necessary to find a solution to distinguish legal requirements from non-legal requirements. Once all requirements have been extracted, a diagnosis (F6, F7 and F8) is launched to identify quality defects (e.g. contradictions and redundancies, ambiguities, etc.) to avoid over-specification with unnecessary requirements and misinterpretations during the survey phase. The cleaning of requirements defects requires another visual, the *quality view*, to illustrate contextual potential redundancies and contradictions. Once cleaned, the requirements are used to infer implicit attributes such as the business (e.g. mechanics, IT, etc.) and functional *vs.* non functional categories (F12). Such classes ease the retrieval of requirements (F12) whose value needs to be estimated from the OEM (F14) and the integrator (F15) perspectives. The estimation of decision-making criteria results in either a basic requirement that is non negotiable from the point of view of the integrator or a requirement that needs to be negotiated (F15). The negotiation phase can be approached as a constrained optimisation problem where integrator's constraints need to be weakened to find a solution belonging to the OEM's feasibility space that is maximum in value but that was originally outside of the scale of constraints [22].

3.2   Implementation of the Framework - "HOW"

In the previous section we detailed what functions the framework must perform to fulfil its mission. Now we shall explain how the functions can be implemented.

To extract the textual content and the metadata we use a specific parser according to the extension of the uploaded StRS. The parser Apache Tika[10] for .doc (Word), .odf (OpenOffice) and .pdf; the parser Apache POI[11] for .xls (Excel) and to extract figures that potentially are graphical requirements; and a simple XML parser (JDOM[12]) for SysML requirement diagrams.

The Stanford CoreNLP[13] toolkit offers a variety of natural language processing (NLP) functions such as tokenisation, sentence splitting, POS-tagging and lemmatisation allowing the identification of sentences. A binary knowledge engineering classifier classifies the sentences as requirements or non-requirements based on prescriptive word matching (shall, must, should, require, have to, need, want, desire, etc.)[3]. As previously explained, any XML parser can do the job for a semi-structured SysML specification. The extraction of textual cross-references to applicable documents is an information extraction problem. We can solve this challenge by building a probabilistic sequence model that is either discriminative such as Conditional Random Fields (CRF) and Maximum Entropy Markov Models (MEMM), or discriminative such as Hidden Markov Models (HMM). Stanford CoreNLP and the Java library Mallet[14] embed the CRF algorithm. A feature function that takes in as input a requirement statement, the position i of a term in the current statement, the class of the current token, and the class of the previous token can be used to build a linear-chain CRF. By defining two classes, *class A* corresponding to strings consisting in a blend of a few capital letters and digits such as "ISO900" or "CS25" standing for prescriptive document titles, and *class B* corresponding to chunks usually used to refer to content in external documents such as "in accordance with", "as specified in", "as set out in", it is likely that a term belonging to *class A* in the sequence model will be a cross-reference given the fact that the previous term belongs to *class B*. In other words, if we find a chunk such as "as specified in" followed by a term that mixes a few capital letters and digits such as "CS25", then we infer that the second term is a reference to an external document. Once extracted, cross-references are displayed to require the user to upload the referred applicable documents which, in their turn, will be processed to extract the requirements they prescribe. While uploading the required applicable documents, the user can manually set a binary (*legal* vs. *non-legal*) switch so as to specify whether it is a legal document. If it is set as a legal document, then the extracted requirements are classified as key legal requirements.

To diagnose quality defects (e.g. redundancies, contradictions, ambiguities) that pollute specifications and often lead to wrong decisions we use natural

---

[10] https://tika.apache.org/.
[11] https://poi.apache.org/.
[12] http://www.jdom.org/.
[13] http://nlp.stanford.edu/software/corenlp.shtml.
[14] http://mallet.cs.umass.edu/.

language processing techniques. To identify redundancies and contradictions we, at first, carry out a thesaurus-based lexical semantic disambiguation of keywords (nouns, verbs, adjectives and adverbs). The identification of the meaning of keywords enables us to reliably select a subset of similar requirements thanks to a sentence-level similarity function. Then, we use the POS-tagger of Stanford CoreNLP to find negations (e.g. no, not, not, 't, etc.) and numerical values (e.g. 40, 50) in the statements, and we look for the antonyms of each keyword by querying the thesaurus WordNet[15]. An analysis of the numerical dependencies in each requirement with the Stanford CoreNLP dependency analyser[16] enables us to only keep the statements that include digital values related to a physical dimension (e.g. $40\,N$ or $50\,K$). With ad-hoc algorithms we build: (1) pairs of requirements that contain physical numerical values, (2) pairs of requirements with a negation and requirements without a negation, and (3) pairs of requirements whose keywords are antonyms. Finally, we combine the similarity function with these numerical, negation and antonymy pairs. If a pair of requirements has a similarity score that is higher than the threshold (e.g. 0.8), then there is potentially a contradiction or a redundancy. Such an approach increases recall rather than accuracy. Interactive visuals representing clusters of similar and potentially contradictory requirements facilitates the cleaning of quality defects. This interactive *quality view* also depicts all the defects due to the infringement of best practices (e.g. ambiguities, incompleteness, etc.) in requirement writing.

Well-defined requirements are the basis for inferring new implicit attributes that help a domain-expert to retrieve requirements that belong to his domain of expertise. One attribute is the business category (mechanical, IT, etc.) a given requirement belongs to. This attribute can be inferred with supervised statistical learning text categorisation algorithms. The Support Vector Machine (SVM) algorithm is usually recognised as the best algorithm for text categorisation. Furthermore, Knauss and Ott (2014) demonstrated that a semi-supervised SVM model outperforms a supervised approach [18]. However, instead of building a time-consuming training set with annotated requirements as was done in [18], we propose to train a multi-class SVM model with sentences from domain-specific (mechanics, electronics, etc.) dictionaries and handbooks. In addition, either a formal linguistic analysis implemented with the syntactic meta-language Backus-Naur Form (BNF)[16] or a supervised machine learning decision tree [23] can be implemented to infer another implicit attribute that categorises the statements as *functional* or *non-functional*. These attributes coupled with the Apache Lucene[17] search engine, and the visualisation of semantic relationships (synonyms, hypernyms, hyponyms, etc.) among requirements are functionalities of the *survey view* that enable domain experts to retrieve the most relevant requirements according to their profile during the estimation phase.

Once assessed, quantitative decision-making criteria can be analysed with principal component analysis, whereas qualitative variables can be analysed

---

[15] https://wordnet.princeton.edu/.

[16] http://nlp.stanford.edu/software/stanford-dependencies.shtml.

[17] https://lucene.apache.org/core/.

with multiple correspondence analysis. A *decision-making view* communicates the results of the statistical multivariate analysis by uncovering unanticipated interesting patterns in the data set. These patterns ease the identification of a subset of added-value requirements that motivate business analysts' decisions.

4 Conclusion and Future Work

In this paper, we have presented a collaborative requirement mining framework that supports OEMs willing to distil a large set of requirements. Its computational capabilities and interactive visuals should help analysts to gain insight and discover opportunities in a massive set of requirements. Computational capabilities include the automated extraction of requirements and relationships, the inference of implicit attributes, the analysis of requirements' quality, a statistical multivariate analysis, and the capitalisation and reuse of information and decisions made. On the other hand, five interactive visuals should improve exploration through contextual views illustrating requirements and their interdependencies and multidimensional views depicting the numerous attributes that make up each requirement and relationship. Furthermore, the originality of this framework is to focus on the contractual phase that brings a system integrator and OEM(s) in one single collaborative digital environment.

The prototyping of a web application is under development. The MVC design pattern JSF 2[18] has been selected. The graph database Neo4j[19] has been chosen to store requirements and relationships in a property graph data model. The Object-Graph Mapping Spring Data Neo4j[20] makes it possible to work with annotated POJO entities. Finally, the JavaScript library D3.js[21] has been adopted to create the web-based interactive visuals.

References

1. Houdek, F.: Managing large scale specification projects. In: 19th International Working Conference on Requirements Engineering Foundation for Software Quality, REFSQ 2013, Essen, Germany, 8–11 April 2013 (2013)
2. The Standish Group: Chaos manifesto report (2013)
3. Sawyer, P., Rayson, P., Garside, R.: REVERE: support for requirements synthesis from documents. Inf. Syst. Front. J. **4**(3), 343–353 (2002)
4. Thomas, J., Cook, K.: Illuminating the Path: Research and Development Agenda for Visual Analytics. IEEE Press, Los Alamitos (2005)
5. Reddivari, S., Rad, S., Bhowmik, T., Cain, N., Niu, N.: Visual requirements analytics: a framework and case study. Requir. Eng. **19**(3), 257–279 (2014)
6. Cooper, Jr., J.R., Lee, S-W., Gandhi, R.A., Gotel, O.: Requirements engineering visualization: a survey on the state-of-the-art. In: 4th International Workshop on Requirements Engineering Visualisation, pp. 46–55. IEEE, Altanta (2010)

---

[18] https://javaserverfaces.java.net/.
[19] http://neo4j.com/.
[20] http://projects.spring.io/spring-data-neo4j/.
[21] http://d3js.org/.

7. Coatanéa, E., Mokammel, F., Christophe, F.: Requirements models for engineering, procurement and interoperability: a graph and power laws vision of requirements engineering. Technical report, Matine (2013)
8. Lash, A.: Computational representation of linguistics semantics for requirements analysis in engineering design. MSc thesis, Clemson University (2013)
9. Zeni, N., Kiyavitskaya, N., Mich, L., Cordy, J.R., Mylopoulos, J.: GaiusT: supporting the extraction of rights and obligations for regulatory compliance. Requir. Eng. **20**(1), 1–22 (2015)
10. de Marneffe, M., Rafferty, M., Manning, C.: Finding contradictions in text. In: 46th Annual Meeting of ACL, Columbus, OH, pp. 1039–1047 (2008)
11. Carlson, N., Laplante, P.: The NASA automated requirements measuring tool: a reconstruction. Innov. Syst. Softw. Eng. **10**(2), 77–91 (2014)
12. Christophe, F., Mokammel, F., Coatanéa, E., Nguyen, A., Bakhouya, M., Bernard, A.: A methodology supporting syntactic, lexical and semantic clarification of requirements in systems engineering. Prod. Dev. **19**(4), 173–190 (2014)
13. Génova, G., Fuentes, J.M., Llorens, J., Hurtado, O., Moreno, V.: A framework to measure and improve the quality of textual requirements. Requir. Eng. **18**(1), 25–41 (2013)
14. Kiyavitskaya, N., Zeni, N., Mich, L., Berry, D.M.: Requirements for tools for ambiguity identification and measurement in natural language requirements specifications. Requir. Eng. **13**(3), 207–239 (2008)
15. Körner, S.J., Brumm, T.: Natural language specification improvement with ontologies. Semant. Comput. **3**(4), 445–470 (2009)
16. Lamar, C.: Linguistic analysis of natural language engineering requirements. MSc thesis, Clemson University (2009)
17. Yang, H., de Roeck, A., Gervasi, V., Willis, A., Nuseibeh, B.: Analysing anaphoric ambiguity in natural language requirements. Requir. Eng. **16**(3), 163–189 (2011)
18. Knauss, E., Ott, D.: (Semi-) automatic categorization of natural language requirements. In: Salinesi, C., van de Weerd, I. (eds.) REFSQ 2014. LNCS, vol. 8396, pp. 39–54. Springer, Heidelberg (2014)
19. Zhang, A., Auriol, G., Eres, H., Baron, C.: A prescriptive approach to qualify and quantify customer value for value-based requirements engineering. Comput. Integr. Manuf. **26**(4), 327–345 (2014)
20. Achimugu, P., Selamat, A., Ibrahim, R., Mahrin, M.N.: A systematic literature review of software requirements prioritization research. Information Softw. Technol. **56**(6), 568–585 (2014)
21. Felfernig, A., Ninaus, G., Grabner, H., Reinfrank, F., Weninger, L., Pagano, D., Maalej, W.: An overview of recommender systems in requirements engineering. In: Maalej, W., Thurimella, A.K. (eds.) Managing Requirements Knowledge, pp. 315–332. Springer, New York (2013)
22. Cheung, J., Wong, J., Forrester, J., Eres, H.: Application of value-driven design to commercial aero-engine systems. In: 10th AIAA Aviation Technology, Integration, and Operations (ATIO) Conference, Fort Worth, TX (2010)
23. Hussain, I., Kosseim, L., Ormandjieva, O.: Using linguistic knowledge to classify non-functional requirements in SRS documents. In: Kapetanios, E., Sugumaran, V., Spiliopoulou, M. (eds.) NLDB 2008. LNCS, vol. 5039, pp. 287–298. Springer, Heidelberg (2008)

An Information Integrated Method and Its Application of Virtual Factory Using BIM

Bao Jinsong[1](✉), Zhu Ying[2], and Xia Ziyue[3]

[1] School of Mechanical Engineering, Donghua University, Shanghai, China
bao@dhu.edu.cn
[2] School of Mechanical Engineering, UM-SJTU Joint Institute, Shanghai Jiao Tong University, Shanghai, China
[3] UM-SJTU Joint Institute, Shanghai Jiao Tong University, Shanghai, China
{zhuyingchina, ziyue.xia}@sjtu.edu.cn

Abstract. Virtual factory has great influence on the competitiveness of the enterprise production during the design and operation stages, especially on the new factory layout, the factory reconstruction and workshop decision. The paper presents a method of the information modeling for virtual factory based on building information modeling (BIM), including the architectural elements, the integrated digital expressions of the equipment elements and the workshop control elements (geometry, physics and function etc.). It organically combines the solid geometric models, physical properties, rules and some other building and semantic information. This method can realize the modeling, simulation and evaluation (MSE) of manufacturing system. The paper presents a virtual factory integrated method of manufacturing marine product, combined with BIM, and realizes a prototype system to visualize the marine virtual factory based on BIM.

Keywords: Virtual factory · BIM · Information modeling · Marine product · System simulation

1 Introduction

Due to the diversification of customization product with uncertainties and rapid changes in market demands, the main problem faced by manufacturing business is to realize an efficient response of the design and the production systems to these demands.

Nowadays, managers and engineers usually apply Virtual Factory (VF), also called as Digital Enterprise Technologies as the decision support tools to deal with the problems above. The virtual factory concept is managing critical data and business process with numeric structure through information and communication technologies [1], which provides good opportunities to the plan and production control system. However, despite the fact that virtual factory enables the modeling, analysis and evaluation of the production system with perfect conditions, too many uncertainties in reality, such as instabilities of machine and changes of requirements, still result in differences among the perfect plans, the actual production and the theoretical results, and lead to great trouble in the VF-based production plans and control decisions.

© Springer International Publishing Switzerland 2015
Y. Luo (Ed.): CDVE 2015, LNCS 9320, pp. 115–123, 2015.
DOI: 10.1007/978-3-319-24132-6_14

Discrete event simulation (DES) is an important technology for evaluating the production system of different respects, in which Manufacturing Execution System (MES) is applied to store the change of controlled elements and the state of change events. Comparing data information stored in MES with the one from DES realizes evaluation and judgment of production systems, and reinstatement of some possible states and parameters of system elements at the same time.

A virtual factory includes not only the architectural elements, but also the integrated digital expressions of the equipment elements and the workshop control elements (like geometry, physics and function) [2]. Traditional geometric information model is able to show the appearance of virtual factory realistically and satisfy the requirements for scene roaming. But this is far from enough to reveal and combine the virtual factory's internal laws and deal with decision simulation. Take Tecnomatix Plant of Siemens for instance. This software focuses on describing engineering simulation models, yet performs poorly in representing actual 3D structures.

Building information model (BIM) is based on 3D digital technology, including geometrical entities information, physical properties, rules and some other building and semantic information. It consists of various engineering data models with related information of a construction-engineering project [3]. Additionally, IFC is a type of open data standard proposed by Building SMART to realize the internal building information expression, share and application. And this has been an international standard (ISO16739).

Based on existent researches and theories, virtual factory is mainly used to plan plant area, such as virtual factory and process model project operated by the industrial virtual reality institute of UIC, and field monitoring and management [4]. Bodner and McGinnis [5] take the advantage of visual process to support the model detection and the performance Evaluation of Production Systems, as well as the optimization. Debevec etc. [6] presented process optimization method using virtual factory. Tekai etc bring a virtual factory data model to support performance evaluation of production system. The model considers only a few properties of production process and is hard to reveal a more complex dynamic production process. Briefly, such an application aims at structured data during production process, while many unstructured data also have considerable effects on production activities but have not been solved. On other hand, there are some scholars study IFC-based modeling. They mainly apply this to simulation [7] and collaborative engineering fields [8] in urban or building constructions, and rarely use the modeling method to the design and management of the production system or virtual factory modeling. Besides, the unstructured data modeling methods in a virtual environment is still lacked for the moment, as well as the researches on the monitoring and feedback from the production of the cooperating manufacturing system. Of that the Pointools developed by the Bentley offers a better system of an integrated 3D scan-point cloud, used for the collision analysis for transportation and prediction of interactions.

Currently, offshore companies have more excess capacity, and has driven many shipyards to turn to the offshore market to shore up their revenue base [9]. To optimize production processes, improve product quality and shorten manufacturing cycle time using VF technology, might be a right way. This paper focuses on a virtual factory modeling and simulation method combined with BIM and IFC, considering not only the building structures of a factory, but also the equipment and MES formed in the equipment room with various data produced.

2 Multidisciplinary Information Integration Using BIM and IFC

2.1 Multidisciplinary Information for MSE of Virtual Factory

Modeling, simulation and evaluation (MSE) of manufacturing system need multidisciplinary information in context of manufacturing cycle time. There are three main catalogs: constraints information for factory layout, manufacturing processes' information; presentations information, which include static and dynamic data from simulation or produced during manufacturing processes, equipment's runtime information; management and decision information, as Fig. 1.

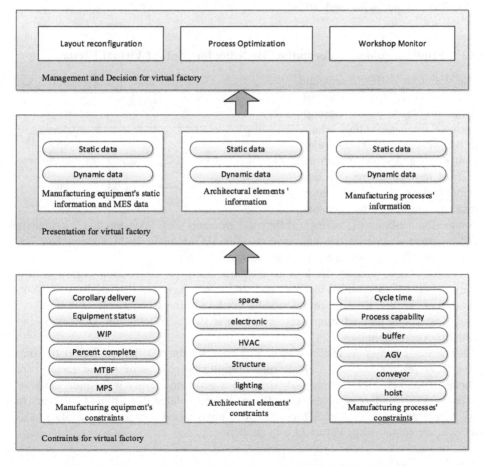

Fig. 1. Three catalogues multidiscipline information of virtual factory

Manufacturing equipment's information includes static and dynamic data. Static properties of equipment are size, type and so on. And dynamic datum are normal collected by MES, such as the information of corollary delivery, the equipment status, MTBF, WIP, percent complete and the MPS (Master Production Schedule). Through the description of both static and dynamic data, the environment of the manufacturing scene and the condition of the MES can be got easily and accurately.

Architectural elements' information includes all the related elements of the factory, like the space of the manufacturing area, the electronic parts, the main characters of HVAC, the structure of the layout and the lighting in the scene.

Besides these, the information about the production process is also necessary to present a virtual factory. This consists of the cycle time, process ability, buffer condition, and the status of the logistics like the AGV, conveyor, hoist and so on.

With the three aspects used to describe a virtual factory, the constraints for the virtual factory can be built. These constraints form the layout, making the factory meet physical behavior. Thus obtained model would realize the visualization of information and data analysis. And the management and decision for the factory can also be provided to support the evaluation.

2.2   Multidisciplinary Information Modeling for MSE of Virtual Factory

The definition of IFC's semantic information is quite powerful, containing substantial descriptions of the construction details. It uses classes, attributes, rules, constraints and so on, which are defined through Express, to describe various engineering information, including the semantic

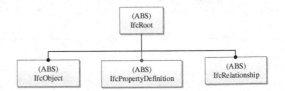

Fig. 2. The hierarchy of IFC base class

connection relations among different elements of construction, complete BIM-supported descriptions and storage. The IFC-standard IFC4 version has 766 entities and 391 classes like enumerations and choice.

Among these classes, IfcRoot is the base class of the schema object in IFC framework. All the entities in core layer and upper layer are derived from IfcRoot. Moreover, the IFC models are described according to the schema objects in the three broad categories derived from IfcRoot, which is IfcObjectDefinition, IfcRelationship and IfcPropertyDefinition.

The Fig. 2 shows the relations among IfcRoot, IfcObjectDefinition, IfcRelationship and IfcPropertyDefinition. And all multidisciplinary objects of virtual factory are encapsulated here. IFC format uses describe a geometric entity with three kinds of expressions: boundary representation (B-rep), sweep volume (Sweep) and constructive solid geometry (CSG). And 3D-measurement point cloud data as well as 3D spatial models are contained in virtual factory modeling.

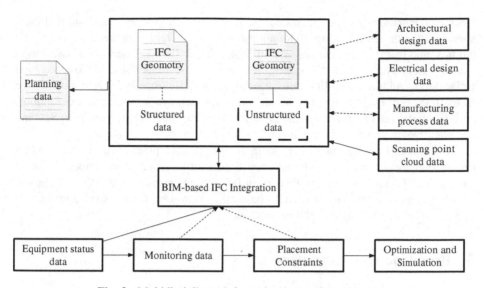

Fig. 3. Multidisciplinary information integration with IFC

And the BIM-based data integration can be divided into structured data and unstructured data. In fact, all data are also produced static and dynamic processes. It is really difficult to combine them.

Structured data are the enterprise-managed data (including equipment condition data recorded by MES), generally stored in the database or described with XML. The other is unstructured data, recording 3D spatial data, point cloud data, video monitoring type or 3D entity modeling data.

Through unifying framework for BIM, these two types of data can be integrated, and provide the optimization of virtual factory layout and equipment simulation. And Fig. 3 shows such unification.

IfcObject is an abstract superclass deriving from

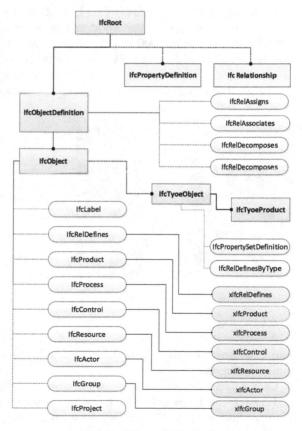

Fig. 4. IFC association class

IfcObjectDefinition. Its six subclasses are IfcProduct, IfcProccess, IfcControl, IfcResource, IfcActor and IfcGroup. IfcRelationship is used to represent the relations among entities, and that between entities and attributes. It has six basic derivative association classes: IfcRelAssigns, IfcAssociates, IfcDecomposes, IfcDefines, IfcConnects and IfcDeclares. Additionally, IfcPropertyDefinition and IfcPropertySetDefinition derive from IfcPropertyDefinition. They are the sets or a series of attributes and definitions, and have derivative classes such as IfcPropertySet, IfcPreDefinedPropertySet and IfcQuantitySet, which is shown in IFC2 × 4 [10].

IFC format is quite appropriate to the description of plant structure, but has no description about the equipment and control element information in factory. Figure 4 shows the IFC association class. Classes in IFC can be extended, creating new classes, which retain characteristics of the IFC base class. A series of classes (xIfc prefix) are inherited the members of the IfcObject class.

3   Prototype and Its Implement

3.1   A Prototype System for a Marine Product Factory

Shanghai Zhenhua Heavy Industry Co., Ltd. (ZPMC) is one of the largest heavy-duty equipment manufacturers in the world and owns 26 transportation ships of capacity from 60,000 DWT to 100,000 DWT, delivering products to all over the world. In the past, the low efficient manual work was the main productivity and the layout was in a mess. However, using automatic equipment like welding robotics, new layouts should be adopted. The comparison between the layouts shows in Fig. 5.

Fig. 5. Comparison between the layouts

A prototype system (SVF) is developed for ZPMC's Offshore Drilling Platform factory to smooth the process of the manufacturing process and enhance the efficiency of the production.

On the data layer, the database of the workshop site is established on the basis of BIM and IFC-data modeling and connected with the data layer, combined with upstream Research and Design Development database, Production Process database and Fault Diagnosis to Product Line database at downriver position. Then these are integrated into the platform database through the interface, abstracting all the hardware equipment, network equipment, storage device, operating system, and database and application software into the service resources. Different kinds of sophisticated resources are unified into one type to simplify the objects of the system integration and reduce complexity of the service components.

Faced with a large number of hardware and software resources in a virtual factory and sophisticated business-expansion requirements, the platform requires a new framework for system integration because the regular system integration takes the hierarchical-management method which relies on the continuously increasing hierarchies to refine the service application and

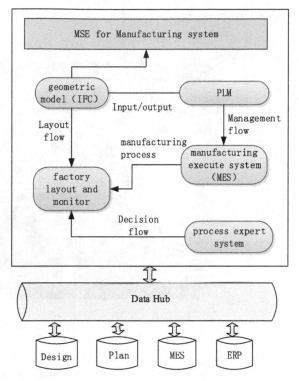

Fig. 6. The framework of system platform

however, such a method would complicate the system, leading to the hard expansion. To enhance the expandability of the virtual factory system platform, the platform architecture is designed into a three-layer structure, as shown in Fig. 6.

3.2 Development of Prototype

The virtual factory prototype is developed using open source graph engine (Openscenegraph, http://www.openscenegraph.org) and MongoDB database. The prototype provides a relatively concise simulation environment and adopts the virtual reality technology, making the simulation process more understandable and the simulation effects more intuitive. The users can modify the simulation objects in real time. As shown in Fig. 7, the whole system simulation is an interactive 3D simulation process, mainly shown and controlled by the simulation interface, which constrained by BMI and equipment properties and manufacturing processes. The virtual factory plan and simulation system mainly realize a virtual simulation platform used for a virtual factory. Its structure consists of the interface layer, the application layer and the data exchange layer. There are four steps to apply the prototype:

Firstly, many models, such as machine tools and other auxiliary equipment, will be stored in model vault. Those models can be drag in a 2D layout drawing.

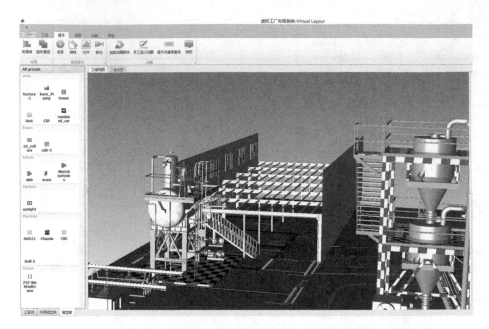

Fig. 7. Prototype and its GUI

The necessary factory equipment models are added into the virtual scenes, set the attributes and the states of the corresponding equipment and build up a relatively complete virtual factory workshop through the scene-editing module. With scenes, we can control various states of the system simulation and realize the interactive 3D simulation through the simulation-control module of the interface layer.

Secondly, the proper positions of equipment are calculated and constrained by information of IfcObject. All equipment is in their right position.

Thirdly, the system would simulate the current factory planning according to the layout, the behavior logic attribute and the connection relations of the facility among the whole workshop. In the simulations, the users can observe its rationality in real time, immediately modifying the geometric properties and behavior properties of the experiment. After the simulation is finished, the system can export data information of the simulation results, and evaluate the simulation process and results with system analysis module.

Finally, the users can optimize the design, improve the layout scheme, re-plan the workshop according to the evaluation and continue evaluating the new results. Repeating these simulations and planning processes will achieve a more reasonable planning result.

4   Conclusions

The paper combines the characteristics of the marine product development process, virtual and other digital technologies, designs a 3D integration design and the production link of the virtual factory, and puts forward a modeling, simulation and evaluation method for the intelligent plant. These four key factors include data preparation, data generation, system extension and client's design on the system platform, visualization of the data and their transformation into 3D scenes, and improvements for the effectiveness of the system compared with the emulation technology. And the processing algorithm raised in the paper enables effectiveness higher for the extraction of mass data in future.

Acknowledgements. Supported by the Natural Science Foundation of China (51475301).

References

1. Yushun, F.: The connotation and implementation method of the total solution to enterprise information. Comput. Integr. Manuf. Syst. **5**, 1 (2004)
2. Yang, X., Malak, R.C., et al.: Manufacturing system design with virtual factory tools. Int. J. Comput. Integr. Manuf. **28**(1), 25–40 (2015)
3. Lee, H.W., Oh, H., Kim, Y., et al.: Quantitative analysis of warnings in building information modeling (Bim). Autom. Constr. **51**, 23–31 (2015)
4. Zetu, D., Banerjee, P.: Integrated vision system for virtual factory. Cirp J. Manuf. Syst. **29** (3), 265–269 (1999)
5. Bodner, D.A., Mcginnis, L.F.: A structured approach to simulation modeling of manufacturing systems. In: Proceedings of the 2002 Industrial Engineering Research Conference, p. 471. Orlando, FL, USA (2002)
6. Debevec, M., Simic, M., Herakovic, N.: Virtual factory as an advanced approach for production process optimization. Int. J. Simul. Model. **13**(1), 66–78 (2014)
7. Terkaj, W., Urgo, M.: Virtual factory data model to support performance evaluation of production systems. In: Proceedings Of Osema 2012 Workshop, 7th International Conference On Formal Ontology In Information Systems, pp. 24–27. Graz, Austria (2012)
8. Stascheit, J., Koch, C., Hegemann, F., et al.: Process-oriented numerical simulation of mechanized tunneling using an Ifc-based tunnel product model. In: Proceedings of the 13th International Conference on Construction Applications of Virtual Reality. London, UK (2013)
9. Ryu, H.-G., Kim, S.-J.: Case study of concrete surface design and construction method for freeform building based on bim -focused on tri-bowl Korea. J. Korea Inst. Build. Constr. **12** (3), 347–357 (2012)
10. Guangqin, Z.: Comments on Chinese shipbuilding enterprises moving into the ocean engineering equipment market. Shanghai Shipbuild **1**, 55–58 (2011)

Global Stiffness and Well-Conditioned Workspace Optimization Analysis of 3UPU-UPU Robot Based on Pareto Front Theory

Dan Zhang$^{(\boxtimes)}$ and Bin Wei

University of Ontario Institute of Technology, Oshawa, ON, Canada
{Dan.Zhang,Bin.Wei}@uoit.ca

Abstract. In this paper, an approach based on the Pareto front theory is employed to conduct the multi-objective optimization of the global stiffness and well-conditioned workspace of 3UPU-UPU parallel mechanism. The inverse kinematic and Jacobian matrix of the 3UPU-UPU mechanism are first calculated. Then the stiffness model of the mechanism is derived and the sum of the diagonal elements of the stiffness matrix is used as a criterion to evaluate the global stiffness. Secondly, the Monte Carlo method is used to derive the global condition index of the mechanism which later is used as a criterion to evaluate the well-conditioned workspace of the mechanism. Normally, increasing the workspace of the mechanism will deteriorate the stiffness, here the global stiffness and well-conditioned workspace of the mechanism are optimized simultaneously based on the Pareto front theory, and the optimized results are displayed and compared.

Keywords: Global stiffness · Well-conditioned workspace · Parallel robot · Optimization · Modelling

1 Introduction

Parallel mechanisms have been widely used in the past decade, especially in parallel robotic machine tools [1], micro-instruments [2], medical devices [3–6], entertainment equipment [7], automotive realm [8] and mine industries [9, 10], due to parallel mechanisms possess high stiffness, high payload capacity, good acceleration characteristics and high precision. These attributes all attribute to the structure of parallel mechanisms, i.e. the moving platform connected to the base by several parallel limbs.

Parallel mechanisms have their own disadvantages, especially the small workspace. Scholars tried to optimize the workspace of the parallel mechanisms to make it bigger, but the stiffness of the parallel mechanism is affected while optimizing the workspace, i.e. optimizing one objective will deteriorate the other. In reality, these two performances are both needed to be considered since high stiffness can lead to high precision and large workspace means the end-effector can reach different parts of the workpiece when conducting manufacturing, for example.

There are several methods for multi-objective optimization, such as Pareto front theory, particle swarm optimization method, the weighting objective method, etc., and these

© Springer International Publishing Switzerland 2015
Y. Luo (Ed.): CDVE 2015, LNCS 9320, pp. 124–133, 2015.
DOI: 10.1007/978-3-319-24132-6_15

methods have been successfully applied to the multi-objective optimization applications. Konak, etc. [11] proposed the multi-objective optimization using genetic algorithms. Gao [12] used Pareto front method to multi-optimize system stiffness, dexterity and manipulability of a parallel manipulator. Zhang, etc. [13] used particle swarm optimization method to multi-optimize the dexterous stiffness and reachable workspace of a parallel manipulator. Lara-Molina, etc. [14] multi-optimized dexterity, payload transmission capacity and dexterity uniformity of Steward Gough parallel manipulator over the required workspace based on the multi-objective evolutionary algorithm. Here the Pareto front theory is used to simultaneously optimize the global stiffness and well-conditioned workspace of the 3UPU-UPU mechanism since these two performances are important in the applications. The sum of the diagonal elements of the stiffness matrix is used as an objective function to evaluate the global stiffness. The global condition index is used as an objective function to evaluate the well-conditioned workspace of the mechanism. The result shows that the optimal solution is not just one solution, but rather several solutions which we call them non-dominate solutions. Finally the optimized results are displayed and compared.

2   Inverse Kinematic and Jacobian of 3UPU-UPU Mechanism

Figure 1 is the kinematic scheme of 3UPU-UPU mechanism. The moving platform is connected to the fixed base by three identical actuated limbs and one central passive limb. Each actuated limb consists of a fixed U joint, a moving link, an actuated prismatic joint, another moving link and another U joint attached to the platform from base to platform. The central passive limb consists of a fixed U joint, a moving link, a passive prismatic joint, another moving link and another U joint attached to the platform. B_i and P_i $(i = 1, 2, 3)$ represent the centers of the U joints. $B_1B_2B_3$ and $P_1P_2P_3$ are both equilateral triangles. According to Kutzbach-Grubler formula, this mechanism has three translational degrees of freedom. For the purpose of analysis, two Cartesian coordinates systems $O(X, Y, Z)$ and $P(x, y, z)$ are attached to the center of the base and platform, respectively. The X axis of the fixed coordinate is perpendicular to B_1B_3 and in the plane

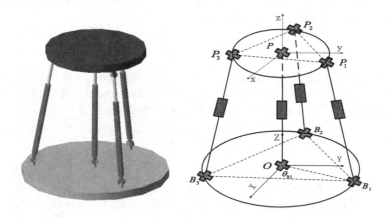

Fig. 1. 3UPU-UPU mechanism

of the base, Z axis is perpendicular to the base and towards up, Y axis is according to the right hand rule. The same rule applies to $P(x, y, z)$. R_p and R_b are the radii of circumcircle of the platform and base, respectively. θ_{bi} are the angles between the points of attachment on the base and X axis, and θ_{pi} are the angles between the points of attachment on the platform and x axis, respectively.

The position vectors of point B_i with respect to the fixed frame are expressed by b_i, the position vectors of point P_i with respect to the moving frame and fixed frame are expressed by p'_i and P_i, respectively. The coordinates of point P with respect to the fixed frame is expressed by ^OP, thus we can have the following,

$$
p'_i = \begin{bmatrix} x'_i \\ y'_i \\ z'_i \end{bmatrix} = \begin{bmatrix} R_p \cos \theta_{pi} \\ R_p \sin \theta_{pi} \\ 0 \end{bmatrix}, b_i = \begin{bmatrix} b_{ix} \\ b_{iy} \\ b_{iz} \end{bmatrix} = \begin{bmatrix} R_b \cos \theta_{bi} \\ R_b \sin \theta_{bi} \\ 0 \end{bmatrix}, P_i = \begin{bmatrix} x_i \\ y_i \\ z_i \end{bmatrix}, {}^OP = \begin{bmatrix} u \\ v \\ w \end{bmatrix},
$$

$$
\theta_{bi} = \begin{bmatrix} \theta_{b1} \\ \theta_{b2} \\ \theta_{b3} \end{bmatrix} = \begin{bmatrix} \pi/3 \\ \pi \\ 5\pi/3 \end{bmatrix}, \theta_{pi} = \begin{bmatrix} \theta_{p1} \\ \theta_{p2} \\ \theta_{p3} \end{bmatrix} = \begin{bmatrix} \pi/3 \\ \pi \\ 5\pi/3 \end{bmatrix}
$$

$$
P_i = {}^OP + Qp'_i (i = 1, 2, 3) \tag{1}
$$

Subtract b_i from both sides of above equation, one obtains:

$$
P_i - b_i = {}^OP + Qp'_i - b_i \tag{2}
$$

where Q is the rotation matrix of the moving frame with respect to the fixed frame. Taking the Euclidean norm on both sides of Eq. (2), one obtains:

$$
\|P_i - b_i\| = \|{}^OP + Qp'_i - b_i\| = \rho_i \tag{3}
$$

where ρ_i is the length of the ith limb. The solution of the inverse kinematic problem for this mechanism is completed and can be written as follows,

$$
\rho_i^2 = (P_i - b_i)^T (P_i - b_i) \tag{4}
$$

The Jacobian matrix maps the output velocity, i.e. the moving platform velocity to input velocity, i.e. actuated joint velocities. The Jacobian matrix for the manipulators can be determined by time differentiating Eq. (4) as follows,

$$
B\dot{\rho} = At \tag{5}
$$

where

$$
J = B^{-1}A = \begin{bmatrix} u - R_b \cos \theta_{b1}\rho_1 & v - R_p \sin \theta_{p1} - R_b \sin \theta_{b1}\rho_2 & w + R_p \cos \theta_{p1}\rho_3 \\ u - R_b \cos \theta_{b2}\rho_1 & v - R_p \sin \theta_{p2} - R_b \sin \theta_{b2}\rho_2 & w + R_p \cos \theta_{p2}\rho_3 \\ u - R_b \cos \theta_{b3}\rho_1 & v - R_p \sin \theta_{p3} - R_b \sin \theta_{b3}\rho_2 & w + R_p \cos \theta_{p3}\rho_3 \end{bmatrix}
$$

3   The Global Stiffness and Workspace of the Mechanism

High stiffness is the merit of the parallel manipulators; high stiffness can lead to high precision. The stiffness of a parallel manipulator at a given point of its workspace can be characterized by its stiffness matrix. The diagonal elements of the stiffness matrix represent the pure stiffness in each direction [15] and the sum of leading diagonal elements of the stiffness matrix is defined as the global stiffness [16]. The disadvantage of parallel manipulators is the limited workspace. Parallel manipulators designed for maximum workspace volume may cause poor dexterity and manipulability. Here the global condition index [17] is used to optimize the workspace which will result in a well-conditioned workspace by maximizing a global condition index of the mechanism.

3.1   Global Stiffness of the Mechanism

In order to obtain the optimal stiffness in each direction, one can write an objective function as follows with stiffness element to maximize [15],

$$y = \eta_1 K_{11} + \eta_2 K_{22} + \eta_3 K_{33} \tag{6}$$

For i = 1, 2, 3, K_{ii} represents the diagonal elements of the mechanism's stiffness matrix, η_i is the weight factor for each directional stiffness, which characterizes the priority of the stiffness in this direction. Here the sum of diagonal elements of stiffness matrix is used as an objective function to evaluate the global stiffness. The stiffness model of the mechanism is established by using traditional method which is the calculation of the Jacobian matrix.

$$K = J^T K_J J \tag{7}$$

K_J is the joint stiffness matrix of the mechanism, with $K_J = diag[k_1, k_2, k_3], k_i(i = 1, 2, 3)$ is a scalar representing the joint stiffness of each actuator. Particularly, in the case for which all the actuators have the same stiffness, i.e. $k_1 = k_2 = k_3 = k$, then (7) will be reduced to:

$$K = J^T K_J J = k J^T J \tag{8}$$

The objective function for optimization is: $y = \eta_1 K_{11} + \eta_2 K_{22} + \eta_3 K_{33}$.

3.2   Global Condition Index of the Mechanism

The global condition index is defined as follows,

$$\eta = \int_W \frac{1}{k} dW \tag{9}$$

where k is the condition number of the Jacobian matrix of the mechanism. Solving Eq. (9) analytically is too much work to do that compels us to use a numerical solution technique like Monte Carlo method. The general procedure of the method are as follows: firstly, a large number of points are selected randomly in the possible workspace of the mechanism; secondly, it needs to be checked whether it falls within the workspace of the manipulator, this is done by solving inverse kinematic for each limb to see whether the limb length satisfies the limb limits; thirdly, calculate the kinematics condition index, which is the summation of the reciprocal of the condition number for each point that falls within the workspace of the mechanism; finally, the global condition index can be determined by multiplying the volume V of the possible workspace and kinematics condition index, after that dividing by the total number of points n_{total} which we previously selected, then one obtains the following:

$$\eta = \frac{V \cdot \sum_i \frac{1}{k_i}}{n_{total}} \tag{10}$$

4 Optimization for Stiffness and Workspace

Multi-objective optimization problems consist of optimizing several objective functions simultaneously which are different from that of single-objective optimization. In the single-objective optimization, the solution of the optimization aims to obtain the best solution over all other alternatives. In the multi-objective optimization, it requires to find all possible tradeoff solutions among many objective functions which are conflicting to each other. Normally, when the workspace of the mechanism becomes bigger, the stiffness of the mechanism will become smaller. Here the optimization for global stiffness and well-conditioned workspace of the mechanism is studied. Two objectives for optimization are global stiffness evaluation criteria and workspace evaluation criteria which are given blow:

(1) Objective functions
     Global stiffness evaluation criteria—objective function 1:

$$y = \eta_1 K_{11} + \eta_2 K_{22} + \eta_3 K_{33}$$

Here it is assumed the priority of the stiffness in each direction is the same: $\eta_1 = \eta_2 = \eta_3 = 1$. The bigger the value, the better the global stiffness has. Minimize $-y$ is equivalent to maximize y.
Workspace criteria—objective function 2:

$$\eta = \frac{V \cdot \sum_i \frac{1}{k_i}}{n_{total}}$$

The bigger the value, the larger the well-conditioned workspace has. Minimize $-\eta$ is equivalent to maximize η.

(2) Design variables
The design variables for multi-objective optimization are given as:

$$s = [R_p, R_b, u, v, w]$$

(3) Constraints
Their bounds are set as follows according to the practical requirements:

$$\begin{cases} R_p \in [0.20, 0.50]m \\ R_b \in [0.60, 0.90]m \\ u \in [-0.5, 0.5]m \\ v \in [-0.5, 0.5]m \\ w \in [0.2, 1.2]m \end{cases}$$

Using matlab optimization toolbox and some parameters and options are set as follows: Population size: 50; Maximum of generations: 66; Selection strategy: Tournament; Tournament size: 2; Crossover type: Intermediate; Crossover ratio: 1; Mutation function: Adaptive feasible; Pareto front population fraction: 0.7. Run the solver and then the Pareto front is obtained as follows.

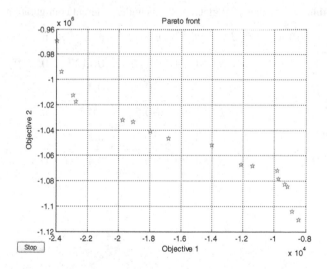

Fig. 2. Pareto optimal frontier sets between stiffness and workspace criteria

The Pareto front of the global stiffness and global condition index is illustrated in Fig. 2. From the figure, it is obvious that the global stiffness and global condition index are conflicting to each other. The optimal solution is not one solution but rather several solutions which we call them non-dominate solutions. Four typical objective values and their corresponding design variable values from the above several solutions are listed in Table 1. Designers can choose one specific value obtained above according to their own design requirements.

Table 1. Pareto front typical solutions for objective values and corresponding design variables

y	η	R_p	R_b	u	v	w
−9772	−1072181	0.292	0.868	0.260	0.250	0.289
−23641	−993961	0.441	0.778	0.181	0.173	0.239
−19737	−1032054	0.428	0.832	0.189	0.338	0.251
−23938	−969626	0.440	0.769	0.177	0.172	0.239

For the purpose of analysis, selecting one optimized result as an example for analyzing, i.e. $u = 0.1767, v = 0.1722, w = 0.2391$, and the global stiffness mapping can be obtained along with change of R_p and R_b as shown in Fig. 3. It is obvious that when $R_p = 0.5$, $R_b = 0.79$, the global stiffness reaches the maximum value 29918. Before optimization, $R_p = 0.3$, $R_b = 0.7$, $u = −0.3$, $v = 0.4$, $w = 0.8$, the sum of stiffness is 4454.2. The stiffness sum is improved 6.7 times after optimization. Through a number of experiments, some of the results are listed in Table 2, from which one can also see that when $R_p = 0.5$, $R_b = 0.79$, $u = 0.1767$, $v = 0.1722$, $w = 0.2391$, the global stiffness has the maximum value.

Table 2. The values of global stiffness under different configurations

Global stiffness	R_p	R_b	u	v	w
29918	0.5	0.79	0.1767	0.1722	0.2391
4454.2	0.3	0.7	−0.3	0.4	0.8
3813.2	0.2	0.6	−0.5	−0.3	0.5
8178.5	0.4	0.8	0.3	0.2	0.6
9560.9	0.5	0.79	0.3	0.4	0.5

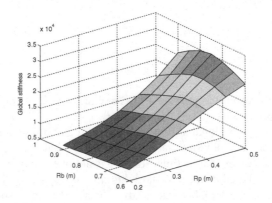

Fig. 3. Global stiffness mapping of the mechanism when u, v, w are fixed

The well-conditioned workspaces before optimization and after optimization are shown in Figs. 4 and 5, respectively. One can see that the well-conditioned workspace has become larger after optimization. From the above analysis, one can see that when the radius of moving platform equals to 0.5 m, the radius of base equals to 0.79 m and the coordinates of the center point P of moving platform with respect to the fixed frame are 0.1767 m in X direction, 0.1722 m in Y direction and 0.2391 m in Z direction, the global stiffness has the maximum value 29918 N/m, and also the well-conditioned workspace has become larger.

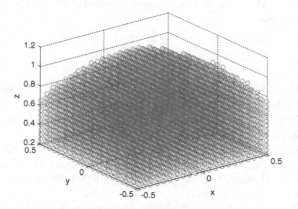

Fig. 4. Workspace of the mechanism after optimization

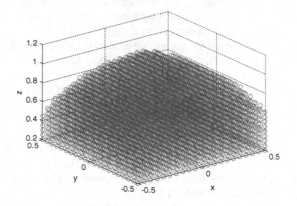

Fig. 5. Workspace of the mechanism before optimization

5   Conclusion

This paper focuses on the global stiffness and well-conditioned workspace optimization of 3UPU-UPU parallel mechanism. The Jacobian matrix of the mechanism is first determined and then the stiffness model of the 3UPU-UPU mechanism is derived and the sum of the diagonal elements of the stiffness matrix is used as a criterion to evaluate the global stiffness. Furthermore, the global condition index of the mechanism is determined based on the Monte Carlo method and later used as a criterion to evaluate the well-conditioned workspace of the mechanism. The global stiffness and well-conditioned workspace of the mechanism are optimized simultaneously based on Pareto front theory. Finally the optimized results are displayed and compared, and showed that the global stiffness and well-conditioned workspace have increased after optimization.

Acknowledgements. The authors would like to gratefully acknowledge the financial support from the Natural Sciences and Engineering Research Council of Canada (NSERC) and Canada Research Chairs program.

References

1. Zhang, D., Bi, Z.M., Li, B.Z.: Design and kinetostatic analysis of a new parallel manipulator. Robot. Comput. Integr. Manuf. **25**, 782–791 (2009)
2. Zhang, D., Gao, Z., Fassi, I.: Design optimization of a spatial hybrid mechanism for micromanipulation. Int. J. Mech. Mater. Des. **7**, 55–70 (2011)
3. Gorie, N., Dolga, V., Biomechatronics recovery systems for persons with disabilities. In: Proceedings of International Conference on Innovations, Recent Trends and Challenges in Mechatronics, Mechanical Engineering and New High-Tech Products Development – MECAHITECH 2011, vol. 3 (2011)
4. Castelli, G., Ottaviano, E.: Modelling, simulation and testing of a reconfigurable cable-based parallel manipulator as motion aiding system. Appl. Bion. Biomech. **7**(4), 253–268 (2010)
5. Castelli, G., Ottaviano, E.: Modeling and simulation of a cable based parallel manipulator as an assisting device. In: Computational Kinematics: Proceedings of the 5th International Workshop on Computational Kinematics. Springer, pp. 17–24 (2010)
6. Pan, M.: Improved design of a three-degree of freedom hip exoskeleton based on biomimetic parallel structure. Master Thesis, University of Ontario Institute of Technology, Canada (2011)
7. Huang, X.G., He, G.P., Tan, X.L.: An introduction to parallel robot mechanism. J. North China Univ. Technol. **27**(3), 25–31 (2009)
8. Yu, H.J.: Research on parallel robot based flexible fixtures for automotive sheet metal assembly. PhD thesis, Harbin Institute of Technology (2010)
9. Zhang, Y.W., Wei, B., Wang, N.: Kinematic performance analysis of 3-SPS-S spatial rotation parallel mechanism. Trans. Chin. Soc. Agri. Mach. **43**(4), 212–215 (2012)
10. Zhang, D., Gao, Z.: Hybrid head mechanism of the groundhog-like mine rescue robot. Robot. Comput. Integr. Manuf. **27**, 460–470 (2011)
11. Konak, A., Coit, D.W., Smith, A.E.: Multi-objective optimization using genetic algorithms: a tutorial. Reliab. Eng. Syst. Saf. **91**, 992–1007 (2006)
12. Gao, Z.: Spatial three degree-of-freedom parallel mechanisms: configurations, performances and applications. PhD thesis, University of Science and Technology of China (2009)
13. Zhang, D., Gao, Z.: Forward kinematics, performance analysis, and multi-objective optimization of a bio-inspired parallel manipulator. Robot. Comput. Integr. Manuf. **28**(4), 484–492 (2012)
14. Lara-Molina, F.A., Rosario, J.M., Dumur, D.: Multi-objective design of parallel manipulator using global indices. Open Mech. Eng. J. **4**, 37–47 (2010)
15. Zhang, D.: Parallel Robotic Machine Tools. Springer, Berlin (2009)

16. Hu, X.L.: Design and analysis of a three degrees of freedom parallel kinematic machine. Master thesis. University of Ontario Institute of Technology (2008)
17. Stamper, R.E., Tsai, L.W., Walsh, G.C.: Optimization of a three DOF translational platform for well-conditioned workspace. In: Proceedings of the IEEE International Conference on Robotics and Automation. New Mexico, pp. 3250–3255 (1997)

A Hadoop Use Case for Engineering Data

Benoit Lange and Toan Nguyen[(⊠)]

INRIA Rhône-Alpes, 38334 Saint-Ismier, France
{benoit.lange,toan.nguyen}@inria.fr

Abstract. This paper presents the VELaSSCo project (Visualization for Extremely LArge-Scale Scientific Computing). It aims to develop a platform to manipulate scientific data used by FEM (Finite Element Method) and DEM (Discrete Element Method) simulations. The project focuses on the development of a distributed, heterogeneous and high-performance platform, enabling the scientific communities to store, process and visualize huge amounts of data. The platform is compatible with current hardware capabilities, as well as future hardware.

Keywords: Hadoop · HPC · Commodity nodes · Visualization · Hive · Hbase

1   Introduction

For a long time, scientists have tried to understand natural phenomena. In the earlier days of science, researchers described natural phenomena with experimentations. Later, theories have been proposed by scientists to describe phenomena (Newton's laws, Maxwell's equations…). And, at the beginning of the 1980s, computational models have been developed to validate theories. These computational models are used with computer simulations. Computational models and IT hardware have evolved and bring now understanding to a higher level. With modern architectures, a computation takes only a couple of hours: but with efficient computations come huge amounts of data. In most cases, this quantity of information is managed easily, because some parts of the datasets are deleted. This is called filtering, which removes some elements which are none relevant, intermediary time-steps, etc. Unfortunately, this leads to important loses of information, and final analyses are not optimal anymore. To increase the accuracy of the analyses, it is necessary to store all the information produced, instead of deleting parts of it.

This paper is related to the European VELaSSCo project (Visualization for Extremely Large-Scale Scientific Computing). The goal is to provide a storage platform for large datasets produced by engineering simulations. This paper introduces the VELaSSCo architecture and the components of the final platform.

Section 2 is an overview of related work on Big Data. Section 3 presents the VELaSSCo project and its requirements. Section 4 details its architecture, layers and components. Section 5 concludes the paper.

© Springer International Publishing Switzerland 2015
Y. Luo (Ed.): CDVE 2015, LNCS 9320, pp. 134–141, 2015.
DOI: 10.1007/978-3-319-24132-6_16

2 Related Work

Big Data solutions have already been developed and widely discussed in many research papers. Nowadays, many application fields have adopted this paradigm, but the data produced by engineering applications has not yet been well evaluated regarding to the Big Data problematic.

Three dimensions are commonly used to represent Big Data (3Vs rule): Volume, Velocity and Variety [1, 2, 3]. Volume is related to size of datasets (bytes, number of records, etc.). Velocity concerns the acquisition of information (batch, real-time, etc.). And, Variety is linked to the data format (structured, unstructured, etc.).

Google is one of the major Big Data actors. They have developed a computational model specifically adapted to web search; the tools have been presented in different papers: [4] concerns the MapReduce programming model (MR), [5] deals with Big-Table and [6] introduces its own virtual File System (Google FS). Other groups have developed some alternative solutions. One of these tools is Hadoop. It is an open-source and the most used Big Data framework[1], which supports all the requirements describe in the Big Data literature. The earlier implementation of this platform includes a specific file system named HDFS (Hadoop Distributed File System) [7] and the MapReduce [8] computational model. This framework is highly extensible, and many plugins have been developed: one example is HBase, presented in [9, 11]. It is a Hadoop implementation of BigTable.

Alternative software have also been developed, e.g., Dryad[2]. It provides a more complex model than the traditional MapReduce model. With Dryad, it is possible to add intermediary layers between the Map and the Reduce phases. Microsoft originally developed this software from scratch. But now, to fit with most of existing BigData infrastructures, Microsoft provides also a Hadoop implementation of Dryad. This implementation is based on YARN [10]. YARN is part of the second release of Hadoop. It is the task manager for Hadoop. It splits the *JobTracker* in two separate functions: *RessourceManager* and *ApplicationManager*. Hadoop computations have thus been improved, and MapReduce is not anymore the only computational model for Hadoop. The new Hadoop framework can run on up to 10.000 nodes.

3 The VELaSSCo Project and Goals

By 2020, complex simulations will produce more data than ever before and IT systems used by the scientific communities need to evolve accordingly. Nowadays, the scientists use mainly HPC facilities to run large simulations. Cloud systems are evolving and starting to offer some HPC cloud infrastructures. But they do not yet offer performance in par with current HPC facilities. However, in the near future, cloud providers will offer new kinds of services based on HPC nodes instead of commodity nodes. These future systems will achieve high performance figures.

---

[1] http://cloudtimes.org/2013/11/06/idc-report-hadoop-leads-the-big-data-analytics-tool-for-enterprises/.

[2] http://research.microsoft.com/en-us/projects/dryad/.

In these new systems, the bottleneck will not be on computations but on I/O operations. With current engineering solvers, to avoid latency in I/O operations, the stored data is explicitly reduced by the users. The research in this project aims to avoid this filtering by storing all the information produced.

The European Union is funding the VELaSSCo project, in the Seventh Framework Programme (FP7). It groups researchers and engineers from different fields to reach a common goal: provide an innovative and efficient platform to manipulate engineering data produced by simulations. Different industry partners (ATOS and JOTNE) and laboratories/universities (UEDIN, Fraunhofer IGD, SINTEF, CIMNE and INRIA) are involved in the project. The goal is to provide an efficient storage, analytics and visualization platform, specially designed for engineering data.

The platform is supported by Big Data software, in order to handle large datasets produced by simulation engines. The goal is to deal with FEM and DEM simulations. These applications produce huge amounts of data, with complex data structures, e.g., spherical particles, none spherical particles, etc.). The second requirement concerns analyses. In order to provide specific information to the users, some analyses need to be executed on the platform, for example extract splines, iso-surface, level of details, etc. These analyses must be supported by our architecture and fit with computational models of HPC, but also cloud infrastructures. Finally, the platform needs to be specifically designed using a user centric paradigm (focused on real-time visualization). When the users perform rendering queries, the response times need to be short. Other requirements and the preliminary design have been described in [11].

From all these specificities and regarding the extensibility of Hadoop, we selected this framework as the foundation of our software stack. In the next section, we describe how we plan to use it. We combine Hadoop with existing plugins and also provide new pieces of software to respond to the needs of the project.

4   The VELaSSCo Solution

As stated in the previous section, the foundation of the platform is Hadoop. This software stack can be deployed on any kind of IT architecture with some advantages for commodity nodes. But currently, most scientific communities have their own HPC facilities, based on high-end computers. Further, Hadoop is not well suited for this kind of hardware. The project goal is therefore to provide a flexible Hadoop distribution to support efficiently a large variety of IT infrastructures. In this section, we present a global overview of the VELaSSCo architecture (Fig. 1). The architecture is decomposed into layers. Four layers are presented: simulation, storage, engine and client.

The first layer named *simulation* already exists. This layer is in charge of the production of data. Simulations are executed on specific nodes and the produced data is stored locally (on the HPC FS). These files contain tabular data with different time steps information from the simulations. The simulation software already exist and they produce very large amounts of information. All the time-steps are not stored because this would require too much storage space. Another issue comes from I/O operations, which are slow. With a DEM simulation, a scientist can produce 1 Petabyte of data with 10 millions particles and 1 Billion of time-steps. After the production of data, it is

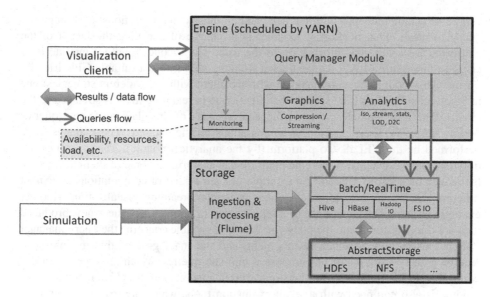

Fig. 1. VELaSSCo architecture

necessary to store the results in the storage layer. A Flume agent is in charge of this task.

Three modules compose the *storage* layer: the ingestion (extract information), query (communication part) and storage modules. The ingestion module is in charge of gathering data from the simulation layer. This module is also used to format data and store these new elements into the correct storage repositories. This strategy is based on a Flume agent, specially designed for our datasets (where simulations are run). Then, the agent sends to the Batch/real-time module (purple box), which is composed by different "I/O query software". This module can be decomposed into different Hadoop extension: Hive, Hbase or the traditional HDFS I/O (Hadoop Distributed File System) query engines. We also have included the standard I/O operations from an operating system, to ensure read and write operations on most existing file systems. These different accesses enable to support automatic benchmarking. This part will be discussed at the end of paper. To select the desired file system, it is necessary to specify in the Hadoop configuration file this parameter. This configuration impacts directly the *AbstractStorage* module.

The third layer is related to the *client* part. In this project we target two visualization tools: IFX[3] (developed at IGD Fraunhofer) and GID[4] (from CIMNE). We extend these tools to enable connections and gathering of information with the future versions of the VELaSSCo platform. This part will be managed using Thrift.

The last layer is named *engine*. Four modules compose this layer: a query manager, a monitoring module, a graphical module and an analytic module. This layer is in

---

[3] http://www.i-fx.net.

[4] http://www.gidhome.com.

charge of communications with the user, and all these communications go through the query manager. The monitoring module, is in charge of checking the health of the platform, and sends this information to the user. The second (graphic) module is in charge of translating RAW data extracted from the platform to a suitable GPU friendly format. This module can communicate with the client with two different strategies: one in batch (chunks of data are send to the client), one in real time (data is streamed to the client). The third module concerns the analysis part of the platform. Some queries performed by the users imply new computations on the datasets. These analyses are performed by the VELaSSCo platform (by the analytics module). The user does not only execute these analyses, and the platform can also trigger some of them to increase the access on specific datasets. An example of such a kind of computations is: extract different resolutions of a model in order to enable streaming visualization. Another example is: extract an iso-surface of a selected part of a model. All these new produced data are directly stored into the platform. The final module concerns the query manager (QM). This module is under development, and the main goal of this module is to receive a query from a user, decompose it into sub-queries, which are able to interact with all available queries (from the storage layer), analytics or graphics modules. This module is also equipped with a set of evaluation tools, which are executed automatically (when no computation is running on the platform) to evaluate the best storage and access (using Hive, HBase or HDFS) strategy for a data set. This evaluation is configured by previous analyses of users. This QM is extendable to support more query engines or analytics operations.

5   Preliminary Results

In order to validate the VELaSSCo approach, we performed some preliminary tests [11]. Two scenario have been used for this evaluation. The visualization tool asks for all data from a data set, and second, asks for a subset (a filtering based on particle ID) of the dataset. The dataset is composed of information produced by simulations stored into a column-oriented format. Each file contains the particle id, location, acceleration, etc. For the complete extraction, the tool asks the platform for all data from a specific dataset. For the read query, only a subset of data (identify by particles id) is extracted.

For the evaluation, we use a single node with an Intel® Core™ i7-2620 M Processor, (with 2 physical cores) and 8 GB of memory, running Fedora Core 20. For our experiments, we compare three alternatives: (1) a myHadoop installation (which supports Hadoop 2.x) on a bare metal node, (2) our simplified architecture deployed on three VirtualBox (version 4.3.14) machines, and (3) a simplified distribution with three Dockers (version 1.1.2) containers.

Here, we only deal with simple queries (extract data directly from the storage module), and we have made a comparison on existing extensions of Hadoop. The main idea is to find the most effective way to extract content from one of the three data access systems: NFS Gateway (linked to HDFS), Hbase and Hive.

Using the NFS Gateway to read all data and read a specific part of a dataset, we show that NFS gateways have the same performance on both solutions. For the second benchmark, we compare Hbase read with the same hardware parameters. For read operations (sub-selection on the data set), on a small distribution (from 1,000 to 100,000 particles), all three methods need the same amount of time to gather a subset of records. But, when the number of particle is higher (1,000,000), VirtualBox is not adequate and the containers is the fastest solution. For the second test (gather all data from a dataset), a similar pattern appears. The best solution is the use of 3 containers. These evaluations are presented in Figs. 2 and 3.

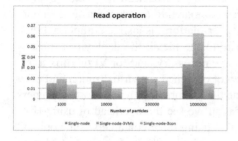

Fig. 2. Read operation for Hbase.

Fig. 3. Read all operation for Hbase.

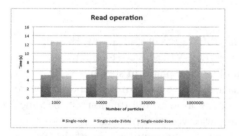

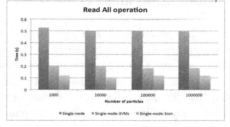

Fig. 4. Read operation for Hive.

Fig. 5. Read all operation for Hive.

For the third benchmark, our experiments are performed with the Hive plugin. Hive is a data warehouse solution built on top of the Hadoop platform. It facilitates queries by providing a high level language called HiveQL. For read operations, the best solution is the architecture with containers, tied to the bare to the metal solution (Fig. 4). Usage of pure virtual machines is not efficient. For the read-all operations, 3 containers provide the best architecture (Fig. 5). The bare metal solution is not really efficient in this case, because Hadoop does not use efficiently multi-threading capabilities. Thus, for this purpose, it is more efficient to use a solution based on containers.

Another advantage is that Hive and Hbase can be combined, and Hive can query a Hbase data set easily. This is important, because from these previous tests, a mixed solution will be necessary to extract information as fast as possible. Indeed, Hbase has to be used for select operations, while Hive is more efficient to gather a complete dataset. Another concern is how to increase the computation capabilities: with containers, the solution can reach the highest performance, when compared to bare to the metal or using VirtualBox. The NFS Gateway is not the most efficient solution, but it provides a simple way to deal with Hadoop data. The most useful feature with this gateway is the ease of data accesses: with Hbase and Hive, it is necessary to use a specific protocol based on Thrift. However, the Thrift compiler produces all necessary classes to communicate with these plugins.

From these results, it appears necessary to adopt a container virtualization approach to increase the performance of the Hadoop platform and to avoid important modifications on the whole framework. Containers reduce the overhead for such a kind of virtualization. The system is drastically reduced compared to a virtual machine engine. Moreover, the time needed to deploy our container platform is also less important than the time needed for virtual boxes. For the bare to the metal, the deployment time is 1.7 s, while for the container distribution 8.8 s are necessary, and for VirtualBox it is a big 188.2 s. Unfortunately, all IT systems are not designed for virtualization and even less for containers. Finally, we tried to evaluate the performance using more containers for read and read all operations. In this evaluation we see the overhead of using Hive and Hbase at the same time. And we can see that using three containers is the optimal solution. Results are produced faster than with the other methods. For this test, Hive is used to create the Hbase table.

6 Conclusion and Perspectives

This paper provides an overview of the VELaSSCo project and a new Hadoop distribution, which has been designed to answer the VELaSSCo requirements. This European project aims to develop a new kind of storage platform specifically designed to store, manipulate and visualize scientific data. Because modern simulation software used by the scientific communities produce enormous information, it becomes increasingly difficult to deal the corresponding large volumes of data.

A specific architecture is defined which supports the requirements of the project regarding computation, and also the available hardware. The platform is composed by existing and new software. The architecture is organized using a layered approach: simulation, storage, client and engine. The simulation part is related to the production of data. The client layer is the access interface of the platform. The storage layer is in charge of different storage methodologies. It is extensible by new storage and access libraries. The last part concerns the engine part. It is in charge of the communications with the client and data layers. It decomposes complex queries provided by the users into specific parts. These sub-queries gather information from the storage layer and apply computations on the data sets, and finally provide a GPU friendly format of the extracted data sets to support efficient visualization.

The platform is currently under development and different parts need to be evaluated. We are developing an automatic evaluation tool, which measures the best storage and access strategies for a specific query regarding a data set. We also plan to extract information from this platform in real time.

Acknowledgments. This work is supported in part by the EC for the FP7 project VELaSSCo, project number 619439, Call FP7-ICT-2013-11. We thank all the members of the consortium:

CIMNE (SP, Coordinator), University of Edinburgh (UK), SINTEF (No.), Fraunhofer IGD (D), JOTNE (No.) and ATOS (SP) for their invaluable contributions and for many fruitful discussions.

References

1. Fan, W., Bifet, A.: Mining big data: current status, and forecast to the future. ACM SIGKDD Explor. Newslett. **14**(2), 1–5 (2013)
2. Laney, D.: 3d data management: controlling data volume, velocity and variety. META Group Res. Note **6**, 70–76 (2001)
3. Dean, J., Barroso, L.A.: The tail at scale. Commun. ACM **56**(2), 74–80 (2013)
4. Dean, J., Ghemawat, S.: Mapreduce: simplified data processing on large clusters. Commun. ACM **51**(1), 107–113 (2008)
5. Chang, F., Dean, J., Ghemawat, S., Hsieh, W.C., Wallach, D.A., Burrows, M., Chandra, T., Fikes, A., Gruber, R.E.: A distributed storage system for structured data. ACM Trans. Comput. Syst. (TOCS) **26**(2), 4 (2008)
6. Ghemawat, S., Gobioff, H., Leung, S.T.: The file system. In: ACM SIGOPS Operating Systems Review, vol. 37, no. 5, pp. 29–43. ACM (2003)
7. Borthakur, D.: The hadoop distributed file system: architecture and design. Hadoop Proj. Website **11**, 21 (2007)
8. Lam, C.: Hadoop in Action. Manning Publications Co., New York (2010)
9. Vora, M.N.: Hadoop-HBase for large-scale data. In: 2011 Computer Science and Network Technology (ICCSNT), vol. 1, pp. 601–605. IEEE (2011)
10. Vavilapalli, V.K., Murthy, A.C., Douglas, C., Agarwal, S., Konar, M., Evans, R., Graves, T., Lowe, J., Shah, H., Seth, S., Saha, B., Curino, C., Malley, O.O, Radia, S., Reed, B., Baldeschwieler, E.: Apache hadoop yarn: yet another resource negotiator. In: 4th Annual Symposium on Cloud Computing (SOCC 2013). ACM, New York, USA (2013)
11. Lange, B., Nguyen, T.: Bigdata architecture for large-scale scientific computing, In: 2014 International Conference on Advances in Big Data Analytics (ABDA), pp. 181–184, Las Vegas, USA (2014)

Crowdsourced Clustering of Computer Generated Floor Plans

David Sousa-Rodrigues[1], Mafalda Teixeira de Sampayo[2](✉),
Eugénio Rodrigues[3], Adélio Rodrigues Gaspar[3], and Álvaro Gomes[4]

[1] Faculty of Maths, Computing and Technology, Centre of Complexity and Design,
The Open University, Milton Keynes, UK
david.rodrigues@open.ac.uk
[2] Department of Architecture, CIES, Lisbon University Institute, Lisbon, Portugal
mafalda.sampaio@iscte.pt
[3] Department of Mechanical Engineering, ADAI, LAETA,
University of Coimbra, Coimbra, Portugal
[4] Department of Electrical and Computer Engineering, INESC Coimbra,
University of Coimbra, Coimbra, Portugal

Abstract. This paper identifies the main criteria used by architecture specialists in the task of clustering alternative floor plan designs. It shows how collective actions of respondents lead to their clustering by carrying out an online exercise. The designs were randomly pre-generated by a hybrid evolutionary algorithm and a questionnaire was posed in the end for the respondents to indicate which similarity criteria they have used. A network of designs was then obtained and it was partitioned into clusters using a modularity optimization algorithm. The results show that the main criterion used was the internal arrangement of spaces, followed by overall shape and by external openings orientation. This work allows the future development of novel algorithms for automatic classification, clustering, and database retrieval of architectural floor plans.

Keywords: Architecture · Network theory · Crowdsourcing · Clustering · Floor plan design · Online survey

1 Introduction

With the advent of computer-aided design, the computer has become more than a mere drawing tool or structural properties calculator. It also takes part in assisting building practitioners during the creative process, by allowing the exploration of potential solutions in the daily architectural practice. In Sect. 2 a brief review of how the field is engaging with these new tools is presented, namely how algorithms are used to generate designs, to classify, and may be used to retrieve architectural documents from databases. The development of such algorithms requires a profound knowledge of the way human practitioners of architecture perceive, understand, group and classify those same documents. The aim of this

© Springer International Publishing Switzerland 2015
Y. Luo (Ed.): CDVE 2015, LNCS 9320, pp. 142–151, 2015.
DOI: 10.1007/978-3-319-24132-6_17

study is to understand what are the collective actions of architecture practitioners when grouping floor plan designs. To this effect an online survey was conducted in which participants were asked to select similar floor plan designs and to answer a questionnaire indicating the similarity criteria used. The resulting answers were mapped to a network of floor plan designs co-selection and were clustered by a modularity optimization algorithm (Sect. 3). The findings of this study (Sect. 4) can help in the development of query mechanisms for database retrieval of floor plans and the implementation of clustering mechanisms to aggregate results from generative design methods. Besides these applications, the understanding of how architecture practitioners solve this complex problem may help to develop specific programs for the teaching of architecture. The limitation and implications of this work are broad and range from the pedagogic level to the development of new algorithms and databases (Sect. 5).

2 Related Work

One of the early architectural tasks in the building design process is space planning. Architects seek to accommodate all requirements and preferences into architectural floor plans during the synthesis phase, which are determined during the analytical phase. This is a time-consuming trial-and-error process with its associated costs. The resulting design is much dependent on the past experience of the architect and often based on already built examples. As the rooms' configuration is essentially a combinatorial problem, medium to large design programs—list of functional spaces, topological relations, and geometric constraints—can easily reach a number of alternative design solutions that are impossible to be drafted by humans in the traditional way. For this reason, since 1960 s researchers have been developing computer-based approaches to help practitioners [1,2]. These approaches have tried to resolve specific design problems such as area assignment [3], partitioning of a boundary [4–6], allocation of rooms [6–10], design adaptation [11], or the hierarchical construction of different elements [12]. If the earlier approaches looked to enumerate all possible configurations, which led researchers to face the cumbersome problem of the exponential growth of possible solutions for design programs with more than 8 spaces, recent studies tried to find only the most promising solutions. To achieve this, evolutionary computation techniques were used, as these have shown capabilities to deal with ill-defined and complex problems, and demonstrated to produce surprisingly novel solutions applied to the generation of architectural floor plans [13].

Online surveys have been used in several applications and are a method of data collection that conveys several advantages, namely they provide access to many individuals who share specific interests and professions that would otherwise be difficult to contact. Surveys also save time as they do automated collection of responses and allow researchers to work on other tasks while data is being collected [14]. When properly developed and implemented, a survey portrays the characteristics of large groups of respondents on a specific topic and allows assessing representativeness [15]. Several types of surveys are available; e.g. questionnaire and interview formats, phone survey, and online surveys, which can be coupled with inference engines that act and direct the survey according to respondents' answers [16, 17].

The use of surveys in architectural environments has been conducted in many aspects of the discipline. They have been used in the establishing ground truths in perceptual understanding of floor plans for the characterization of shapes, lines and texture [18, 19]. Feedback to architects is being given by surveys of architecture virtual immersive experiments that aim to understand physiological signals of emotions, namely fear, in space perception [20, 21]. Several studies have been proposed that include the participation of the crowd and are bottom-up learning processes, e.g. peer assessment [22] where students mark each other' work. In this study the process of grouping floor plans is investigated to understand the criteria used by the students and other practitioners during the grouping process.

3   Methods and Materials

3.1   The Online Survey

An online survey was setup as an exercise to collect information on how the respondents perform the clustering task. There are many online tools for conducting surveys [14, 15], but none can handle the special problem posed by using architectural documents. Therefore, it was decided to develop a web application for the experiment (Fig. 1). To understand the perception and criteria of the target population, a post experiment questionnaire was presented to participants. Individuals whose daily activities are related to building design were chosen as the target group; i.e. architects, architecture students, civil engineers, and urban planners. As the target group is well delimited, the selection of participants was conducted through University communities of architecture students and former students, and also through the professional affiliation contact lists. This ensured that the majority of the participants in this study were related to the subject or if their present professional occupation is not related to architecture, at least they received training in architecture.

From a total of 72 generated floor plans, twelve were randomly selected and displayed in a web interface. The user was asked to drag-and-drop to a specific area in the screen the floor plans that he considered similar. Each respondent repeated this iteration ten times. The 72 floor plans were generated using the Evolutionary Program for the Space Allocation Problem (EPSAP algorithm) [7–9]. This algorithm is capable of producing alternative floor plans according to the user's preferences and requirements set as the building functional program. The solutions generated were for a single-family house with three bedrooms, one hall, one kitchen, a living room, one corridor and two bathrooms. One bathroom and all bedrooms are connected to the corridor. The remaining spaces are connected to the hall. The kitchen presents an internal door connecting it to the living room. One of the bathrooms serves the public areas of the house, while the

Clustering of Floor Plans

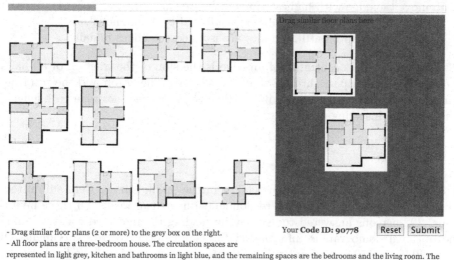

- Drag similar floor plans (2 or more) to the grey box on the right.   Your **Code ID: 90778**   [Reset] [Submit]
- All floor plans are a three-bedroom house. The circulation spaces are
represented in light grey, kitchen and bathrooms in light blue, and the remaining spaces are the bedrooms and the living room. The
entrance door is facing the north quadrant.

Fig. 1. Users drag-and-drop floor plans into the shaded area according to similarity

other connects to the corridor of the private area of the house. All inner rooms
have doors of 90 cm width, the exception being the living room doors that are
140 cm. Except for the circulation areas and one of the bathrooms; all areas
have at least one window. The hall has an exterior door facing north. No other
restrictions were imposed. At the end of the online survey, a final questionnaire
was presented with a list of possible criteria and the user could chose which he
used or to provide written alternatives. After submission the exercise ended and
the user was redirected to the home page.

3.2 Network Science Analysis of the Collected Data

A normalized matrix depicting the fraction to times each pair of floor plans was
co-selected is constructed. This matrix is understood as an adjacency matrix
where the entries represent the weights of the connections between two designs.
The results present some background uncertainty and it is necessary to define
a minimum threshold for the entries of the matrix. The threshold value was
tested to identify the structure of the selection process, which represented the
floor plan's network. This network—undirected and weighted—is partitioned
with the edge betweenness community detection algorithm [23]. This is a divisive
hierarchical mechanism that aims to find communities by maximizing the value of
modularity—networks with high modularity have dense intra cluster connections
but sparse connections between vertices of different clusters. The algorithm for
creating the dendrogram proceeds in the following manner [23]:

1. Calculate the edge betweenness in the network.
2. Remove the edge with highest value of betweenness.
3. Recalculate betweenness for all edges affected by the removal.
4. Repeat from step 2 until all nodes are isolated (no edges remain).

The betweenness centrality of an edge is the sum of the fraction of all-pairs shortest paths that pass through that edge [24–26]. The graph and the resulting partition are characterized according to diverse properties—average path length, density, and clustering coefficient.

4   Results

A total of 609 invitations to participate in the online survey were submitted. The survey was available for the respondents during two weeks. Of those invitations, 202 persons answered the survey by reading the informed consent, filling the optional demographic information form and initiated the experiment. Of those 202 only 110 carried out the 10 iterations asked and filled the final criteria questionnaire. In total, the respondents performed 1257 iterations. Of the participants that registered, 92 did not conclude the exercise. The average number of iterations made by those 92 persons was 1,7. The pool of participants inhabits mainly in Portugal and the ages range between 18 and 50 years old.

By varying the threshold of the fraction of co-selections of floor plan designs, it is possible to verify that the initial dense network presents low modularity, high density of edges, and small average path length (Fig. 2). It also presents a high clustering coefficient, which is indicative of many triangles in the network. The

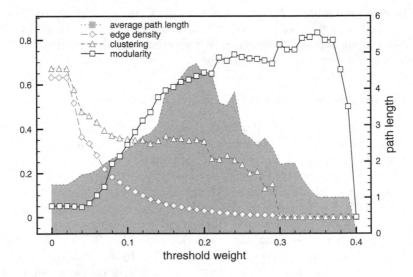

Fig. 2. Floor Plan Design Network properties: clustering, density, modularity (left axis) and average path length (right axis).

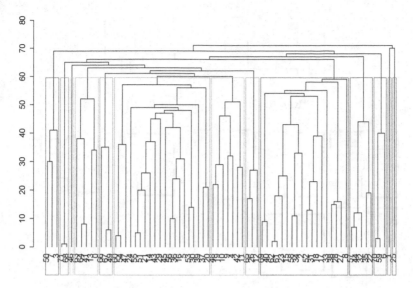

Fig. 3. Dendrogram of the clustering identifying the resulting clusters.

increase of the threshold leads to higher average path length, lower edge density, and lower clustering coefficient. Modularity starts rising until a threshold of 0,36. The average path length peaks around a threshold of 0,19 and a value of 4,6 and after starts decreasing again as a result of the fragmentation of the resulting network were many isolated nodes emerge.

Due to this fragmentation, a threshold of 12 % was chosen. This still ensured a modularity value of 0,44 and an average path length of 2,7. The clustering resulted in 13 clusters (Fig. 3). It is clear from the dendrogram that this clustering present some isolated nodes, namely $\{1, 25, 46\}$. The distribution of the floor plan design clusters was $\{20, 18, 7, 5, 5, 3, 3, 3, 3, 2, 1, 1, 1\}$.

The clusters present good internal consistency, meaning that upon inspection they are coherent with the criteria reported by the users. This can be seen in the three examples of the clusters obtained from the clustering process in Figs. 4, 5, and 6.

The survey co-criteria analysis indicates that two criteria are often selected together by participants, *by interior spaces* and *by circulation spaces* (Table 1). On a second level, the participants considered criteria related to the overall *shape*

Fig. 4. Cluster of plans $\{0, 13, 41, 63, 64\}$

Fig. 5. Cluster of plans {3, 7, 50}

Fig. 6. Cluster of plans {4, 9, 10, 11, 19, 42, 48}

Table 1. Criteria co-selection. Diagonal entries represent frequency of each criterion. Intersections of the lower triangle indicate frequency of co-selection of two criteria.

75	by interior spaces				
22	41	by shape general			
20	18	36	by shape mirrored		
17	18	18	29	by shape rotated	
47	19	20	12	63	circulation spaces
13	7	7	3	12	18	exterior openings

(either considering cases where mirroring or rotations occurred) and in a third tier respondents considered the existence of *external openings*. This clearly shows that users favor the interior space organization as the most important feature in defining similarity of floor plans.

5   Conclusion

The results, as shown in Table 1, indicate that architecture practitioners give higher importance to the interior configurations of spaces than the overall building shape. This information is important for future development of ICT-mediated strategies for architecture education and professional practitioners. They will also impact other applications such as floor plan design database retrieval—by identifying the encoding features used by human practitioners that can then be implemented in the encoding of database records—and aggregation of similar solutions that result from generative design methods—releasing humans from the tedious and repetitive task of grouping similar floor plans, and allowing for concise typological presentation of floor plans in automated ways.

The execution of online surveys is not free of problems. Sampling issues might be present, as the respondents are not monitored and some misbehavior can happen; e.g. double answering [14]. The minimization of these problems was achieved by assigning a unique five-digit code to each participant that matches the answers in the dataset with the IP address. The problem "lurkers" was minimized by contacting each participant directly, that is people who do not participate but have access to the survey [14].

The response rate was around 30 %. Although many online surveys have low response rates, they try to increase by some incentive mechanisms, e.g. financial incentives, prizes, coupons, or books. However, in this case that was not an issue. No incentive mechanism was implemented in this experiment for the completion of the survey. The personal contact of the researcher with each participant made the participation in the survey a matter of personal and professional respect. However, the effective completion rate was small, as 92 participants did not complete the survey (18 %). These limitations are not exclusive to this kind of online survey technique [14, 15].

These results, namely the criteria reported by the respondents, can be incorporated in machine learning algorithms to perform clustering tasks in ways that mimic experts' actions. Also, the obtained clustering results will be used as a ground truth or benchmark for new clustering algorithms that deal with perceptual clustering of floor plan designs.

Acknowledgements. Sousa-Rodrigues, D. was partially supported by project Topdrim FP7-ICT-2011-8/318121. Rodrigues, E., Gaspar, A.R., and Gomes, Á. were partially supported by project *Automatic Generation of Architectural Floor Plans with Energy Optimization* (GerAPlanO), QREN 38922, CENTRO-07-0402-FEDER-038922 and framed under the *Energy for Sustainability Initiative* at University of Coimbra.

References

1. Liggett, R.S.: Automated facilities layout: past, present and future. Autom. Constr. **9**(2), 197–215 (2000)
2. Steadman, P.: Generative design methods and the exploration of worlds of formal possibility. Architect. Des. **84**(5), 24–31 (2014)
3. Gero, J.S., Kazakov, V.A.: Evolving design genes in space layout planning problems. Artif. Intell. Eng. **12**(3), 163–176 (1998)
4. Mitchell, W.J., Steadman, J.P., Liggett, R.S.: Synthesis and optimization of small rectangular floor plans. Environ. Plan. B **3**(1), 37–70 (1976)
5. Quiroz, J.C., Louis, S.J., Banerjee, A., Dascalu, S.M.: Towards creative design using collaborative interactive genetic algorithms. In: Evolutionary Computation 2009, pp. 1849–1856. IEEE, May 2009
6. Koenig, R., Knecht, K.: Comparing two evolutionary algorithm based methods for layout generation: dense packing versus subdivision. Artif. Intell. Eng. Des. Anal. Manuf. **28**(03), 285–299 (2014)

7. Rodrigues, E., Gaspar, A., Gomes, Á.: An evolutionary strategy enhanced with a local search technique for the space allocation problem in architecture, part 1: methodology. Comput. Aided-Des. **45**(5), 887–897 (2013)
8. Rodrigues, E., Gaspar, A., Gomes, Á.: An evolutionary strategy enhanced with a local search technique for the space allocation problem in architecture, part 2: validation and performance tests. Comput. Aided-Des. **45**(5), 898–910 (2013)
9. Rodrigues, E., Gaspar, A., Gomes, Á.: An approach to the multi-level space allocation problem in architecture using a hybrid evolutionary technique. Autom. Constr. **35**, 482–498 (2013)
10. Michalek, J.J., Choudhary, R., Papalambros, P.Y.: Architectural layout design optimization. Eng. Optim. **34**, 461–484 (2002)
11. Garza, A.G.D.S., Maher, M.L.: GENCAD: a hybrid analogical/evolutionary model of creative design. In: Gero, J.S., Maher, M.L. (eds.) Computational And Cognitive Models Of Creative Design V, pp. 141–171. Key Center of Design Computing and Cognition, University of Sidney, Sydney (2001)
12. Virirakis, L.: GENETICA: a computer language that supports general formal expression with evolving data structures. IEEE Trans. Evol. Comput. **7**(5), 456–481 (2003)
13. Kalay, Y.E.: Architecture's New Media: Principles, Theories and Methods of Computer-Aided Design. The MIT Press, Cambridge (2004)
14. Wright, K.B.: Researching internet-based populations: advantages and disadvantages of online survey research, online questionnaire authoring software packages, and web survey services. J. Comput.-Mediated Commun. **10**(3), 00–00 (2005)
15. Evans, J.R., Mathur, A.: The value of online surveys. Internet Res. **15**(2), 195–219 (2005)
16. Urbano, P., Sousa-Rodrigues, D.: The advantage of using rules in online surveys. Revista de Ciências da Computação **III**(3), 38–49 (2008)
17. Urbano, P., Sousa-Rodrigues, D.: Rule based systems applied to online surveys. In: IADIS WWW/Internet Conference. Freiburg, Oct 2008
18. Sousa-Rodrigues, D., de Sampayo, M.T., Rodrigues, E., Gaspar, A.R., Gomes, Á., Antunes, C.H.: Online survey for collective clustering of computer generated architectural floor plans. arXiv preprint arXiv:1504.08145 (2015)
19. de las Heras, L.P., Fernandez, D., Fornes, A., Valveny, E., Sanchez, G., Llados, J.: Perceptual retrieval of architectural floor plans. In: 10th IAPR International Workshop on Graphics Recognition (2013)
20. Dias, M.S., Eloy, S., Carreiro, M., Proença, P., Moural, A., Pedro, T., Freitas, J., Vilar, E., d'Alpuim, J., Azevedo, S.: Designing better spaces for people: virtual reality and biometric sensing as tools to evaluate space use. In: Gu, N., Watanabe, S., Erhan, H., Haeusler, M.H., Huang, W., Sosa, R. (eds.) Rethinking Comprehensive Design: Speculative Counterculture, Proceedings of the 19th International Conference of the Association of Computer-Aided Architectural Design Research in Asia, Hong Kong (2014)
21. Dias, M.S., Eloy, S., Carreiro, M., Vilar, E., Marques, S., Moural, A., Proença, P., Cruz, J., d'Alpuim, J., Carvalho, N., Azevedo, A.S., Pedro, T.: Space perception in virtual environments - on how biometric sensing in virtual environments may give architects users's feedback. In: Thompson, E.M. (ed.) Fusion - Proceedings of the 32nd eCAADe Conference, Newcastle upon Tyne, England, UK, vol. 2, pp. 271–280, September 2014
22. de Sampayo, M.T., Sousa-Rodrigues, D., Jimenez-Romero, C., Johnson, J.H.: Peer assessment in architecture education. In: International Conference on Technology and Innovation, Brno, Czech Republic, September 2014

23. Girvan, M., Newman, M.: Community structure in social and biological networks. Proc. Natl. Acad. Sci. USA **99**, 7821–7826 (2002)
24. Anthonisse, J.M.: The rush in a directed graph. Technical report, Stichting Mathematicsh Centrum, Amsterdam (1971)
25. Freeman, L.C.: A set of measures of centrality based on betweenness. Sociometry **40**(1), 35–41 (1977)
26. Brandes, U.: A faster algorithm for betweenness centrality*. J. Math. Sociol. **25**(2), 163–177 (2001)

Collective Intelligence Support Protocol

A Systemic Approach for Collaborative Architectural Design

Alexandru Senciuc[1(✉)], Irene Pluchinotta[2,3], and Samia Ben Rajeb[4]

[1] Independent Researcher, Cachan, France
alexandru.senciuc@gmail.com
[2] DICATECh, Technical University of Bari, Bari, Italy
[3] LAMSADE-CNRS, Université Paris-Dauphine, Paris, France
[4] LUCID, Université de Liège, Liège, Belgium

Abstract. The collaborative architectural design process can be difficult to generate and maintain, especially when consisting of large teams, time constraints and long distance as it requires a higher sense of working together. However, a formal description of collaborative design as a system made of elements, agents, sub-systems and relationships could open a path to potentially improve production efficiency and stream collective intelligence. The CISP is a first attempt methodology to support collaborative design based on the empirical analysis of a single case study involving a multi-disciplinary team competing in an international architectural idea competition. The methodology operates through interdependencies on three layers: organization, planning and shared workspace. By articulating methods, tools, team members and project phases, the CISP fosters an integrated design system and a fluent design process.

Keywords: Collective intelligence · Collaborative design · Systemic approach · Decision support system

1 Introduction

Collaborative design is a creative and complex domain that faces multiple challenges today. Designers regularly define and/or frame the problem, they adopt holistic thinking, and they sketch, draw, and model possible ideas throughout the design process [1]. Specifically, collaborative design is an activity that requires participation of individuals for sharing information and organizing design tasks and resources [2] and it is a process of managing multiple perspectives [3]. Most architectural projects involve large numbers of participants that design and produce together a complex object that is one of a kind. Often, participants do not work together regularly, as teams are organized on a project basis [4]. As Kvan [5] points out, design collaboration requires a higher sense of working together in order to achieve a creative result. It is a far more demanding activity than simply completing a project as a team. Especially when dealing with a multidisciplinary team, the lack of shared understanding reduces the quality of the final

© Springer International Publishing Switzerland 2015
Y. Luo (Ed.): CDVE 2015, LNCS 9320, pp. 152–161, 2015.
DOI: 10.1007/978-3-319-24132-6_18

product [6]. What is more, it is critical for geographically distributed designers, through remote collaboration, to accurately perceive other team members' activities with a high level of awareness as if they were working in the same room [7]. In addition, designers must work fast, as competition in the marketplace drives short design cycles and are expected to constantly challenge the limits of known solutions and venture into unknown territories [1]. In this context, a collaborative architectural design process is generally difficult to generate and maintain, especially in an environment consisting of large teams, short deadlines and long distance. Thus, it seems interesting to understand how collaborative design methodologies can help designers form a collective intelligence that would be able to face ever-shifting challenges. This paper is based on an empirical analysis of a single case study involving a multidisciplinary team that competed in an international architectural idea competition with over 1700 entries and that received an award. The main objective of the current research is to make the first step towards identifying a systemic methodology that allows fostering collective intelligence. The question of the research is: how does a large multidisciplinary team harness collective intelligence in order to design an architectural project in a constraining spatiotemporal situation? The challenge gave rise to a Collective Intelligence Support Protocol (CISP) for architectural design, based on a systemic approach. This tentative starts from the assumption that collective architectural design is a highly complex system that consists of a multitude of elements linked together by interdependencies. A systemic approach is methodical, repeatable and learnable through a step by step procedure [8], clarifying the interdependencies of the members in a collaborative project [5]. Through the formal description of the CISP the present research seeks to understand the structure and the macro behavior of a system through its internal sub-models.

2   Collaborative Architectural Design System

The definition of a system can have several hues. For the aim of this research, it is useful to remember that a system can be defined as a set of two or more elements where: (i) the behavior of each element has an effect on the behavior of the whole; (ii) the behavior of the elements and their effects on the whole are interdependent; (iii) and while subgroups of the elements all have an effect on the behavior of the whole, none has an independent effect on it [9]. Additionally, groups or organizations are dynamic systems, adapting and evolving with their multiple parts that interact with one another and with the environment [10–12]. Indeed, as collaborative design process complexity continuously increases, design has to integrate a great number of expertise [13] and using systems concepts offers a way of rationalizing aspects of existing practice and of suggesting directions for improvement [14–16]. In fact, systems theory can be summarized as a knowledge framework that focuses on structures, relationships, and interdependence between elements [17]. Furthermore, design context is project-based, defined considering time product, process aspects, and also the human, social and organizational aspects [18]. Within collaborative design, agents gather around a common objective related to an architectural project, in order to exchange information and share knowledge, with high-level coordination activities. In system theory, these elements of purpose, interdependencies, structure, techniques and information must be coordinated and integrated by the managerial system, in order to maximize value for the organization [11, 19, 20]. The previous observations suggest that the collaborative design process can be seen as a dynamic system in which involved agents form an organization with a common objective, exchanging information and sharing knowledge with high levels of coordination, by focusing on structures, relationships and interdependencies. Besides, organizations can be understood in terms of their decision process [21] and supporting it facilitates more effective group interaction, leading to greater decision-making effectiveness [22, 23]. Historically, the concept of decision support system emerged in the 1970s when it was proposed for models providing assistance in dealing with semi-structured and unstructured problems [24–26]. In this regard, collaborative design is a term that denotes more than just cooperation or coordination. In cooperation participants do not have a common goal but rather work together to achieve mutual benefits [4] through informal relationships [5, 27]. Coordination consists of more formal relationships as well as a structure of compatible missions. It requires division of roles, some planning and the establishment of communication channels [27]. However, collaboration occurs when several agents are working together in a planned way in the same production process or in different but connected production processes [28]. In collaboration, the common mission is the bounding element to which participants are committed [5]. Therefore, agents may share fully or partially overlapping goals and coordination is needed in order for them to work together harmoniously [29, 30]. Hence, within the general structure of collaborative design process there are interdependencies between collaborative and cooperative moments, which are organized in an alternating chain from the first sketch to final render.

Continuity between these moments, as well as teamwork efficiency, require an element that can be identified as "collective intelligence". The term defines the capacity of groups of individuals to act collectively in ways that seem intelligent in regards to certain objectives [31]. Furthermore, in order to organize the design process, the collective intelligence could be associated with the ability of the agents group to work with each other, with subsystems as well as with the main system. The research seeks to develop a methodology that supports collective intelligence in the architectural design process.

3   Collective Intelligence Support Protocol (CISP)

The general idea of the CISP sparked from several initial hypothesis regarding collaborative design in architecture [32]. The aim is to support collective intelligence in order to generate a shared architectural design and to provide managerial structure in response to spatiotemporal constraints. Specifically, the CISP seeks to: (i) create an organizational structure within the team, assign specific roles to members by defining the set of relationships between sub-systems, (ii) plan phases and deadlines for the design process timeline, (iii) configure a shared workspace for exchanging ideas (both online and offline) and for supporting collective decision making, (iv) develop a common ground between team members, (v) maintain the necessary adaptability throughout the collective design process. The CISP sees collaborative architectural design as a system of interconnected sub-systems (e.g. team members, layers), interacting with each other and with the system in which they operate, in order to create and produce a common architectural project. The methodology operates on three layers of the teamwork: organization, planning and shared work space. By working with each layer individually and by connecting them between each other, the CISP can respond simultaneously to management and creativity issues in architectural design.

The CISP methodology has been progressively developed in parallel to the case study and has resulted into the formalization of the three layers, based on continuous empirical feedback from team activity.

3.1 Organization Layer

The organization layer assigns specific roles and types to team members, generates a set of relationships and creates sub-teams. The structure is created through collective decision and can be continuously adapted throughout the design process. It is used to implement the planning of the design process and to construct the shared workspace. Using a systemic approach, when the architectural project is identified, a number of functionally specific and modular system components can be developed. This decomposition allows each agent (or sub-team) to use its best knowledge for solving a particular problem. In the organization layer, agents need to coordinate and collaborate with one another to ensure that interdependencies are properly managed.

Within the case study, team members were initially selected to cover all the particular aspects of the design theme. Each agent's background was scanned to define their member type and role in order to manage interdependencies within the team. Team types and roles created a shared awareness of the potential interactions between members as well as of individual production capacities in order to avoid the polarization of viewpoints and the incapacity of a group to create a joint basis for communication and action. Firstly, the following member types have been defined: (i) the Designer is the agent involved in the development of the project idea, proposing new design alternatives; (ii) the Researcher explores and provides knowledge to support the team's design process; (iii) the Consultant is the agent who delivers expert advice and specialized information in a particular topic; (iv) the Producer is the agent member of the team that produces parts of the project render, based on the collaborative decision. Secondly, the role distinction between coordinator and member creates a hierarchy decomposition that distributes responsibilities, decisions and tasks. In particular: (i) the (Overview) Coordinator is responsible for promoting the project and managing all the activities relating to his/her agency, in order to achieve the previously set objectives; (ii) the Member agent is part of a specific team and produces information relative to its targets. To support the design process, the organizational layer of the protocol implemented a dual layout: vertical and horizontal. The horizontal organization layout encouraged creative interaction (Fig. 1) (i.e. designing, project decision-making). Each member had the same decisional legitimacy and collaboration methods and tools were used to channel team activity towards a common architectural project. On the other side, the role of the vertical organization layout was to maintain design process efficiency (Fig. 1). Members' distribution into sub-teams created task dispersion and simplified objectives for each team as well as for its members. Every team had a dominant role in a corresponding phase of the planning layer. The type attribute that has been assigned to each member referred to their background but also to their possible contribution in the team (Table 1). Moreover, team members were distributed into four teams and each team received a leading role in decision-making throughout the timeline of the design process. Three of the four teams cover the main tasks of a design process: research, exploration and production (Table 2).

Table 1. Team members' background, type and role

Code	Background	Member type	Member role
AS	Collaborative design architect	Designer, Researcher	(O) coordinator
RG	Architect and BIM specialist	Designer, Consultant	Coordinator
TM	Business and marketing specialist	Consultant	Coordinator
IP	Environmental engineer	Researcher, Consultant	Coordinator
HG	3D visualization specialist	Designer, Producer	Member
AN	Computational design specialist	Designer, Producer	Member
AR	Architect and landscape specialist	Designer	Member
CS	Urban strategist	Designer, Consultant	Member
SB	Collaborative design researcher	Consultant	Coordinator
IY	Motion graphic designer	Designer, Producer	Member
AT	Architect and graphic designer	Producer	Member

Table 2. The four teams of the competition

Name	Goals	Input	Output
T0 Organization	Organize the collaborative design process	Organization and planning decisions	Collaboration and cooperation methods
T1 Research	Knowledge support and common ground	Design theme and general orientations	Knowledge mapping and knowledge insight
T2 Exploration	Creating and developing project	Knowledge mapping and insight	Project idea and development alternatives
T3 Production	Producing project and render documents	Project idea and alternatives	Render documents

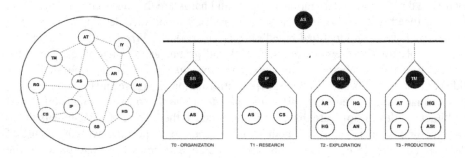

Fig. 1. Horizontal layout (left) and vertical layout (right) of the team in the case study

3.2 Planning Layer

The planning layer distributes team activity throughout the time frame of the design process. As an evolution from first sketch to final render, planning is used to create temporal sequences that prioritize tasks. Temporal particularities may also have an impact on the organization and shared workspace layers. At a detail level, the planning layer distributes team activity into a chain of alternating collaborative and cooperative moments. They use horizontal and vertical organizational layouts and ensure a continuity of articulation from one phase to the other. Collaborative moments are associated to synchronous distance or in-presence meetings while cooperative moments are linked with asynchronous meetings or individual work.

Within the case study, the planning layer consisted of three phases corresponding to the three teams: research, exploration and production. The goal of each phase was the same as the goal of the corresponding sub-team (Table 2). During a particular phase, all team members worked for the same tasks while the leading team carried the responsibility for delivering the necessary output. As a consequence, interdependencies between members changed over time, as leading teams rotated from one phase to the other. Furthermore, design theme specificities established the time attribution per phase. However, research and exploration phases overlapped almost completely while exploration and production overlapped much less in the process timeline. Hence, design process has been focused significantly more on idea development (research and exploration phases) than project production.

3.3   Shared Workspace Layer

The shared workspace layer provides team members with the necessary framework where the interactions take place in order to produce the project. It seeks to support common knowledge between members, build a common set of work and communication tools as well identify a physical and virtual space for collaborative work. The workspace is made of two elements: a set of tools and a set of methods.

Within the case study, the set of tools consisted of already developed and market available design and collaboration software and hardware that allowed team members to work together or individually in project production and idea development. Several tool types have been identified based on type of work: (i) *Virtual workspace* gathers digital tools for lightweight textual, verbal and graphical information exchange for cooperative and collaborative moments; (ii) *Physical workspace* uses physical tools (idea boards, post-it's and prints) to support information exchange and to produce physical format output (sketches); (iii) *Individual design tools* consist in precision digital architectural design software that are used to produce the final render documents in the architectural project. The set of methods is designed to support the evolving nature of the collaborative design process: changing interdependencies from one phase to the other, adapting to specific requirements of collaborative and cooperative moments, ensuring decisional continuity from vertical to horizontal layout and vice versa. Several method types have been defined, based on nature of collaborative work: (i) *ShareLab*[1] is a methodology that allows to manage the collaborative design process in presence or distance synchronous meetings; (ii) *Collaborative decision-making methods* encourage the participation of agents in the decisional process and try to formalize a common understanding, which supports information exchange and cooperation; (iii) *Coordination methods* are a set of guidelines that ensure the continuity between collaborative and cooperative moments through the generation of team activity awareness using meeting reports, workspace instructions and tool use charter.

---

[1] The ShareLab has been defined in Ben Rajeb S., Senciuc A., Pluchinotta I. (2015). "ShareLab support for collective intelligence. 1 deadline, 11 designers, 1 project". Currently under review in the COLLA 2015 conference.

4   Conclusions

Describing collaborative architectural design as a system made of agents, sub-systems and relationships opens a path to support the design process from first sketch to final render. In the case of the international architectural idea competition, the CISP provided the necessary methodology for an integrated design system connecting organizational, planning and shared workspace elements. Fostering collective intelligence enabled an adaptable process that took into account the teamwork complexities and allowed to deliver a shared project idea within the available spatiotemporal constraints. Some notable case study observations and limitations on the CISP are presented hereafter. At first, the protocol was procedural, imposing a large number of formalized interactions between team members, but gradually naturalized into the design process, evolving and adapting along with it. Within the organization layer, sub-team coordinators of the vertical layout changed their role, becoming simple sub-team members. Therefore, while sub-team distribution was maintained, the vertical layout relied mainly on the overall coordinator for ensuring continuity of the design process. From the planning layer point of view, the design process split into two main parts: idea development (including the research and exploration phases) and project render (including the production phase). As a consequence, the two parts used distinct CISP configurations: (i) during idea development the horizontal organization layout, virtual and physical workspace tools, ShareLab and collective decision making methods were dominant; (ii) during project render the vertical organization layout, individual tools and coordination methods were dominant. Within the shared workspace layer, the design process required extensive knowledge sharing between agents as well as intensive coordination between collaborative and cooperative moments. For this reason, virtual and physical workspace tools as well as ShareLab and coordination methods have been adapted to include the above-mentioned interactions. The present research is simply a first iteration that is aimed at formalizing a protocol capable of supporting collective intelligence within collaborative architectural design and at obtaining preliminary feedback this in regard. Further developments seek to: (i) improve methodology through research development within future case studies, (ii) develop the methodology towards other stages of the architectural project that include non-expert agents (i.e. clients, stakeholders); (iii) integrate innovative collaborative design technologies (i.e. BIM, building information modelling) and an agent-based modelling approach (multi-agent systems).

Acknowledgement.   The Researchers would like to address a warm thank you to the members of the TarTar Team for agreeing to take part in this case study.

References

1. Goldschmidt, G., Rodgers, P.A.: Design thinking approaches of three different groups of designers based on self-reports. Des. Stud. **34**, 454–471 (2013)
2. Chiu, M.L.: An organizational view of design communication in design collaboration. Des. Stud. **23**, 187–210 (2002)

3. Detienne, F.: Collaborative design: managing task interdependencies and multiple perspectives. Interact. Comput. **18**, 1–20 (2006)
4. van Leeuwen, J.P.: Computer support for collaborative work in the construction industry. In: Proceedings of the International Conference on Concurrent Engineering, Madeira, Portugal (2003)
5. Kvan, T.: Collaborative design: what is it? Autom. Const. **9**, 409–415 (2000)
6. Dong, A.: The latent semantic approach to studying design team communication. Des. Stud. **26**, 445–461 (2005)
7. Wang, X., et al.: Mutual awareness in collaborative design: an augmented reality integrated telepresence system. Comput. Ind. **65**, 314–324 (2014)
8. Forrester, J.W.: System Dynamics: The Foundation Under Systems Thinking. Cambridge, Sloan School of Management, MIT (1999)
9. Skyttner, L.: General Systems Theory: An Introduction. Macmillan Press, London (1996)
10. Ashmos, D., et al.: The systems paradigm in organization theory: correcting the record and suggesting the future. Acad. Manage. Rev. **12**(4), 607–621 (1987)
11. Amagoh, F.: From perspectives on organizational change: systems and complexity theories. Innov. J. Public Sect. Innov. J. **13**(3), 1–14 (2008). Article 3
12. Martinelli, D.P.: Systems hierarchies and management. Syst. Res. Behav. Sci. **18**(1), 69–82 (2001)
13. Robin, V., Rose, B., Girard, P.: Modelling collaborative knowledge to support engineering design project manager. Comput. Ind. **58**, 188–198 (2007)
14. White, L.: Changing the "whole system" in the public sector. J. Organ. Change Manage. **13**(2), 162–177 (2000)
15. Rhee, Y.: Complex systems approach to the study of politics. Syst. Res. Behav. Sci. **17**(6), 487–491 (2000)
16. Stewart, J., Ayres, R.: Systems theory and policy practice: an exploration. Policy Sci. **34**(1), 79–88 (2001)
17. Katz, D., et al.: The Social Psychology of Organizations. Wiley, New York (1978)
18. Ostergaard, K., Summers, J.D.: A taxonomic classification of collaborative design processes. In: International Conference on Engineering Design (2003)
19. Randolph, A., et al.: Managing Organizational Behavior. Irwin, Boston (1989)
20. Montuori, L.: Organizational longevity. Integrating systems thinking, learning and complexity. J. Organ. Change Manage. **13**(1), 61–73 (2000)
21. Simon, H.A.: Administrative Behavior: A Study of Decision-Making Processes in Administrative Organization, 4th edn. Macmillan Co, New York (1947)
22. Shim, J.P., et al.: Past, present, and future of decision support technology. Decis. Support Syst. **33**, 111–126 (2002)
23. Warkentin, M.E., et al.: Virtual teams versus face-to-face teams: an exploratory study of a web-based conference system. Decis. Sci. **28**(4), 975–996 (1997)
24. Gorry, G.A.: Scott Morton, M.S.: A framework for management information systems. Sloan Manage. Rev. **13**(1), 55–70 (1971)
25. Anthony, R.N.: Planning and Control Systems: A Framework for Analysis. Harvard University Graduate School of Business Administration, Boston (1965)
26. Simon, H.A.: The New Science of Management Decision. Harper and Brothers, New York (1960)
27. Mattessich, P.W., Monsey, B.R.: Collaboration: What makes it work. Amherst H. Wilder Foundation, St. Paul (1992)
28. Wilson, P.: Introducing CSCW - what is it and why we need it. In: Computer-Supported Cooperative Work, Brookfield, VT, Ashgate Publishing (1994)

29. Malone, T.W., Crowston, K.: What is coordination theory and how can it help cooperative work systems? In: Proceedings of the Conference on Computer-Supported Cooperative Work, Los Angeles (1990)
30. Malone, T.W., Crowston, K.: The interdisciplinary study of coordination. ACM Comput. Surv. **26**(1), 87–119 (1994)
31. Malone, T.W., Laubacher, R., Dellarocas, C.N.: Harnessing crowds: mapping the genome of collective intelligence. MIT Center for Collective Intelligence Working Paper, Cambridge (2009)
32. Senciuc, A., Lecourtois, C.: Exploring collective architectural conception: cooperation, coordination and collaboration via basic online tools. In: Luo, Y. (ed.) CDVE 2013. LNCS, vol. 8091, pp. 51–55. Springer, Heidelberg (2013)

Collaborative Shopping with the Crowd

Andreas Mladenow[1(✉)], Christine Bauer[2], and Christine Strauss[1]

[1] Department of eBusiness, University of Vienna, Vienna, Austria
{andreas.mladenow,christine.strauss}@univie.ac.at
[2] Department of Information Systems and Operations,
Vienna University of Economics and Business, Vienna, Austria
chris.bauer@wu.ac.at

Abstract. The ubiquity of information and communication technologies (ICT) stimulate collaborative shopping and bring together customers with similar interests around the world to perform cooperative and collective online shopping. As a result, various models of collaborative online group buying are emerging. This paper analyses the phases of interaction during the shopping processes and provides a systematic categorization of the online group buying based on the top-down/bottom-up crowd-shopping models. In addition, this paper discusses recent developments and challenges of group buying in order to contribute to future research directions within the field of collaborative online group buying.

Keywords: Crowdsourcing · Collaboration · Crowd-Shopping · Online group buying · Group buying 2.0 · Social shopping · Cooperative decision making · Collaborative information seeking · Business model

1 Introduction

When shopping, users increasingly achieve satisfaction in terms of user experience through the entire shopping process [1, 2]. To reach a satisfying user experience, many users carry out the shopping process in groups, either collectively or in assigned roles [3]. This phenomenon is primarily known as "group buying" and "collective buying" and can be observed in business-to-business (B2B) contexts as well as in business-to-consumer (B2C) shopping transactions [4, 5].

The motivations to engage in group shopping are manifold and include financial aspects such as discounts as well as quality and service aspects such as the opportunity to obtain additional services or adapted package solutions [6]. Vendors, in addition to buyers, benefit from group buying [7]. For example, vendors can take advantage of group buying by realizing increased sales figures due to higher demand, generating profits despite lower prices due to higher quantities sold, realizing cost-effective transactions due to lower communication and bargaining costs compared to having to deal with a great many of individual buyers, etc.

The advancement of information and communication technologies (ICT) is an important enabler that significantly supports and improves the entire process of group buying, including group forming, discussion, bargaining with vendors, decision making,

© Springer International Publishing Switzerland 2015
Y. Luo (Ed.): CDVE 2015, LNCS 9320, pp. 162–169, 2015.
DOI: 10.1007/978-3-319-24132-6_19

post-purchase services, etc. As a result, online group buying has flourished recently and numerous intermediaries have emerged that provide platforms for transactions in the entire business process of group buying (e.g., LivingSocial, Groupon, Dianpin, Meituan). Interestingly, large, renowned companies such as Google [8] and Facebook [9] failed with their online group buying concepts, Google Offer and Facebook Deal, respectively, while new players on the market are very successful. For instance, China's Tuan800.com achieved a turnover of 5.94 billion USD with 71 million group buying customers in 2013 [10].

Beside the use of specific online group buying platforms (intermediaries), which is essentially a top-down approach, ICT also enables users to form and manage a cooperative crowd via various communication channels (bottom-up approach). Interestingly, this top-down type of online group buying, which has existed for a long time before intermediaries for online group buying emerged, is far less researched than bottom-up group buying [4].

These two types of group shopping vary tremendously in communication, coordination, and collaboration. Particularly the interaction and non-interaction phases alternate in varying degrees and compositions throughout the online group shopping processes. Consequently, the required support of ICT in these phases varies, as well. However, this aspect has not yet been systematically approached in research. Against this background, we will fill this research gap by addressing the interaction challenges and opportunities of online group buying, for which we – as a basis – also provide a systematic typology of the online group buying types based on the top-down/bottom-up crowd-shopping aspect of online group buying.

The remainder of this paper is structured as follows: The next section provides a theoretical background on the group buying phenomenon. In Sect. 3, we identify and differentiate the various types of online group buying with the crowd. Built on this, we identify, visualize and discuss the interaction phases for each of the presented types of online group shopping. In Sect. 4, we discuss our findings with challenges and opportunities and, in Sect. 5, we conclude with a summary of our work and point to future research opportunities.

2 Theoretical Background

In this section, we first provide details on group buying, then continue with outlining how the Internet is currently leveraged to improve this phenomenon.

2.1 Group Buying

Group buying, also referred to as collective buying, is a shopping strategy in which individuals form a collective to obtain better conditions for purchases than they would obtain as individuals [5]. Benefits achieved from collective bargaining include, for instance, volume discounts, better product quality, additional services, or customized package solutions [4, 5].

The main motivation to participate in a group-buying collective is the financial aspect [11]. When a group buys higher quantities of items, volume discounts can be agreed upon during the negotiation process between the collective and the vendor [5]. Furthermore, when a large group is willing to buy the same product or service, the collective may obtain additional services or customized package solutions under better conditions due to the group's increased bargaining power [5]. In addition, there is an incentive for uninformed customers to cooperate with intermediaries that often have a better understanding of the market and thus use their skills for the benefit of the customer [12].

One advantage for the vendor lies in the potentially increased sales figures, which may be realized, and in the resulting financial flexibility. Cash flow and, thus, liquidity may increase significantly. Therefore, the vendor may generate profits despite lower prices compared to traditional retailing strategies [13]. Furthermore, a deal with a group buying collective may be a tremendously cost-effective business transaction: On average, the marketing costs, as well as those costs incurring from allocation of sales staff, are lower than in transactions with individual customers. In the latter case, the purchase intention is never as extensive as in the case with group buying participants. This means that in transactions with individual customers, higher communication costs and personnel costs are needed to ultimately convince the prospective customer to purchase a product or service.

Group buying incorporates two main elements: the generic process of shopping [14], and the socializing effects in the social network [15]. Over the Internet, however, group buying offers manifold design possibilities and a broader scope: while the traditional prospective customer is limited to his/her friends, family, and acquaintances, the online collaborative shopper has access to a large group, i.e. his/her social web network.

2.2 Fostering the Crowd for Collaboration Online

Due to the evolution of social aspects of online shopping in recent years, many new social web services have popped up in the last years, allowing users to participate in the web sphere [15, 16]. Online retail and e-commerce environments are also affected by this trend. Nowadays, a user may recommend products, leave comments, rate vendors or publish a wish list. This is often called *social shopping* or *social commerce*. Customers may participate and interact online with other users. New shopping concepts are constantly emerging as the mass of potential customers grows.

The online group buying concept uses the capabilities of the Internet by bringing many people together to compare prices and negotiate jointly with suppliers. The participants search jointly for a suitable vendor, a fitting product, as well as an accurate model, and they assess processes in the pre-acquisition phase jointly. Thereby, each individual may contribute in the provided forums or chat rooms. In this respect, group buying embodies a form of cooperative teamwork among the participants.

3   Online Group-Buying Models Using the Crowd

3.1   Online Group-Buying Models Based on Initiation of the Process

Early online group-buying business models were launched in the 1990s. Mercata.com, LetsBuyIt.com, Mobshop.com, and other Websites brought together users with similar product interests to receive sales discounts. The rationale behind these vendor-based models offering specific "deals" is the following: the more users who are willing to buy a specific product or service, the lower the price. In this dynamic price-level model, the purchase is not initiated by potential customers, but by the companies or suppliers themselves. The customer therefore receives a prepackaged offer, which he or she may either accept or decline within a certain period of time. Thus, the vendors provide no possibility for negotiation.

In contrast, examples such as Jasmere demonstrate that so-called group buying discounts, i.e. quantity discounts, are granted by allowing consumers to pool their demand to increase the purchase volume. In this model, pricing is based on the number of participating customers throughout the entire offer period. The more customers who are willing to accept the current price, the faster the next lower price level is reached. This bottom-up model enables a better price for the entire group of participating customers. Furthermore, this model may offer a useful extra service for customers who do not yet agree with the current price offered since there is an option to accept the offer at a lower price level and pre-register one's interest.

Beginning in 2008, a novel group-buying model evolved: Groupon.com offers mainly location-based deals such as restaurant menus, tickets, and training lessons. The offered special discounts have a fixed price; there is a minimum number of required customers that has to be exceeded per day in order to obtain the discounts, which may be redeemed after payment [17, 18].

Apart from these vendor-initiated group-buying models, there are demander-initiated models involving the crowd. These models, which originated in Asia [19, 20], bring together consumers who plan to buy a specific product or service. The crowd participants may enjoy discounted pricing through collective bargaining. They have the opportunity to meet on an online forum or on specific websites, which might speed up the process of crowd formation. TeamBuy.com.cn is the current market leader in this segment, bringing merchants and customers together. Another prominent example of consumer-to-consumer group-buying platform is Jiazhang100.com. Table 1 illustrates different types of shopping with the crowd models covering both, vendor-initiated as well as demander-initiated group buying.

3.2   Phases of Interaction and Non-Interaction

In the following section, we outline in detail and compare the processes of the traditional, vendor-initiated model of group buying and the processes involved in the collaborative crowd-shopping experience. The phases of interaction and non-interaction of the crowd vary between these two online group-buying models and demonstrate two variations for each model.

Figure 1(a) illustrates the simplified process of the traditional vendor-initiated model of group buying. The user accesses the platform, optionally pays an admission fee or subscription rate (step 1), evaluates the offer such as "daily deals" in the Groupon model [21] (step 2) and, in case the user wants to purchase the item, accepts the deal (steps 3). Cooperation between the crowd participants occurs only by accepting the offered deal. No further interaction of the crowd participants is necessary.

Table 1. Shopping with the crowd models

	Traditional group-buying exchange (top-down approach)	Collaborative crowd-shopping experience (bottom-up approach)
Exchange is…	• Vendor-initiated	• Demander-initiated
Deals are…	• Pre-defined • Voucher based	• Initiated by the crowd for the purchase of specific products
Interaction is…	• Organized by intermediaries to make profits and/or companies to promote brands	• Formed by the crowd in order to increase the benefit for participating customers
Occurrence of Collaboration	• Collaborative decision making during few phases of shopping process only	• Collaborative information seeking and decision making during whole shopping process
Products are…	• Mainly location-based • "Daily deals"	• Determined by the crowd with no restriction
Group Buying is based on…	• Time-limited "grouponing" with fixed prices (coupons) or • Dynamic price mechanism model	• Collaboration between group buyers and time-limited negotiations/dialogue with vendor

Figure 1(b) illustrates the process for vendor-initiated group buying with dynamic offers (e.g., dynamic pricing where the price drops the more customers buy the product or services). A user accesses the platform; (step 1), evaluates the deals (step 2), and accepts the offer if interested (step 3). Some platforms offer the possibility to restrict the acceptance of the offer to a "maximum price level". The user is notified about the purchase if within the set price restriction on the determined point in time (step 4). Similar to version 1(a), interaction is reduced to the joint acceptance of an offer and the potential of recommending an offer to other users.

Figure 1(c) illustrates the first version of a simplified demander-initiated group-buying process. A "crowd" is formed by the users (e.g., parents with similar interests; e.g., Jiazhang100.com.) (step 1). This step includes the online-search for potential group members on an online forum or directly on an online group-shopping platform. The user evaluates the offers (with fixed pricing) at the platform provider (step 2). Finally, an offer is accepted, if it is of interest to a user (step 3).

Figure 1(d) illustrates the second version of simplified demander-initiated group-buying process, which is the most interactive one. The process begins with crowd formation; the crowd may access an online platform or forum (step 1). The crowd then searches

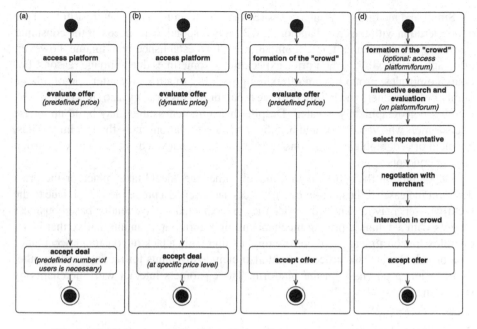

Fig. 1. Traditional group buying (a/b) vs collaborative crowd shopping (c/d)

interactively for potential group members, potential merchants, and/or deals on the open market (step 2). The crowd can communicate and discuss with other potential buyers online, and can jointly assess different brands. Next, a group representative (or several group representatives) is typically interactively selected for negotiations (step 3). This representative or representatives negotiate(s) with the selected merchant on the group's behalf; this phase of the process may also take place offline in the merchant's premises (step 4) [22]. Then the group discusses the available deals so that the group representatives may agree to accept or to decline the offer that has been negotiated (step 5). Finally the merchant's offer is accepted to the agreed conditions if convenient (step 6).

4 Discussion

Group buying allows companies to serve solvent customers in larger quantities and – as a consequence – to generate additional profit margins. A disadvantage for the vendor arises due to the increased influence of customers on pricing negotiations in a group buying setting. As a result, unit contribution margins may be lowered. After all, suppliers still can set prerequisites in the price negotiations, e.g., a certain price requires a certain number of sales. One difficulty with this approach from the perspective of a supplier might arise in determining the correct group size without deterring potential customers by quoting unrealistic sales volumes in negotiations. Therefore, consumers are motivated to distribute product information to other people if the required number of potential buyers has not been reached [23]. The success for both parties of the group-buying schemes, thus, depends largely on the efficiency of consumers as sales aids.

Small and medium-size enterprises (SMEs) show an increased interest in this type of cooperation with the crowd and often willingly respond to the needs of the consumer groups regarding pricing. Larger companies with an established brand name, however, often appear inflexible in their price expectations, sometimes due to image reasons. For many companies, group buying offers the possibility to attract the attention of a large number of consumers and build a positive reputation. This strategy also suits companies, which are geographically isolated. Despite their remoteness they may build up a base of customers who value good and beneficial business relations more than vicinity. Thus, physical or geographical conditions/restrictions may be leveled out in context of group buying concepts.

Depending on the group-buying model, either the "deal" takes place or the price discount increases if the number of customers has reached a predefined level. Due to the fact that users may not know the price they are expected to pay, vendor-based business models with a dynamic pricing mechanism might turn out as an alternative that is too complex for consumers and therefore might suffer from a lack of consumer acceptance on a broader basis. This process might also include discounts for recommending other users to join a purchase on the platform. The customers interact with merchants by redeeming the "deal".

5   Conclusion

In recent years, there has been an upswing concerning collaborative online group buying. To date, many aspects that could help to understand, explain and operationalize this phenomenon have not been explored through research. Interestingly, while there has been a trend towards pre-defined vendor-initiated "daily deals" in countries such as the USA, in other countries, platforms such as China's market leader Teambuy, where forum members initiate crowd-shopping activities, have flourished.

These types of group shopping vary tremendously with regard to communication, coordination, and collaboration among participants. This paper focuses on phases of the entire process of group buying including online intermediaries which speed up the process in both directions. The suggested model categorization provides a basis for future research, as a systematic approach is essential to an understudied research field like online group buying. Analyzing different phases of interaction as well as providing a categorization will help to improve the involved shopping process and the underlying notion of the different business models.

References

1. Kauffman, R.J., Lai, H., Ho, C.T.: Incentive mechanisms, fairness and participation in online group-buying auctions. Electron. Commer. Res. Appl. **9**(3), 249–262 (2010)
2. Cho, N., Park, S.: Development of electronic commerce user-consumer satisfaction index for internet shopping. Ind. Manage. Data Syst. **101**(8), 400–406 (2001)
3. Shin, D.H.: User experience in social commerce: in friends we trust. Behav. Inf. Technol. **32**(1), 52–67 (2013)

4. Liu, Y., Sutanto, J.: Online group-buying: literature review and directions for future research. ACM SIGMIS Database **46**(1), 39–59 (2015)

5. Wang, J.J., Zhao, X., Li, J.J.: Group buying: a strategic form of consumer collective. J. Retail. **89**(3), 338–351 (2013)

6. Chen, W.Y., Wu, P.H.: Factors affecting consumers' motivation in online group buyers. In: 2010 6th International Conference on IEEE Intelligent Information Hiding and Multimedia Signal Processing (IIH-MSP), pp. 708–711 (2010)

7. Yu, M., Lang, K., Pelaez, A.: Evaluating electronic market designs: the effects of competitive arousal and social facilitation on electronic group buying. In: 47th Hawaii International Conference on System Science, pp. 4148–4157 (2014)

8. Blumenthals. http://blumenthals.com/blog/2014/03/05/google-shuts-down-self-serve-offers-product/

9. Forbes. http://www.forbes.com/sites/tomiogeron/2011/08/26/facebook-shutting-down-deals-service/

10. Lee, E.: 2013 China's Group-buying Turnover Rockets 67.7 % YOY to 35.88 Billion Yuan. http://technode.com/2014/01/15/2013-group-buying-turnover-rockets-68-percent-yoy-in-china/

11. Sharif-Paghaleh, H.: Analysis of the waiting time effects on the financial return and the order fulfillment in web-based group buying mechanisms. In: Proceedings of the 2009 IEEE/WIC/ACM International Joint Conference on Web Intelligence and Intelligent Agent Technology, Vol. 1, pp. 663–666. IEEE Computer Society (2009)

12. Jing, X., Xie, J.: Group buying: A new mechanism for selling through social interactions. Manage. Sci. **57**(8), 1354–1372 (2011)

13. Leitner, P., Grechenig, T.: Collaborative shopping networks: sharing the wisdom of crowds in E-commerce environments. In: BLED 2008 Proceedings, p. 21 (2008)

14. Hu, M., Shi, M., Wu, J.: Simultaneous vs. sequential group-buying mechanisms. Manage. Sci. **59**(12), 2805–2822 (2013)

15. Mladenow, A., Bauer, C., Strauss, C.: Social crowd integration in new product development: crowdsourcing communities nourish the open innovation paradigm. Glob. J. Flex. Syst. Manage. **15**(1), 77–86 (2014)

16. Bauer, C., Mladenow, A., Strauss, C.: Fostering collaboration by location-based crowdsourcing. In: Luo, Y. (ed.) CDVE 2014. LNCS, vol. 8683, pp. 88–95. Springer, Heidelberg (2014)

17. Edelman, B., Jaffe, S., Kominers, S.D.: To Groupon or not to Groupon: The Profitability of Deep Discounts, Harvard Business School. NOM Unit Working Paper 11–063 (2011)

18. Dickinger, A., Kleijnen, M.: Coupons going wireless: determinants of consumer intentions to redeem mobile coupons. J. Interact. Mark. **22**(3), 23–39 (2008)

19. Chung, W., Chen, L.: Group-buying e-commerce in China. IT Prof. **14**(4), 24–30 (2012)

20. Zhang, J.J., Tsai, W.H.S.: United we shop! Chinese consumers' online group buying. J. Int. Consum. Mark. **27**(1), 54–68 (2015)

21. Luo, X., Andrews, M., Song, Y., Aspara, J.: Group-buying deal popularity. J. Mark. **78**(2), 20–33 (2014)

22. Tan, W.K., Tan, Y.J.: Online or offline group buying? In: 2010 Seventh International Conference on Fuzzy Systems and Knowledge Discovery, vol. 6, pp. 2853–2857 (2010)

23. Xie, G., Zhu, J., Lu, Q., Xu, S.: Influencing factors of consumer intention towards web group buying. In: 2011 IEEE International Conference on Industrial Engineering and Engineering Management (IEEM), pp. 1397–1401. IEEE (2011)

G-Form: A Collaborative Design Approach to Regard Deep Web Form as Galaxy of Concepts

Radhouane Boughammoura[✉], Lobna Hlaoua,
and Mohamed Nazih Omri

Research Unit MARS, Faculty of Sciences of Monastir, University of Monastir,
Monastir, Tunisia
Radhouane.Boughammoura@gmail.com, Lobna1511@yahoo.fr,
MohamedNazih.Omri@fsm.rnu.tn

Abstract. Deep web is growing rapidly with multitude of devices and rendering capability. Despite the richness of deep Web forms, their rendering methodology is very poor in terms of capacity of expression. Hence, user has no indication about the richness of query and query capability when he interprets this interface. In this paper we propose a new rendering approach of deep Web forms which is easy to interpret by user and reflects the exact meaning of query. We have evaluated our algorithm on standard dataset and compared it to a well known state of the art algorithm. Our approach has proved good performances with respect to standard measures.

Keywords: Collaborative design · Query interpretation · Galaxy of concepts · Pertinence of a concept

1 Introduction

Deep web is the part of Web which is not reachable via hyperlinks [3, 4]. It is hidden behind Web forms which give access to deep Web databases [3, 5]. Information on databases is really a big treasury and more than 90 % of information in Web comes from deep Web. In addition, this information is very rich in terms of quality of service offered to internet users [6–10]. We aim by our job to reveal deep Web to novice internet users via new, simple, and easy-to-use web forms.

Novice users regard Web forms as source of inspiration in order to understand exact meaning of query. Nowadays design methodology don't help novice users understand correct query as they have no background about semantic value of query [1, 2]. In this paper we propose a new design methodology approach Galaxy-Form (G-Form) which is based on query's schema (see Fig. 1).

We present in the following section a brief related works. In Sect. 3 we explain the motivation of our new approach G-form and we present its principle. In Sect. 4, we present the experimental evaluation and analysis of the results. We finally conclude in Sect. 5.

© Springer International Publishing Switzerland 2015
Y. Luo (Ed.): CDVE 2015, LNCS 9320, pp. 170–174, 2015.
DOI: 10.1007/978-3-319-24132-6_20

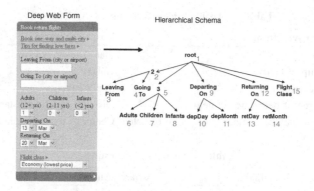

Fig. 1. Deep Web form and its hierarchical schema

2 Related Work

Z-Forms [3] are the most used information retrieval query interface in Web. The first drawback is that all fields are rendered in the same interface. When the number of fields is big query becomes very complex and novice users find difficulty to pursue his interpretation till the end. The second drawback is in line segment which covers an entire line and forms hence one semantic entity of fields. However in many cases, more than one semantic entity may appears in one line. Ko-Chiu [12] proposes a new approach for affective surfing in the visualized interface of a digital library for novice users (children). When novice users search for information [1, 2], they have specific directions but they do not have specific search target. These novice users have no special training or beliefs regarding search strategies [13, 14]. A visual interface based on navigation experience is used to help users build mind maps. This interface stimulates curiosity of novice users in order to enhance information retrieval experience.

3 Affinities Between Deep Web Form and Galaxy

G-Form is deep Web form which is inspired from Galaxy. First, we will present affinities between galaxy and deep Web form, and then we explain the way galaxy form is buid (Table 1).

Hypothesis: *Novice users regard deep web form like they regard cosmic universe.*

Deep Web form is regarded as cosmic universe where stars are fields and galaxy is group of fields. When novice users regard deep Web form, they move by regard from one semantic entity to another entity as astronaut move from one planet to another or from one galaxy to another. If distance is a measure of this cosmic travel, pertinence is the measure of relevance between fields. Center of mass of the galaxy correspond mean average pertinence of group of fields. Degree of pertinence in G-Form corresponds exactly to Depth First Search (DFS) traversal of schema elements. DFS identify order of visiting of schema elements. In Fig. 1, we have indicated under each schema element its degree of pertinence.

Table 1. Analogy deep Web form vs Galaxy

Deep Web form	Cosmic universe
Field	Star
Group of fields	Galaxy
Super-group of fields	Super-galaxy
Degree of pertinence of field	Distance separating stars
Mean average pertinence of group of fields	Center of mass of galaxy

Table 2. Experimental results

Domain	Airfare	Auto	Books
#extracted	214	102	108
#extracted and pertinent	146	78	70
#total_entities	200	105	110
Precision	0,68	0,76	0,64
Recall	0,73	0,74	0,63

4   Experimental Results

Our evaluation methodology is as follows. We build G-Form for every schema of Web form available on dataset (ICQ [11]). Then we simulates user clicks on different stars in the Web form. Then we count number of correct entities (group, super-group of fields). An entity is considered as correct if it is semantically coherent. For example, entity {Adults, Children, and Infants} is a correct entity as it describes number of passengers. While entity {Time, Adults, Children} is not correct because Date of flight and Number of passengers overlap. We count for each G-Form number of extracted entities, number of extracted entities which are correct, and then we measure precision (P), recall (R), and F1 of the algorithm.

With regard to the results shown in Table 3, we notice that, the two sets of results corresponding to the two approaches follow the same pace. This phenomenon can be explained by the fact that process of rendering of fields is based on query schema which is common to the two approaches. These results also show that performance of our approach is always better than the performance of Z-Form (Table 2).

Table 3. Comparison between the two approaches G-Form and Z-Form

	Domain	P	R	F1
G-Form	Airfare	**0,68**	**0,73**	**0,70**
	Auto	**0,76**	**0,74**	**0,75**
	Book	**0,64**	**0,63**	**0,64**
Z-Form	Airfare	0,66	0,70	0,67
	Auto	0,72	0,71	0,71
	Book	0,62	0,60	0,60

$$R = \frac{number\ of\ extracted\ entites}{total\ number\ of\ entites\ in\ the\ Web\ form} \tag{1}$$

$$P = \frac{number\ of\ extracted\ pertinent\ entities}{number\ of\ extracted\ entities} \tag{2}$$

$$F1 = \frac{2RP}{R+P} \tag{3}$$

5 Conclusion and Future Work

In this paper we have proposed an essay to resolve the complexity of query in deep Web forms. We propose a new design approach G-Form inspired from galaxy. It offer to novice users an easy- to-use deep Web forms and reveals clearly the exact meaning of query even if its schema is complex. There is a strong analogy between galaxy and deep web form with respect to structure and granularity of entities in each concept. G-Form is better than Z-Form which is well known state of art algorithm. Z-Form lacks design expressivity because there is no background concerning the semantic value of query, while our approach is based on hierarchical schema which reveals clearly the semantic of query. Our approach is clearly outside performance of Z-Form with respect precision, recall, and F1 measures of performance.

References

1. Omri, M.N., Tijus, C., Poitrenaud, S., Bouchon-Meunier, B.: Fuzzy sets and semantic nets for on line assistance. In: Proceedings, 11th Conference of Artificial Intelligence for Applications, pp. 374–379. IEEE (1995)
2. Omri, M.N., Chouigui, N.: Measure of similarity between fuzzy concepts for identification of fuzzy user's requests in fuzzy semantic networks. Int. J. Uncertainty Fuzziness Knowl. Based Syst. 9(06), 743–748 (2001)
3. Wensheng, W., Doan, A.-H., Yu, C., Meng, W.: Modeling and extracting deep-web query interfaces. In: Proceedings of AIIS 2009 (2009)
4. Zhang, Z., He, B., Chang, K.: Understanding web query interfaces: best-effort parsing with hidden syntax. In: Proceedings of SIGMOD 2004 (2004)
5. Vo, L.T.H., Cao, J., Rahayu, W.: Structured content-based query answers for improving information quality. In: World Wide Web, pp. 1–24 (2014)
6. Boughammoura, R., Omri, M.N., Youssef, H.: Fuzzy approach for pertinent information extraction from web resources. J. Comput. e-Syst. 1(1) (2008)
7. Boughammoura, R., Omri, M.N.: Statistical approach for information extraction from web pages. In: Proceedings of International Symposium on Distance Education (EAD 2009) (2009)
8. Boughammoura, R., Omri, M.N.: SeMQI: a new model for semantic interpretation of query interfaces. In: Proceedings of NGNS 2011 (2011)

9. Boughammoura, R., Omri, M.N., Hlaoua, L.: VIQI: a new approach for visual interpretation of deep web query interfaces. In: ICITeS (2012)
10. Boughammoura, R., Omri, M.N., Hlaoua, L.: Information retrieval from deep web based on visual query interpretation. Int. J. Inf. Retrieval Res. 2(4), 45–59 (2013)
11. The UIUC Web Integration Repository, Computer Science Department, University of Illinois at Urbana-Champaign (2003). http://metaquerier.cs.uiuc.edu/repository
12. Wu, K.-C.: Affective surfing in the visualized interface of a digital library for children. Inf. Process. Manage. 51(4), 373–390 (2015)
13. Omri, M.N., Chouigui, N.: Linguistic variables definition by membership function and measure of similarity. In: Proceedings of the 14th International Conference on Systems Science, vol. 2, pp. 264–273 (2001)
14. Omri, M.N.: Fuzzy knowledge representation, learning and optimization with Bayesian analysis in fuzzy semantic networks. In: Proceedings of 6th International Conference on Neural Information Processing (ICONIP 1999) (1999)

Helaba: A System to Highlight Design Rationale in Collaborative Design Processes

Marisela Gutierrez Lopez$^{(\boxtimes)}$, Mieke Haesen, Kris Luyten,
and Karin Coninx

Expertise Centre for Digital Media, Hasselt University - tUL - iMinds,
Wetenschapspark 2, 3590 Diepenbeek, Belgium
{marisela.gutierrezlopez,mieke.haesen,kris.luyten,
karin.coninx}@uhasselt.be

Abstract. Design activities associated to the ideation phase of design processes require mutual understanding and clear communication based on artefacts. However, this is often a challenge for remote and multidisciplinary teams due to the lack of ad hoc tools for this purpose. Our approach is to solve these limitations by explicitly connecting pieces of information related to design rationale, feedback, and evolution with the artefacts that are subject of communication. We propose *Helaba*, a system that creates a shared workspace to support communication revolving around design artefacts and activities within multidisciplinary teams. Helaba supports design communication and rationale, and potentially leads to more satisfying outcomes from the design process.

Keywords: Design · Design rationale · Remote/multidisciplinary communication

1 Introduction

Modern design has evolved into a complex knowledge activity that more often than not involves multidisciplinary teams. However, these teams often lack the tools for efficient collaboration and communication, specifically because the different roles involved also have different work practices and focus, and use domain specific languages.

We tackle two main challenges in communication within a design team and with their stakeholders. First, issues with mutual understanding and clear communication during the ideation phase of the design process, which leads to suboptimal results, loss of time and thus money and sometimes frustrations and difficulties in collaboration. Second, design processes often involve asynchronous and remote communication, which we found has many disadvantages if there is no domain-specific system to mediate and support this type of communication. We discovered that explicitly connecting pieces of information with the artefacts that are the subject of communication can help a great deal to improve this.

In this paper we introduce *Helaba*, a semi-functional prototype that aims to reduce the challenges faced in remote, multidisciplinary design communication. The word Helaba is used in the Flemish spoken language to greet someone, but also to attract the explicit attention of another person and point something out. The Helaba prototype

© Springer International Publishing Switzerland 2015
Y. Luo (Ed.): CDVE 2015, LNCS 9320, pp. 175–184, 2015.
DOI: 10.1007/978-3-319-24132-6_21

focuses on the processes for documenting design rationale and decision-making since they have been acknowledged to support multidisciplinary communication. Section 2 of this paper elaborates on how our prototype relates to previous research.

The concept of Helaba, presented in Sect. 3, is based on previous research where a survey and series of interviews uncovered that designers consider team and customer communication the main issue that influences the quality of their designs and design decisions, rather than technical limitations they might have to deal with [1]. Based on this study, we analysed and mapped internal and external (customer and other stakeholders) communication, both on the design activities and on the artefacts that are subject of these activities.

Rather than creating a system that integrates everything in one single tool (e.g. chat, e-mail), Helaba focuses on the visualization of communication and artefact evolution over time. Because of this focus, Helaba helps to structure, understand and optimize the team communication as well as the rationale that led to certain design decisions. Helaba does not include artefact editing or manipulation and leaves this work to specialized design tools. The focus of Helaba ensures that different disciplines involved in design teams can adopt this tool without moving away from the tools they are familiar with.

Sections 4 and 5 present the lessons learned from three scenarios about the way Helaba supports communication within multidisciplinary, distributed design teams. While this solution is an initial insight that needs further validation, the proposed prototype is a system for "smoothening" communication. It can be integrated into the design process, and is adoptable by both team members and stakeholders. Future steps towards this integration are discussed in Sect. 6.

2 Context and Background

Communication during the early stages of design is often linked to visual artefacts [2, 3]. However, existing systems tend to focus on the support for creating these artefacts, but not on the influence of communication to their evolution [3]. Designers use various practices as workarounds to reduce the burden of managing artefact-based communication, including [1]:

- Crafting textual communication to "point" at specific elements of artefacts. However, designers must invest a significant amount of resources in this task.
- Having multiple channels of feedback and communication. This strategy implies that designers frequently fail to capture ideas together with artefacts, as communication is scattered among different tools.
- Using physical workspaces to convey within multidisciplinary teams, organizing frequent meetings and workshops with stakeholders for reaching common ground. This is difficult in remote teams, as moments of face-to-face meetings are limited.

These practices are consistently mentioned as helpful but often frustrating and a common source of misunderstandings [1]. In this paper we propose a system to address this gap, reflecting on a solution to integrate artefacts and design decisions.

A useful approach for integrating communication and artefacts is by capturing the design rationale. Design rationale is a representation of the reasoning behind the design of an artefact, evolving with the design process by capturing design decisions and how they relate to relevant evaluation criteria [4]. Explicitly documenting design rationale is useful for connecting discussions and communications into artefacts [5]. Furthermore, design rationale is useful when artefacts need to be understood by many people, allowing them to better comprehend the design decisions of others and keep track of previous group decisions [4].

Existing systems for capturing design rationale focus on a variety of methods and approaches. Some of these systems have focused on capturing design rationale based on traceability of requirements [6], argumentation [7], and decision-making processes [8]. While each of these systems propose a valuable approach for capturing design rationale, design practitioners are yet to adopt tools with this purpose [9]. One reason for this is that designers customize existing tools to their own practices [1]. Therefore, efforts should be directed to a solution that can be adapted to a variety of design practices. Helaba extends previous work by proposing a tool for capturing design rationale by connecting pieces of information related to rationale, feedback, and evolution of artefacts to the communication and design activities of multidisciplinary design teams.

Some characteristics of Helaba are inspired by Design Space Analysis (DSA) [4], which is an approach for representing design rationale in a simple and flexible way by opening a space for augmenting the rationale elements. According to [4], DSA uses a semi-formal notation called QOC, which stands for *Question, Options, Criteria*, to outline the design space of artefacts. The elements of the QOC notation are: *Questions*, which identify discussions related to the artefact, *Options*, which provide trade-offs and answers to the Questions, and *Criteria*, which define the evaluation criteria for an Option. Helaba is related to the DSA approach as we adopt the understanding of design rationale as: (i) an artefact that has to be crafted and evolved along the design process, and, (ii) a discussion space for ongoing issues [4]. Furthermore, Helaba's workspace was inspired by the QOC notation, as we represent argumentation of options in relation to its evaluation criteria.

3   Helaba Design Overview

Helaba is a system prototype that supports communication revolving around design artefacts and activities within multidisciplinary teams. A shared workspace that structures and tracks artefacts and design activities is the main component [10]. Three core User Experience (UX) guidelines were used as design rules for Helaba. These UX guidelines are the result from our user studies with design practitioners, which reported the importance of capturing, structuring, and presenting communication within design teams and with stakeholders [1]. The *UX guideline 1* indicates that when design teams communicate, there should exist a connection between the tools for sharing artefacts and for communicating design rationale to facilitate the creation of a common visual vocabulary. *UX guideline 2* points out that when designers share and receive feedback from their team or stakeholders, a shared, activity-oriented workspace should be integrated to trace back the design decisions and rationale behind them. Finally, *UX guideline 3* specifies that when involved in artefact-based communication, designers need to maintain awareness over the evolution of the artefact, having an overview of previous design decisions.

In consideration of these three UX guidelines, our prototype is designed to focus on communication related to the design activities and artefacts. We believe that this will improve documenting the design rationale significantly, and eventually lead to more satisfying outcomes from the design process. Figure 1 is a screen shot of Helaba that demonstrates its features. The images of avatars and the sketches are examples of content created during the design process, which are used for illustrative and expert review purposes, but should not be considered as part of the prototype.

The information captured and presented by Helaba can be decomposed in three different types of information, which each include a set of features and deal with a UX guideline. (i) The intention of the *rationale information* (Fig. 1A), which reflects on UX guideline 1, is to document the reasoning and arguments of the artefact in relation to its evaluation criteria, as suggested in the QOC notation. (ii) *Feedback information* (Fig. 1B) reflects on UX guideline 2 as it organizes general discussions and gathers qualitative and quantitative feedback. (iii) *Evolution information* (Fig. 1C) refers to UX guideline 3 and concerns the metadata of the artefact and timeline for traceability of its evolution.

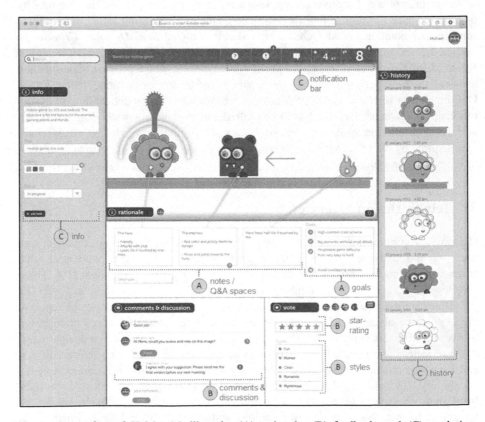

Fig. 1. Screenshot of Helaba labelling the (A) rationale, (B) feedback, and (C) evolution information types and their associated features.

4 Making Design Decisions and Rationale Explicit

For exploring potential uses of Helaba, we observed the ideation processes of a multi-disciplinary team involved in a user interface (UI) design project. The two main reasons to observe this particular team and project are: (i) the multidisciplinary nature of UI design projects, and (ii) the involvement of complex design and technological problems being solved by geographically distributed team members. The observed UI design project involves 6 organizations from both industrial and academic fields distributed across different locations in Europe. The team, formed by 11 professionals, worked towards the common goal of creating a shared UI design for an interactive system.

The analysis of these observations led to the creation of three open-ended and fragmentary narrative scenarios that concentrate on the different communication activities associated to ideation processes. In the scenarios the design team consists of 4 key actors: *Joe* a UX designer, *Pam* a visual designer, *Ann* a software developer, and *Danny* the project manager. Each scenario presented below, which is based on our observations, describes a pitfall in the communications of the team. Following, a description of Helaba's features explain how Helaba can overcome the pitfall for each scenario.

4.1 Documenting Outcomes of Individual Work

> *Joe individually created early UI designs. He focused on designing UIs using Illustrator while making sketches and writing annotations in his notebook and on random pieces of paper. He worked with ease in these individual activities, but lost track of the reasoning behind the evolution of his designs since he had no centralized record of his ideas. This made difficult for Joe to accurately communicate his sources of inspiration and evolution of ideas to his team.*

Joe fell in what we call the *scattered rationale* pitfall, as he does not have a centralized record of how his design came to be. This can create difficulties when transitioning from individual to group work. Helaba can be helpful for capturing the rationale information with two features (Fig. 1A). The *notes* feature supports digital "post-its" that can be used to include textual notes, and pinpoints to specific elements of the design. Individual notes can be transformed into *Q&A spaces*, which are open spaces for discussion, as designers can directly ask questions to specific team members (see Fig. 2). This feature could be useful to integrate communication that currently takes place over e-mails or chat messages. The *goals* feature allows the creation of a customizable checklist containing design guidelines or requirements that serve as criteria for evaluation of the artefact. Criteria can be checked once they are handled in the artefact.

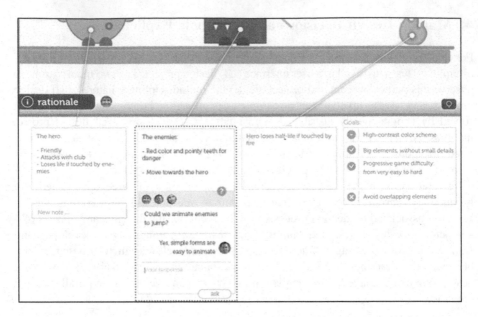

Fig. 2. *Notes* feature with active *Q&A space* and *goals* feature with checked items.

4.2   Communicating Feedback Within Multidisciplinary Teams

Joe organized a VoIP call with screen sharing with Pam and Ann to gather feedback about his UI designs. During Joe's remote presentation, Ann felt it was not the place for asking questions about implementation, while Pam felt her ideas were not valuable enough to interrupt his speech. The outcomes of this meeting were poor for the participants. From Joe's perspective, the reactions of his UI design were positive because he gathered only a few lines of feedback. From Ann's and Pam's perspective, they were not able to express their points of view in full.

The team fell in what we call the *incomplete feedback* pitfall. This means that remote communication often leads to a loss of context of what actually happens. Helaba aims to overcome this pitfall by integrating and facilitating the capture of feedback information (Fig. 1B). The *comments & discussion* feature is a space for global argumentation. Individual comments can be marked to direct an inquiry (*question*) or to bring awareness (*attention*) to a specific team member. The *vote* feature is a space to give feedback in a quick, visual way. Users can vote using a 5 points *star-rating* scale and a *styles* scale, which are user-defined categories that can be used to rate and interpret an artefact. This is illustrated in Fig. 3, where five categories are defined by the designer and open for others to vote, giving designers the opportunity to evaluate the perceptions of their team about the artefact.

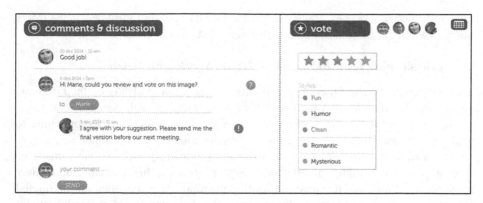

Fig. 3. Left side: *comments and discussion* feature with comments marked as *question* or *attention*. Right side: *vote* feature with *star-rating* scale and *styles* suggestions.

4.3   Communicating Design Decisions to Stakeholders

> *Joe, Pam, Ann, and Danny gathered together for a co-located workshop. Since Danny was not involved in the iterative process for this artefact (scenario 2), he had several remarks about Joe's UI designs. Not having a clear focus, the team discussion started to circle around previously agreed design decisions. This was a critical point of the project, as it could lead to wasting valuable ideas or resources.*

Danny fell in the *multidisciplinary decision-makers* pitfall. The evolution information kept by Helaba can be useful to overcome this pitfall, as Danny was not informed of how to proceed due to misinformation. The features of Helaba that can be useful are (Fig. 1C): *history*, a timeline to record the evolution of an artefact's elements in chronological order. The *notification bar*, that includes a general rating of image, which is a numeric grade (1–9) to qualify the acceptance rate of the image (i.e. *star-rating*) and the adherence to requirements (i.e. *goals*).

5   Discussion

Our approach focuses on supporting communication related with design activities and artefacts. Designers report that most of their collaborative problems are due to problematic communication instead of technical limitations [1]. Despite many different remote communication technologies that are available today, we found that existing solutions fail to support communication on design activities and artefacts. The three pitfalls described in the previous section highlight missing features of current communication tools for designers. Helaba fills this gap as it provides solutions for these pitfalls by structuring the communication following design rules. These rules were obtained from interviews with designers and observing collaborative design activities. To validate our approach, we conducted expert reviews with 8 design practitioners to explore the concept of Helaba. From this early validation with domain experts, we discovered opportunities for refining Helaba, but most importantly, that our approach has the potential to set the ground to create more comprehensive development of communication tools to support design activities. Besides enabling traceability of the design rationale and reflecting on team-based design practices, Helaba solves the pitfalls that were identified as the major causes of work dissatisfaction during our observations and interviews.

5.1   Transitioning from Individual to Group Work with Helaba

Designers invest much of their time and efforts working individually on their designs, but not on documenting the reasoning behind artefacts [5, 10]. Nevertheless, when transitioning from individual to group work, designers must find ways to communicate the design rationale to their team members and stakeholders [5]. A common practice for communicating design rationale is to write the rationale, posting it into e-mails or Basecamp, and embedding the artefact. Designers mention this as inefficient, as they invest plenty of time and resources on crafting the rationale that is often misinterpreted since it is not attached directly to the artefact. This is the *scattered rationale* pitfall.

Helaba creates a centralized workspace to embed rationale information to artefacts by means of notes, comments, discussions and evaluation criteria, enabling the inclusion of informal communication. This information is captured along the design process and shared directly with team members. Currently this information is dispersed and often hard to connect to design artefacts as designers have no explicit support for storing and sharing it. Helaba could solve this issue as illustrated by a domain expert.

> *"[The notes feature is]... very useful to connect to the part I'm talking about. Now I just type long emails, or a document with all comments, and they [team members] have to search what I am talking about. I would use it a lot."* [Graphical designer]

5.2   Integrating Multidisciplinary Points of View with Helaba

In multidisciplinary teams, designers must consider feedback from a variety of perspectives [3–5]. Current practices for gathering feedback include using video conferencing and screen sharing tools for organizing remote, synchronous meetings. However, remote feedback implies a reduction of communication cues and a loss of human and work context (e.g. empathy [12]), which makes it difficult to assess the reactions of others [13]. The risk of this situation is failing to include a variety of points of view. This is the so-called *incomplete feedback* pitfall. To avoid this situation, Helaba creates an open, shared workspace where designers and team members can participate in the argumentation and validation of design decisions in relation to evolving design artefacts. This is illustrated by a domain expert.

> *"At first I thought [the styles feature] was a whimsical thing [...], but it can be used if you want to achieve certain values on your picture... it's a good way to measure people's emotions when they see something."* [Game designer]

5.3   Tracking Down Artefact Evolution with Helaba

Design decisions are communicated to stakeholders, such as project managers or clients, who often do not have design background themselves. Designers frequently struggle to communicate design decisions to these stakeholders, as they might end up expressing rationalizations that have little to do with their actual inspiration [2]. These situations might lead to the *multidisciplinary decision-makers* pitfall, as designers risk having to dismiss novel ideas in favour of more traditional ones, which are easier to interpret for stakeholders [2]. From a designer point of view, this often leads to sub-optimal results.

Helaba allows multidisciplinary teams to annotate artefacts and reflect on the design process and helps to communicate it to relevant stakeholders. As design decisions evolve over time, stakeholders could benefit of being informed about decisions in which they were not involved, or be reminded of past decisions [4]. We envision Helaba could be useful for stakeholders to become aware of the evolution of designs, grasping the efforts invested in the design process, and of other explored but not implemented design choices [11]. This is explained by one of the domain experts.

"[Design processes are] not always friendly in real life, and it's good to keep track of who said what. This is done now by e-mail, but I like [about Helaba] that I can point out [in the artefact]". [Graphical designer & illustrator]

6   Future Work and Conclusion

Our research offers insights in how to support communication revolving around design artefacts and activities and provides a set of solutions, as concrete design concepts and strategies. The work presented in this paper has also a set of limitations on which we elaborate further in this section. The Helaba prototype is validated in an early stage with a limited number of domain experts. The scenarios we use to illustrate how Helaba can support design teams only covers a limited number of situations and is not complete.

Despite these limitations, the early validation with domain experts demonstrated three promising directions for extending the prototype. The first direction is to provide richer communication features within the shared space. For instance, by allowing users to add the reasons behind the votes given in the 5-points *star-rating* scale (see Fig. 3), which enables a space for critical design and discussion. Second, further investigations should be directed to explore the navigation across different versions of an artefact. This includes extending the *history* feature to provide teams with a "big picture" of design processes without being overwhelming. The final possibility to extend the prototype is to support the inclusion of different media, e.g. videos, as the current system prototype only considers images.

To conclude, we found the need to create more comprehensive development of communication tools to support design activities. This is reflected in the fact that despite the many different remote communication technologies available today, existing solutions fail to support comprehensive communication on design activities and artefacts. Helaba fills this gap by providing a shared workspace for teams to integrate communication with the rationale and evolution of design artefacts over time. We believe this has the potential of leading to more satisfying outcomes from design processes.

Acknowledgments. This research is supported by the COnCEPT project, funded by the European Commission 7th Framework ICT Research Programme (project no: 610725). We give special thanks to Karel Robert for his involvement in the creation of Helaba, and to the designers involved in our studies.

References

1. Gutierrez Lopez, M., Haesen, M., Luyten, K., Coninx, K.: Study and analysis of collaborative design practices. In: PIN-C 2015, pp. 176–183 (2015)
2. Eckert, C., Stacey, M.: Sources of inspiration: a language of design. Des. Stud. **21**, 523–538 (2000)
3. Sharmin, M., Bailey, B.P.: Making sense of communication associated with artifacts during early design activity. In: Campos, P., Graham, N., Jorge, J., Nunes, N., Palanque, P., Winckler, M. (eds.) INTERACT 2011, Part I. LNCS, vol. 6946, pp. 181–198. Springer, Heidelberg (2011)
4. MacLean, A., Young, R.M., Bellotti, V., Moran, T.: Questions, options, and criteria: elements of design space analysis. Hum. Comput. Interact. **6**, 201–250 (1991)
5. Reeves, B., Shipman, F.: Supporting communication between designers with artifact-centered evolving information spaces. In: CSCW 1992, pp. 394–401 (1992)
6. Martinie, C., Palanque, P., Winckler, M., Conversy, S.: DREAMER: a design rationale environment for argumentation, modeling and engineering requirements. In: SIGDOC 2010, pp. 73–80 (2010)
7. Shum, S.B., Hammond, N.: Argumentation-based design rationale: what use at what cost. Int. J. Hum Comput Stud. **40**, 603–652 (1994)
8. Lee, J.: SIBYL: a tool for managing group decision rationale. In: CSCW 1990, pp. 79–92 (1990)
9. Schubanz, M.: Design rationale capture in software architecture: what has to be captured? In: WCOP 2014, pp. 31–36 (2014)
10. Houben, S., Bardram, J.E., Vermeulen J., Luyten, K., Coninx, K.: Activity-centric support for ad hoc knowledge work – a case study of co-activity manager. In: CHI 2013, pp. 2263–2272 (2013)
11. Fischer, G.: Social creativity: turning barriers into opportunities for collaborative design. In: PDC 2004, pp. 152–161 (2004)
12. Tan, C.S.S., Luyten, K., van den Bergh, J., Schöning, J., Coninx, K.: The role of physiological cues during remote collaboration. Presence Teleoperators Virtual Environ. **23**, 90–107 (2014)
13. Dourish, P., Bellotti, V.: Awareness and coordination in shared workspaces. In: CSCW 1992, pp. 107–114 (1992)

Cooperative Operating Control for Stimulation of Simultaneously Cultivated Bioprocesses

Mieczyslaw Metzger[1], Witold Nocoń[1(✉)], and Anna Węgrzyn[2]

[1] Faculty of Automatic Control, Electronics and Computer Science,
Silesian University of Technology, ul. Akademicka 16, 44-100 Gliwice, Poland
{mieczyslaw.metzger,witold.nocon}@polsl.pl
[2] Faculty of Faculty of Energy and Environmental Engineering,
Silesian University of Technology, ul. Akademicka 2, 44-100 Gliwice, Poland
anna.wegrzyn@polsl.pl

Abstract. Simultaneous cultivation of microorganisms in the specially designed experimental laboratory plant with five bioreactors system is a difficult problem. An especially important issue is the realization of the biomass biocoenosis stimulation by controlling the ratio of the dosed substrates. Such control requires a constant attendance by a two-person team of experimenters - the process operator and a measurement and analysis expert. In this paper, the necessity to carefully select the appropriate (well-cooperating) two-person teams for the operation of the process is discussed. An architecture of the "human-in-the-loop" control system is presented in which such control is proposed to be applied. The division of work between the cooperating experimenters has been discussed, taking into account its influence on proper cooperation.

Keywords: Cooperative operating control · Stimulation of bioprocesses · Allocation of experimenters' groups

1 Introduction

Cultivation of special types of biomass cultures for small wastewater treatment plants and for experimental studies is often required. One possibility of starting up a wastewater treatment process in a new installation is to use an inoculum of bacterial cultures taken from a different wastewater plant. This inoculum is characterized by a certain biocoenosis, e.g. it consists of specific groups of microorganisms in specific quantities. Once new activated sludge is grown from this inoculum, the biocoenosis of the biomass will gradually change since the biomass adapts to new conditions characteristic of the particular installation. Nonetheless, the initial state of the biomass will influence the future behavior of the obtained activated sludge. Additionally, the adaptation process takes a relatively long period of time. Therefore, an interesting possibility is to stimulate the adaptation process so that an activated sludge possessing the needed characteristic is obtained in a controllable way and in a reasonably short period of time.

© Springer International Publishing Switzerland 2015
Y. Luo (Ed.): CDVE 2015, LNCS 9320, pp. 185–192, 2015.
DOI: 10.1007/978-3-319-24132-6_22

Cultivation of biomass in a single reactor is prone to errors caused by inappropriate substrate dosage, resulting in an incorrectly formed biomass. Therefore, it is advised to adapt a concept of simultaneous cultures (see for example [1]). General review of biostimulation methods can be found in paper [2]. Paper [3] presents on the other hand general discussion of biomass composition.

Amongst the many goals that the biological wastewater treatment process must fulfill, two are the most important (apart from the obvious goal of reducing the amount of organic carbon load in wastewater), that is: (a) biological removal of fats and greases (see e.g. [4]) and (b) biological removal of nitrogen compounds (see e.g. [5]). In our research, a rather complex goal of obtaining different kinds of biomass cultures from the same type of biomass supplements, has been stated. Those two kind of biomass should be able to fulfill goals (a) and (b) respectively.

Cultivation of bacterial communities in different reactors working in parallel is a difficult task for the process operator especially since the modern biotechnology requires not only complex analytical methods but also subtle bioinformatics methods, as is for example the case with fluorescent in-situ hybridization - FISH (see form example [6]). It is also important to correctly integrate all the analytical measurement results with the continuous nature of the control system [7]. It becomes evident, that the operating team running the control of the biostimulation process, requiring advanced analytical methods, must be prepared for effective cooperation. This paper presents an example requiring an excellent cooperation between researchers possessing strongly differing fields of expertise. A system, in which such a cooperative control is performed is also presented.

The paper is organized as follows. In the second chapter a problem of directed biostimulation for the biomass cultivation is presented. The third chapter presents a new pilot-plant installation designed for this specific purpose. A discussion of the selection of research groups being able to carry out a cooperative stimulation of the biomass is presented in the fourth chapter, while the fifth chapter presents the cooperative system and some conclusions.

2   Problem Under Consideration

Figure 1 presents an explanation of the stimulation problem for obtaining a biomass with the desirable biocoenosis from a bacterial supplement. In order to reach goal (a), e.g. obtaining a biomass for the biological removal of fats and greases, the stimulation must be directed towards activation of *Bacillus* and *Pseudomonas* strains. In this case, the directed stimulation requires the manipulation of two substrates: oil – a source of lipids, and peptone – a protein hydrolysate containing mainly organic carbon compounds and nitrogen compounds. In order to reach goal (b), e.g. obtaining a biomass for biological removal of ammonia nitrogen, the *Nitrosomonas* and *Nitrobacter* strains must be activates. In this case, the directed stimulation requires the manipulation of two different substrates: a source of organic carbon, either glucose or sodium acetate, and a nitrogen source in a form of ammonium sulfate.

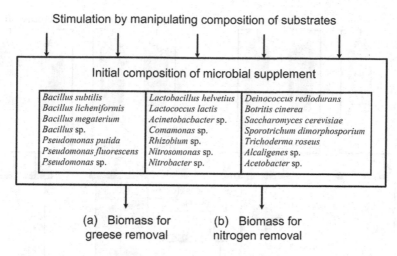

Fig. 1. Biomass culture stimulation directed towards obtaining two different biocoenosis.

3   Experimental Instrumentation for Biomass Culture Stimulation

Experimental laboratory installation dedicated specially for bioprocess stimulation was designed in cooperation with future users, that is by experts of three specializations: automatic control, biotechnology and instrumentation engineering. The installation consists of five continuous stirred tank bioreactors (CSTB) and can be reconfigurated for different research scenarios. Figure 2 presents the most typical architecture.

The CSTB bioreactors have been designed with to overflows each, for two working volumes of 2,5 L and 5 L. By manipulating the valves on the overflow pipes, it is also possible to adapt each CSTB to work in a batch mode or fed-batch mode. This is especially useful during start-up cultures working in the batch testing mode with volumes between 0,5 L and 5 L. It is also possible to gravitationally (without the need of pumps) mix two cultures from reactors CSTB-a and CSTB-b in a third bioreactor CSTB-c. Obviously, other process configuration are available with the employment of pumps.

A key concept for the control of stimulation in the presented process is the dosage of two different substrates (or a mixtures of substrates) into each bioreactor. Such control is possible with the usage of a three-way valve having a flow ratio $r \in [0, 1]$, according to the following formula:

$$Q = rQ_1 + (1 - r)Q_2 \tag{1}$$

What three-way vales are more expensive, it is possible to use two different pumps for flows Q_1 and Q_2, instead of the three-way valve and one pump with flow Q.

Apart from pumps, the installation is equipped with a variety of stationary of manual sensors and transducers. Appropriate nipples allow samples to be collected.

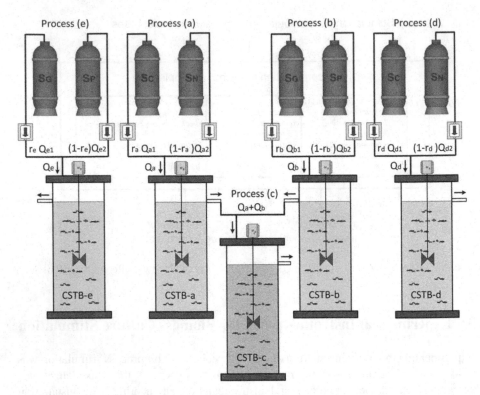

Fig. 2. Example of a typical architecture of five CSTB experimental set-up. Q - flows, r - control rates between dozed substrates.

4   Problem of Allocating Experimenters Groups for Cooperative Stimulation of Bioprocesses

Because of the increasing accuracy and precision of available measuring instruments, but also due to increasing possibilities and functionalities of supervisory software for experimental, control and monitoring purposes, the human factor becomes the weakest link in the whole system.

In the case considered in this paper, the major difficulty is related to the fact that there is a limited number of staff to perform the laboratory experiment, the goal of which is to stimulate the biotechnological process in a proper way. At once, only two experimenters (process operator and measurement specialist) can be involved in the performed experiments.

The experiments are performed cyclically twenty-four hours a day and include various measurement techniques and procedures. Moreover, the complexity of experiments does not allow all the experimenters to perform all the experiments at the same time. Figure 3 graphically presents the problem of experimenters' groups selection.

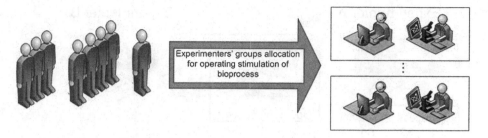

Fig. 3. The allocation of experimenters' groups.

In the classical approach, the pairs of cooperating experimenters are usually chosen arbitrarily. In our case, it is of great importance to select the team members carefully, since the experiments are conducted round the clock, for several days.

Some issues concerning the selection of experimenter's groups have been presented in [8]. In our case, having only a limited number of personnel having different specializations and different working schedule constraints, it has been decided to use our own simulators of simple biological processes in order to initially train the members of two-person working groups. While selecting the experimenter's groups it was also necessary to take researcher's social conditions into account [9].

The most important social conditionings that were taken into account are: possibility of participation in experiments conducted at night, a distance between the experimenter's home and laboratory, and last but not least, the relations between experimenters and their individual preferences for work in a particular group.

5 Human-in-the-Loop Cooperative Operation and Monitoring of Simultaneous Culture of Microorganisms

Carefully selected two-person working groups of experimenters are operating the process in a system presented in Fig. 4. A feedback is clearly indicated in that figure, and the experimenters are part of that feedback. Despite the fact, that their scope of responsibilities is different, it is clearly visible that both are an important part of the feedback loop. Such type of control is called the "Human-in-the-loop" control. In our case, such control is made difficult by the fact that there are two different people in the loop, hence the efficiency of stimulation control is dependent on their effective and strict cooperation.

Additionally, the control is performed in real time, while some of the key analytical measurements are time consuming and results are obtained with a considerable delay, which adds to the difficulty of the whole process operation. In particular, the fluorescent in-situ hybridization technique is time consuming but provides an important almost real-time insight into the biocoenosis of the cultivated biomass. FISH uses fluorescently labelled oligonucleotide probes to detect and estimate the abundance of particular bacterial genera or species [6].

The process operator's (experimenter A) tasks and the issues based on which decisions must be made, can be reasonably easily stated. Those are:

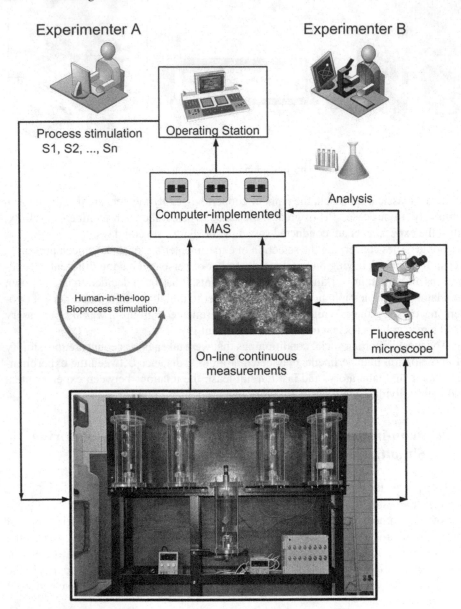

Fig. 4. Cooperative Human-in-the-Loop control for stimulation of microbial cultures cultivated in the system of five continuous stirred tank bioreactors; experimenter A - process operator, experimenter B - technician carrying out analytical measurements, including fluorescent in situ hybridization.

- updating (in the control system) of the available measurement data, including the results of analytical methods, with the minimum time delay (data from the second member of the group - experimenter B),
- verification whether the available measurements are enough to reach the stated goals (a) and/or (b) of the biomass cultivation, and request of additional data from experimenter B if required,
- prediction of the process behavior, based on a process simulator working in a faster-than-real-time mode, e.g. in a accelerated scaled time,
- making decisions about the change of control strategy for the near future (operator control is performed in a piece-wise constant control mode),
- verification of the control strategy with the other member of the group (experimenter B),
- verification of the decision regarding changes in flow ratios between the dosed substrates, and finally
- carrying out of the control action.

The tasks for experimenter B to be carried out, that are important for experimenter A, are as follows:

- drawing of samples from the system for all reactors,
- fixation of cells. This step is performed in order to stop all metabolic activity in the cells, hence to preserve the state of the organism in a state as it was in the reactor, and permeabilisation of the cell's walls in order to enable FISH probes to penetrate the cells,
- hybridization of the samples with FISH probes carefully selected for the detection of the specific microorganisms that are required for the particular control goal (a) and/or (b),
- washing of the samples in order to remove all the probes that did not hybridized to the cells. This step is required in order to see only the probes that hybridized to the cells, and thus be able to detect the organisms sought,
- acquisition of fluorescent microscopy images for different light wavelengths,
- applying image processing analysis in order to quantify the amounts of particular microorganisms in the obtained samples.
- preparation of results that can be directly incorporated into the control system, for experimenter A to be able to make appropriate decisions.

The FISH protocol outlined above requires experimented B to follow a very stringent procedure, that involves working with dangerous chemicals, using freezers, centrifuges, assuring the samples are stored within a narrow range of temperatures and finally microscopic observations. Additionally, a strict time schedule must be maintained for the best results to be obtained. Therefore, careful planning is needed to ensure, that all steps are done in the time frame required. This adds to the overall problem of ensuring a good working environment for the experimenters.

6   Concluding Remarks

The presented analysis of tasks that need to be performed by the experimenters proves, that essential cooperation between the experimenters is of key importance for the successful stimulation control of the biotechnological processes. During the selection of the working group pairs, social constraints have also been taken into account. An additional issue would be an analysis of sociological aspects of the cooperation, but this is a separate topic, requiring additional research in the field of sociology.

Acknowledgments. This work was supported by the National Science Centre under grant No. 2012/05/B/ST7/00096 and by the Ministry of Science and Higher Education under grant BK-UiUA.

References

1. Bougaran, G., Le Déan, L., Ewa Lukomska, E., Kaas, R., Régis Baron, R.: Transient initial phase in continuous culture of Isochrysis galbana affinis Tahiti. Aquat. Living Resour. **16**, 389–394 (2003)
2. Tyagi, M., da Fonseca, M.M.R., de Carvalho, C.C.C.R.: Bioaugmentation and biostimulation strategies to improve the effectiveness of bioremediation processes. Biodegradation **22**, 231–241 (2011)
3. Wagner, M., Loy, A.: Bacterial community composition and function in sewage treatment systems. Curr. Opin. Biotechnol. **13**, 218–227 (2002)
4. Mendoza-Espinoza, L., Stepheson, T.: Grease biodegradation: is bioaugmentation more effective than natural populations for start-up? Wat. Sci. Tech. **34**(5–6), 303–308 (1996)
5. Zhu, G., Peng, Y., Li, B., Guo, J., Yang, Q., Wang, S.: Biological removal of nitrogen from wastewater. Rev. Environ. Contam. Toxicol. **192**, 159–195 (2008)
6. Wagner, M., Horn, M., Daimes, H.: Fluorescence *in situ* hybridization for the identification and characterization of prokaryotes. Curr. Opin. Microbiol. **6**, 302–309 (2003)
7. Nocoń, W., Węgrzyn, A., Polaków, G., Choiński, D., Metzger, M.: Integration of industrial control with analytical expert measurements for cooperative operations. In: Luo, Y. (ed.) CDVE 2014. LNCS, vol. 8683, pp. 80–87. Springer, Heidelberg (2014)
8. Hinds, P.J., Carley, K.M., Krackhardt, D., Wholey, D.: Choosing work group members: balancing similarity, competence, and familiarity. Organ. Behav. Hum. Decis. Process. **81**, 226–251 (2000)
9. Metzger, M., Skupin, P.: Human-in-the-loop simulation based system for more effective allocation and training of experimenters' groups in stimulation of biotechnological processes. In: Advances in Computational Social Science and Social Simulation. Proceedings of the Social Simulation Conference 2014, pp. 47–50 (2014)

Application of the Sequence Diagrams in the Design of Distributed Control System

Dariusz Choinski, Piotr Skupin$^{(\boxtimes)}$, and Piotr Krauze

Faculty of Automatic Control, Electronics and Computer Science, Silesian University
of Technology, ul.Akademicka 16, 44-100 Gliwice, Poland
{dariusz.choinski,piotr.skupin,piotr.krauze}@polsl.pl

Abstract. The paper describes the use of the sequence diagrams in the design
and analysis of the control software for biotechnological process. The goal was
to automate the substrate preparation process. In many situations, a slight change
in the substrate preparation procedure may lead to significant changes in the software performing this procedure. Assuming that the substrate can be prepared in
two different ways (sequential or concurrent preparation of its components), it is
shown that the UML sequence diagrams can be effective in analysis of the possible
scenarios. As a result, one can obtain a control software that is suitable for each
of the possible scenarios, and that can be easily implemented in the hierarchical
distributed control system.

Keywords: UML · Sequence diagrams · Control system design ·
Biotechnological process

1 Introduction

In case of the design of control systems, an important role is played by the sequence
diagrams (subgroup of the behavioral diagrams), which clearly present the operation of
a control application under various scenarios. The UML (Unified Modeling Language)
is an object-oriented modeling approach, which is widely used in the design of information systems. Although, the UML technique is based on the semi-formal notations
[1], the range of its applications is very wide. For instance, the UML techniques can be
used in collaborative product design to define the structure of elements (treated as object
classes) and their relationship [2]. According to Chen and co-workers [2], one of the
major phases in the collaborative product design is the system modeling phase, which
can be realized with the help of UML technique. This phase includes: determination of
the system functionality, identification of use cases, actors and events. In turn, Merlo
and Girard [3] proposed a system supporting engineering design in collaborative environment. In this case, the UML diagrams were used to analyze and design the architecture of the supporting system. The UML technique can also be used in stress testing
methodologies for fault detections of real-time systems as shown, for instance, in [4].
Another interesting example was presented in [5], where the UML-based approach was
used to describe biological systems. The authors presented relationships between

© Springer International Publishing Switzerland 2015
Y. Luo (Ed.): CDVE 2015, LNCS 9320, pp. 193–196, 2015.
DOI: 10.1007/978-3-319-24132-6_23

biological system (biological domain) and the UML environment. From the control system point of view, the UML diagrams can be very helpful in description of the system requirements, modeling of the controlled plant and in analysis of the control system behavior [6].

2   Problem Under Consideration

In order to enforce the appropriate mode of operation of the bioreactor (operation in the range of steady states or in the range of self-sustained oscillations), the biological process has to be properly stimulated. One of the possibilities of induction or elimination of the oscillatory behavior is the manipulation of the substrate content [7, 8]. In practice, due to short durability of substrate, it has to be prepared in small amounts (e.g., every 24 h) and its content can change depending on the desired mode of operation of the bioreactor or other factors influencing the grow of microorganisms (e.g., the change of the content of minerals). Moreover, the substrate can be prepared as a single mixture of required components or separately in single tanks, which allows immediate change of the substrate mixture content. In majority of cases, the preparation of the substrate mixture is described by procedures, which specify the order of mixing of the substrate components and their additional heat treatment (e.g., warming or cooling). Quite often, the substrate is a multiphase mixture which, due to sedimentation, makes the pumping process more difficult [9]. In effect, it may be necessary to prepare the substrate mixture sequentially or concurrently. In the considered case, two scenarios are taken into account: A) the substrate is composed of two basic components that are mixed together and subject to heat treatment according to a strict order; B) there are two separate substrates that have to be prepared simultaneously. Each of these scenarios should be realized by the control application in the hierarchical control system [10].

3   Discussion and Concluding Remarks

The control software is designed for the existing hierarchical Distributed Control System (DCS). Figures 1 and 2 present sequence diagrams corresponding to the Scenarios A and B, respectively. The thickness of arrows is related to each of the substrate components (concentrated products 1 and 2). The actors are the Production Manager and the Production Engineer who cooperate with each other. The Production Manager decides on the content of the substrate mixture and the Production Engineer is responsible for its preparation.

As can be clearly seen, in the Scenario A the structure of the control application is simple and it comprises similar operations (e.g., mixing, warming and cooling) that are performed for the first substrate and then for the mixture of substrates. In the Scenario B the structure is more complex, as both substrates have to be prepared simultaneously. In this case, a change in the system's structure (concurrent production of two single substrates) implies significant changes in the operation of the control application.

The same operations performed in the Scenario A (e.g., cooling or warming) have to be synchronized. For instance, it is not possible to start cooling the first substrate

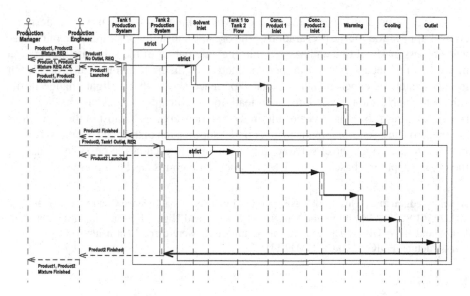

Fig. 1. Sequential preparation of the substrate mixture (Scenario A)

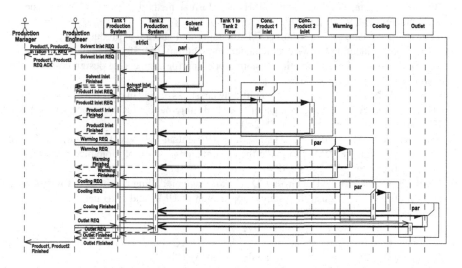

Fig. 2. Concurrent preparation of two single substrates (Scenario B)

before the second substrate is not fully warmed up. The operations that have to be performed concurrently were presented in the combined fragments "par".

Thanks to the use of UML sequence diagrams, the behavior of the designed control application can be analyzed in detail. Such a behavioral synthesis of the control application allows designing a fully functional control system that is suitable for several possible scenarios. Then, the sequence diagrams can be translated into a program for the DCS.

Using the possibilities offered by the UML techniques, our goal was to design a control application for the preparation of the organic substrate for stimulation of biological process. It should be emphasized that the automation of the substrate preparation process is not necessary for a proper conduction of the biotechnological process, but greatly facilitates experimentation. Our experience shows that a slight change in the substrate preparation procedure may lead to significant changes in the software performing this procedure. As a result, in the practical approach, most of the operations is carried out in a semi-automatic manner under supervision of the plant operator. Hence, in order to design a control software that is suitable in each of the possible scenarios, the design approach based on the UML sequence diagrams has been presented.

Acknowledgments. This work was supported by the National Science Centre under grant No. 2012/05/B/ST7/00096 and by the Ministry of Science and Higher Education under grants BK-UiUA and BKM-UiUA. The calculations in this study were carried out using GeCONiI grant infrastructure (POIG.02.03.01-24-099/13).

References

1. Borges, R., Mota, A.: Integrating UML and formal methods. Electron. Notes Theoret. Comput. Sci. **184**, 97–112 (2007)
2. Chen, Y.-J., Chen, Y.M., Chu, H.C.: Enabling collaborative product design through distributed engineering knowledge management. Comput. Ind. **59**, 395–409 (2008)
3. Merlo, C., Girard, Ph: Information system modelling for engineering design co-ordination. Comput. Ind. **55**, 317–334 (2004)
4. Garousi, V., Briand, L., Labiche, Y.: Traffic-aware stress testing of distributed systems based on UML models. In: Proceedings of the 28th International Conference on Software Engineering, Shanghai, pp. 391–400 (2006)
5. Roux-Rouquie, M., Caritey, N., Gaubert, L., Rosenthal-Sabroux, C.: Using the Unified Modelling Language (UML) to guide the systemic description of biological processes and systems. Biosystems **75**, 3–14 (2004)
6. Basile, F., Chiacchio, P., Del Grosso, D.: A two-stage modelling architecture for distributed control of real-time industrial systems: application of UML and Petri net. Comput. Stand. Interfaces **31**, 528–538 (2009)
7. Skupin, P., Metzger, M.: An alternative approach for oscillatory behaviour control in a nonlinear bioprocess. In: Proceedings of the 9th IFAC Symposium on Nonlinear Control Systems (NOLCOS), pp. 253–258, Toulouse (2013)
8. Turek-Szytow, J., Choiński, D., Miksch, K.: Properties of the activated sludge after lipase bioaugmentation. Environ. Prot. Eng. **33**, 211–219 (2007)
9. Choiński, D., Metzger, M., Nocoń, W.: Multiscale three-phase flow simulation dedicated to model based control. In: Bubak, M., van Albada, G.D., Dongarra, J., Sloot, P.M.A. (eds.) ICCS 2008, Part II. LNCS, vol. 5102, pp. 261–270. Springer, Heidelberg (2008)
10. Choinski, D., Nocon, W., Metzger, M.: Application of the holonic approach in distributed control systems designing. In: Mařík, V., Vyatkin, V., Colombo, A.W. (eds.) HoloMAS 2007. LNCS (LNAI), vol. 4659, pp. 257–268. Springer, Heidelberg (2007)

Cooperative Engineering of Agent-Based Process Control Algorithm

Grzegorz Polaków[✉] and Piotr Laszczyk

Faculty of Automatic Control, Electronics and Computer Science,
Silesian University of Technology, Gliwice, Poland
{grzegorz.polakow,piotr.laszczyk}@polsl.pl

Abstract. Process control algorithms constitute a specific software model, as they have well-defined and constant sets of inputs and outputs, and perform calculations cyclically in real time. Therefore, the algorithms rarely are implemented otherwise than embedded in the low level control instrumentation. This paper proposes a departure from this well-known approach in order to apply multi-agent system directly in the control layer. While this novel approach creates few issues requiring resolving, such as the need to develop an agent-based software operating in real time, it also provides the crucial benefit i.e. the possibility of developing the modules of the control algorithm by experts from different fields, which allows for cooperative dynamic engineering of a control algorithm. The resulting methodology allows to include more modern and advanced solutions from various fields of control science than it is possible in the case of the classical approach.

Keywords: Agent system · Cooperative engineering · Process control · Model-based

1 Introduction and Motivation

Nowadays, more and more emphasis is put on effectiveness and energy efficiency of the industrial production processes. So it is virtually impossible to run any process without a properly designed complex system of automatic control [1]. Such a system is built in layers, and the lowest layer (i.e. the regulatory layer) is responsible for direct impact on the process. This layer consists of control algorithms adjusting relevant process parameters.

In the classical approach to the control algorithm is developed once, at the design stage of the control system. At this stage, experts can include additional functionalities in the algorithm e.g. enabling sensor redundancy or values estimation during communication failures. The result is the equation of the algorithm that is later embedded into a hardware controller in the form of cyclically calculated difference equations. In this paper it is proposed to break this static engineering sequence in favour to employing the multi-agent system, which is able to dynamically transform the algorithm equations during the operation of the control system.

© Springer International Publishing Switzerland 2015
Y. Luo (Ed.): CDVE 2015, LNCS 9320, pp. 197–200, 2015.
DOI: 10.1007/978-3-319-24132-6_24

In the classical approach, a sensor failure during the operation of the control algorithm makes the difference equations algorithm invalid and the equations become impossible to calculate due to the lack of relevant data. In the proposed architecture, the algorithm dynamically evolve into a form suitable for further action without absent sensors (this is possible due to the construction of a model-based algorithms). The key benefit is, however, ability to delegate specific tasks that the algorithm includes, to the experts in various fields control theory and computer science. This is particularly important when taking into account the vast knowledge and number of solutions available in this field - there are, for example, complex algorithms of sensor failure detection [2], modern metrology methods, or prediction algorithms. In the classical approach, all this knowledge has to be collected during the development of the regulatory layer, and any later modifications are expensive [3]. In the proposed methodology, the agents can be developed independently by various experts and added/removed from the system asynchronously, even during the operation.

2   The Proposed Architecture

The agent-based programming paradigm is proposed as a method of implementation of the dynamically reconfigurable algorithm. The initial implementation is being developed in NI LabVIEW software using the previous work of authors [4] including the novel real-time pPDC protocol [5], but the final implementation is planned to be developed in the FIPA-compliant SPADE environment, mostly due to the versatility of the Python programming language.

Use of the agent programming methodologies in the process control is relatively uncommon, due to the fact that the discrete nature of multi-agent systems corresponds to the manufacturing processes better than to the continuous ones [6]. It is therefore proposed to implement the control algorithm as an auction, where each single control cycle consists of bidding by agents responsible for communication with hardware measurement sensors. These agents read the measurement data and assess the confidence of the measurements which is an offer in the auction. At the same time the system variables are estimated by the separate agents on the basis of elementary numerical methods, or with more complex methodologies (called software sensors in that case). The confidence of each of the estimated value is also determined and treated as an offer in the auction. The task of the auctioneer agent is to collect the offers, choose the most attractive and reject the unreliable ones, and develop a set of available input values for a single iteration of the algorithm. These set is sent to the solver agent which has knowledge on chosen model-based process control algorithm. Using the set as input the solver agent determines the appropriate equations allowing to calculate the control value, which is then sent to the actuator. The proposed sequence of the communication (with simplifications resulting from omission of details of generating equations agents pool) is shown in Fig. 1.

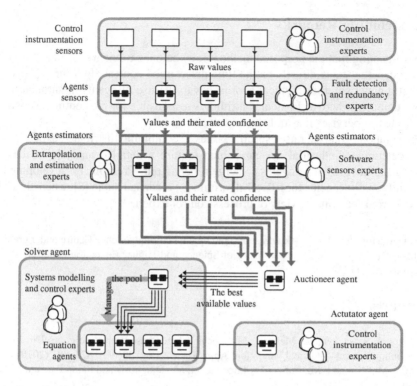

Fig. 1. Data flow in an elementary cycle of the control algorithm in relation to developers' expertise.

With this construction, a clear division of competences of experts is achieved:

- control instrumentation and measurements experts – responsible for obtaining the algorithm's inputs and applying the algorithm's output to the actuator. Their knowledge is used to implement the *control instrumentation sensors* (the only part of the framework which is not a part of multi-agent system) and *actuator agent*. Their knowledge focuses on metrology, industrial instrumentation and I/O interfaces.
- fault detection and redundancy experts – their task is the confidence assessment of the sensors data. The experts embed their knowledge in *sensor agents*.
- Extrapolation and estimation experts – have knowledge about predicting the value of a physical quantity on the basis of its historical progress and are able to determine the level of confidence of the predictions. These tasks are programmed into *estimator agents*.
- Software sensors experts – can determine the interrelationships between physical variables in a dynamic system and predict the changes of one of them on the basis of the others. This knowledge is stored in another group of *estimator agents*.
- Systems modelling and control experts – are familiar with model-based control algorithms and can choose one for the process and derive variants of the algorithm depending on the accessibility of the measured values. This knowledge is embedded in the system through the *solver agent* managing the pool of *equation agents*.

3   Concluding Remarks

It is worth noting that the proposed methodology belongs to the most interesting trend of using agent systems directly as the time-determined control algorithms [6], which makes it a novel solution. Typical approaches to the use of agents in automation are hybrid solutions, where a classical algorithm is responsible for the continuous part and agent system supervises it as in [7].

The solution proposed raises specific issues of combining distributed expertise with a time-determined industrial system, which require a detailed analysis of the time requirements in relation to agents' emergent behaviour. Preliminary development of solver and equation agents for BBAC algorithm [1] is carried out in [8], which describes this work from the point of view of process control expert.

Acknowledgements. This work was supported by the National Science Centre under grant No. 2012/05/B/ST7/00096 and by the Ministry of Science and Higher Education under grants BK-UiUA and BKM-UiUA.

References

1. Czeczot, J., Łaszczyk, P., Metzger, M.: Local balance-based adaptive control in the heat distribution system - practical validation. Appl. Therm. Eng. **30**(8/9), 879–891 (2010)
2. Blanke, M., Kinnaert, M., Lunze, J., Staroswiecki, M.: Diagnosis and Fault-Tolerant Control. Springer, Berlin (2006)
3. Choinski, D., Skupin, P., Szajna, E.: Optimization of engineering design cycles in enterprise integration. In: Luo, Y. (ed.) CDVE 2013. LNCS, vol. 8091, pp. 153–156. Springer, Heidelberg (2013)
4. Polaków, G., Metzger, M.: pPDC blackboard broadcasting in agent-based distributed process control. In: O'Shea, J., Nguyen, N.T., Crockett, K., Howlett, R.J., Jain, L.C. (eds.) KES-AMSTA 2011. LNCS, vol. 6682, pp. 241–250. Springer, Heidelberg (2011)
5. Polaków, G., Metzger, M.: Performance evaluation of the parallel processing producer-distributor-consumer network architecture. Comput. Stand. Interfaces **35**(6), 596–604 (2013)
6. Metzger, M., Polaków, G.: A Survey on applications of agent technology in industrial process control. IEEE Trans. Industr. Inf. **7**(4), 570–581 (2011)
7. Skupin, P., Metzger, M.: The application of multi-agent system in monitoring and control of nonlinear bioprocesses. In: Corchado, E., Snášel, V., Abraham, A., Woźniak, M., Graña, M., Cho, S.-B. (eds.) HAIS 2012, Part III. LNCS, vol. 7208, pp. 25–36. Springer, Heidelberg (2012)
8. Polaków, G., Laszczyk, P., Metzger, M.: Agent-based approach to model-based dynamically reconfigurable control algorithm. In: Fikar, M., Kvasnica, M. (eds.) International Conference on Process Control (PC2015), pp. 375–380, Štrbské Pleso (2015)

An On-Line Model Verification System for Model-Based Control Algorithms

Tomasz Klopot[1], Piotr Skupin[1(✉)], Witold Klopot[1], and Piotr Gacki[2]

[1] Faculty of Automatic Control, Electronics and Computer Science,
Silesian University of Technology, ul.Akademicka 16, 44-100 Gliwice, Poland
{tomasz.klopot,piotr.skupin,witold.klopot}@polsl.pl
[2] PROPOINT sp. z o.o. sp.k., ul.Szobiszowicka 1, 44-100 Gliwice, Poland
piotr.gacki1@propoint1.pl

Abstract. The advanced control algorithms are often based on a mathematical model of the controlled plant and the performance of the control system largely depends on the accuracy of the plant model. However, simplified phenomenological or linear models are often used in practice. Because, the accuracy of these models may differ and vary over time, it is proposed a model verification system. Its main goal is the on-line verification of the accuracy of two plant models. The system is based on a concept of cooperating agents, which are distributed over several controllers. As a result, the proposed solution can be implemented in already existing industrial control systems, where each of the programmable logic controllers (PLCs) performs its basic tasks. The verification system has been implemented and tested on the several distributed PLCs.

Keywords: Agent-based system · Programmable logic controller (PLC) · Distributed control system

1 Introduction

The industrial distributed control systems are sometimes supervised by complex software systems such as SIMATIC PCS7 or Delta V. These systems can support the implementation of advanced control algorithms or they can perform many complex tasks (e.g., verification of the controller's parameters) that have significant impact on the quality of control or process costs. Due to the high demand for computing power, these complex systems are mainly used in the supervisory layer. However, such solutions are expensive and require highly qualified operators. Hence, they are typically used in large industrial sectors (e.g., power stations or refineries) and do not apply to small processes or laboratory facilities. In effect, majority of industrial control systems is based on the simplest control algorithms without additional functionality.

On the other hand, it is well-known that the use of advanced control algorithms in combination with the mathematical model of the controlled plant may lead to a better quality of control [1, 2]. However, the efficiency of the model-based control algorithms largely depends on the accuracy of the mathematical model of the controlled plant. The more accurate the model, the better the controller performance. It should be emphasized

© Springer International Publishing Switzerland 2015
Y. Luo (Ed.): CDVE 2015, LNCS 9320, pp. 201–204, 2015.
DOI: 10.1007/978-3-319-24132-6_25

that the derivation of an accurate mathematical model of the plant is not an easy task, especially for chemical or biological systems [3]. Another factor that makes this difficult is that the process properties can vary over time and the model parameters have to be constantly updated. Hence, simplified phenomenological models derived from mass and energy balances or linear models are often used in model-based control algorithms [4]. The phenomenological models are more accurate than the linear ones in a wide range of operating levels of the controlled plant and they do not require time-consuming identification. In turn, the linear models are defined for a chosen operating point of the plant and their accuracy is limited to a small vicinity of the operating point. In addition, they require estimation of model parameters when switching between several operating points. The results of our study shows that the accuracy of these models may differ and depends on the chosen operating point of the plant. In effect, it also affects the performance of the model-based control algorithm.

Hence, the goal of this study was to design a system, which is responsible for online verification of the accuracy of the plant model. Because, inexpensive Programmable Logic Controllers (PLCs) with limited computing and memory capacities are often used in practice [5], therefore in the proposed solution, the complex calculation procedures are decomposed and distributed over several controllers in the direct control layer.

2   The Agent-Based Verification System

The verification system is based on the concept of a software agent [6, 7]. In the considered case, the "agents" are cooperating procedures distributed over four PLCs (SIMATIC S7-1200) since, the memory capacity of the inexpensive PLCs can be limited (Fig. 1). Moreover, in industrial practice, the control system is often composed of several PLCs that perform some technological tasks. The additional PC with SCADA (supervisory control and data acquisition) software visualizes the controlled process and provides the results of the verification procedure in the supervisory layer.

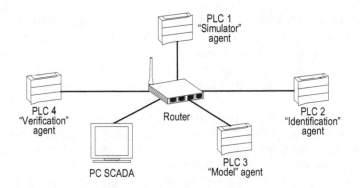

Fig. 1. The architecture of the agent-based verification system

The communication between the PLCs and the PC is realized with industrial Ethernet and TCP/IP protocol. The router was used to connect networking devices.

The procedure realized by the verification system is presented in Fig. 2 and the agents are realized by means of the controllers' function blocks. In the presented case, the real hydraulic plant is simulated in the additional PLC by the "Simulator" agent. For this purpose, a mathematical model of the hydraulic tank was derived and validated against measurement data. The input signals of the model are the inlet flow rate Q_{in} and the valve's opening degree in the output. In turn, the output signals are the liquid level H in the tank and the output flow rate Q_{out}. The simulated variables are sent to other agents every 50[ms].

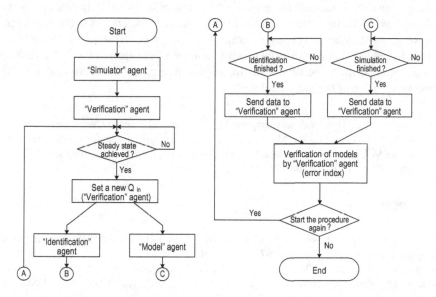

Fig. 2. The verification procedure realized on-line for the simulated plant

The "Verification" agent keeps track of the current liquid level H and waits for the steady state (the operating point) to be achieved by the plant. Then, for identification purposes, the agent determines a new value of the inlet flow rate Q_{in} and sends it to other agents.

The "Identification" agent collects the simulation data received from the "Simulator" agent. Once the steady state is achieved the "Identification" agent determines parameters of the linear model of the plant based on the simulation data. These parameters are then sent to the "Verification" agent. At the same time, the "Model" agent runs a simulation of the plant based on the phenomenological model. The simulated results are sent to the "Verification" agent.

In the final step, the "Verification" agent compares the accuracy of the phenomeno-logical and linear models based on the performance index, which is a function of the identification error, i.e., the difference between the process data (in this case obtained from the "Simulator" agent) and the simulated data. The verification procedure can be realized on-line, and once it is finished, can be repeated again. As a result, the efficiency of the model-based control algorithm can be improved.

3   Concluding Remarks

The agent-based verification system was tested with the use of several inexpensive PLCs (SIMATIC S7-1200) for the simulated hydraulic plant, where the information about the plant dynamics was obtained from its step response data. In the case of real industrial plants, the proposed system is able to obtain the necessary information about the plant dynamics from its input and output signals observed over long time periods, in the same manner as in the case of commercial solutions (e.g., SIMATIC PCS7) [8]. It means that the system can also be used to update parameters in the plant model if the plant properties vary over time, as for instance in the stimulated bioprocesses. Thanks to the distribution of the verification system over several controllers, the proposed solution can be implemented in already existing industrial control systems, where each of the PLCs performs its tasks, while at the same time, calls the cooperating procedures responsible for the on-line verification of the plant model.

Acknowledgments. This work was supported by the National Science Centre under grant No. 2012/05/B/ST7/00096 and by the Ministry of Science and Higher Education under grants BK-UiUA and BKM-UiUA. The calculations in this study were carried out using GeCONiI grant infrastructure (POIG.02.03.01-24-099/13).

References

1. Stebel, K., Czeczot, J., Laszczyk, P.: General tuning procedure for the nonlinear balance-based adaptive controller. Int. J. Control **87**, 76–89 (2014)
2. Klopot, T., Choiński, D., Skupin, P., Szczypka, D.: Metamorphic controller for collaborative design of an optimal structure of the control system. In: Luo, Y. (ed.) CDVE 2014. LNCS, vol. 8683, pp. 230–237. Springer, Heidelberg (2014)
3. Stebel, K., Metzger, M.: Distributed parameter model for pH process including distributed continuous and discrete reactant feed. Comput. Chem. Eng. **38**, 82–93 (2012)
4. Klopot, T., Czeczot, J., Klopot, W.: Flexible function block for PLC-based implementation of the balance-based adaptive controller. In: Proceedings of the American Control Conference, pp. 6467–6472, Montreal (2012)
5. Chmiel, M., Hrynkiewicz, E.: Concurrent operation of processors in the bit-byte CPU of a PLC. Control Cybern. **39**, 559–579 (2010)
6. Jennings, N.R., Sycara, K., Wooldridge, M.: A roadmap of agent research and development. Auton. Agent. Multi-Agent Syst. **1**, 7–38 (1998)
7. Skupin, P., Metzger, M.: Agent-based control of self-sustained oscillations in industrial processes: a bioreactor case study. In: Jezic, G., Kusek, M., Nguyen, N.-T., Howlett, R.J., Jain, L.C. (eds.) KES-AMSTA 2012. LNCS, vol. 7327, pp. 209–218. Springer, Heidelberg (2012)
8. Li, Y., Ang, K., Chong, G.: Patents, software, and hardware for PID control. IEEE Control Syst. Mag. **26**, 42–54 (2006)

Co-construction of Meaning via a Collaborative Action Research Approach

Samia Ben Rajeb and Pierre Leclercq[✉]

LUCID, University of Liege, Liege, Belgium
{samia.benrajeb,pierre.leclercq}@ulg.ac.be

Abstract. This article sets out the four stages of an analytical approach which enables student - designers at the end of their academic career in the domain of design, to "metareflectively" consider their design and collaboration processes. Inspired by collaborative action research approaches, this analytical approach aims to create a space in which the student can learn and co-construct meaning relative to the activity of collaborative design. It plays a role in enabling the learner/designer/observer to take a step back from their activities, both when considering the activity in isolation and in confronting it to others' points of view. This article explains the steps and tools (methodological, theoretical and analytical) involved; it also provides feedback on experiences from 7 different contexts. It shows how the system as a whole enables analysis, interpretation, questioning, and critical and collective reflection of the situation.

Keywords: Conception collaborative · Sciences cognitives · Collaborative design · Analysis of complex activity · Scientific approach · Design sciences · Collaborative action research

1 Introduction

Design careers (architecture, engineering, industrial design, etc.) usually require a training period of five years (three years for a bachelor's degree and a further two years for a master's degree). This training is often centred on the project itself and the designing of it, but it also includes a theoretical element that brings the student into contact with a group of areas and fields necessary to master the complex activity of design. The training is often based on "project-based approach" [1], so the students are as engaged in practical learning as they are in theoretical learning. Throughout their studies, they must learn to conduct their projects via iterative, undetermined, and often multi-faceted processes; they are expected to be creative in order to find a solution to an open, unclearly defined and complex problem which often has to be expressed in words to other collaborators. Without challenging the relevance of such a learning format, which is perfectly adequate for understanding design, this article focuses on the following question: is design teachable in a collective format other than "project workshops", especially when it requires the

© Springer International Publishing Switzerland 2015
Y. Luo (Ed.): CDVE 2015, LNCS 9320, pp. 205–215, 2015.
DOI: 10.1007/978-3-319-24132-6_26

involvement of several participants from the outset of the project (as is the case in the field of architecture and engineering [2]?

To help students take a step back and consider their own design and collaborative processes, this article expounds on a complementary approach to that of the workshop, inspired by collaborative action research methods [3]. In bringing together researcher-guides and learners playing the role of either the designer or observer, all of the participants are "engaged in critical and dynamic reflection on a situation with which they are confronted" [4, p. 78]. The aim is to focus the attention of the learner on the process itself rather than on the object to be designed. This will help learners to consider their own design and collaboration processes metareflectively.

To explain this collective approach, this article first introduces the general modalities of the workshop proposed here, entitled "workshop+". The four component stages are then defined relative to the objectives and methodological, theoretical and analytical tools specific to each step. The various applications, in seven different contexts, which have been conducted to date are then listed. Finally, the feedback from the learners regarding their experiences is put forward; this will detail the input, limitations and perspectives addressed at the end of this implemented educational experience via a collaborative action research approach.

2   General Procedure

Participatory approaches to research are varied but share a common goal, that of balancing experience, action, practical work and analysis of that work [5]. "Action research" is one such approach, marking a break with the classic scientific approaches that separate an action from its analysis, and collective practices from their theoretical generation [6]. Its principal objective is to manage the participants' preoccupations when faced with a situation set by researchers wanting to develop a shared understanding of the situation [7]. An approach is said to be "collaborative" when all the participants (researchers and practitioners, observers and designers) strive to co-construct new meanings relative to their activity. This co-construction occurs through the synergy of their points of view, but also via reflection with others on one's own actions [8]. According to Desgagné [9], this approach is based on a reciprocal relationship of self/co-reflection and self/co-critique and therefore self/co-training with oneself and with the other participants. By integrating it into design training, our approach is inspired by reflections resulting from "collaborative action research". It involves a protocol which incites the participation of several designer/observer/researcher participants. Its educational purpose is not to assess the design project itself (as is the case in project workshops), but rather to describe the process behind it. Neither does it impose a design method; rather, it considers how the design process can be observed, analysed and broken down in order to enable the participants to better take a step back from both the activity and the complexity of the interactions involved. Our premise is that design is a complex process which is difficult to break down, and the outcome of which is thought out, negotiated, assessed, challenged and co-constructed before it even comes into existence. Two questions therefore arise: how can the design process be put into words, and how is the process negotiated and co-thought by the group? To support this approach, tools are put into place to question the collaborative design. They have been defined in such a way that all participants co-construct an integrated meaning and decide together which actions should follow on from that (according to [4] p. 83). This co-construction of meaning for the activity and the fact of being able to take a step back from it therefore occur here *with* the designer, and not *on* the designer. The crossed action of taking a step back from the process is prioritised in the context of this Workshop+. It is composed of four steps, each of which is detailed below; we will expound on their implementation and objectives, and the tools used to enable participants to clarify their thoughts and begin self/co-reflection on their activity will be described.

3   Presentation of the Component Steps of the Analytical Approach

3.1   Step 1: Experiment

Implementation. Here, the learners apply an experimental protocol, previously defined by the researcher-guides. The protocol is constructed according to the formula imposed by the context (long vs. short integration). In order to apply it, each participant in the working group is assigned a role to assume throughout the Workshop+: either as designer (3 designers per group), or as observer (the number of which is defined according to the number of Workshop+ participants).

The protocol is divided into two periods during which the designers – each seated according to the predefined seating plan – respond to the design brief given to them. In the meanwhile, the observers take notes (relative to a shared temporal framework). To begin with, each observer takes notes as instructed by his or her assignment card. Each card is characterised by an attributed theme. The observers are then given pre-defined grids in which to take notes so as to systematise their observations and render their data more explicit, and therefore more easily quantifiable.

Objectives. By imposing a protocol, it is possible to define certain variables such as the seating plan for the designers at the table, the references given, the tools at their disposition, etc. in advance. This imposed organisation also enables the participants to better realise the influence the situation and context have on the design process and collaboration between designers (it should be mentioned that the designers are not told exactly what the observers are commenting on or identifying so as to limit any influence this may have on the designers).

Tools Provided. From a methodological point of view, the protocol is constructed here so as to describe the collective design activity according to 4 categories:

- collaboration (interaction between designers);
- the activity of design (how the object and its representations evolve);
- analogies (particular type of idea generation);
- tools (the means employed to support the process).

The protocol proposes a note-taking system that is adapted to multi-participant interactions in order to gather data. In order to do so, the observers are trained, in private and in advance, on note-taking techniques and the relevance of respecting such a protocol in the context of a scientific procedure. At this stage, only the note-taking grids are given to the observers. Everything is recorded "on the fly" relative to a chronometer in clear display as the single and same temporal point of reference, enabling the observers to synchronise their actions (Fig. 1).

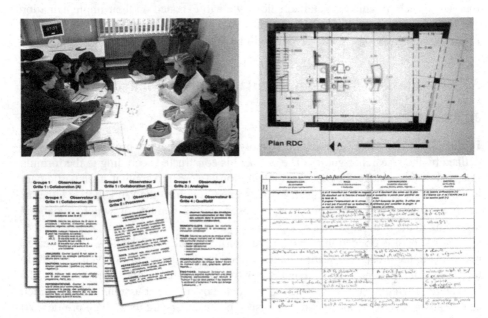

Fig. 1. Protocol and example of a project produced. Assignment cards and note-taking grid.

3.2 Step 2: Transcript

Implementation. For this phase, each group, composed of student-designers and observers, and guided by a researcher-guide, is asked to pool the notes taken, and describe in chronological order the actions carried out by each of the designers during the experiment. Each action bears witness to the design and collaborative operations put into practise by each participant relative to his or her points of view, relevance and references. These actions are then assembled to form key moments, thereby dividing the process into several sequences (for example: general implantation > layout of the ground floor > layout of the first floor > processing of the input > etc.).

Objectives. This stage allows for the student-observers to make eye contact and synchronise the note-taking for a temporal communal description of the collaborative design activity (with the student-designers and researcher-guides). It is through this stage that each participant enters into dialogue with himself or herself, as well as with the other participants, to organise and specify the sequence of events for the activity. By describing each action, the various participants negotiate and strive to understand one another's contributions. This stage requires the participants to leave implicit messages to one side and to be explicit; this sometimes even requires deconstruction/reconstruction of the previous representations that the participants had of their activity [10]. The transcript grid is therefore defined in advance by the researchers so as to propose a reference system which enables the observers to collectively (by consensus) identify the main actions to study. It serves as a basis for discussion with the researcher-guides as it enables the querying of certain criteria defining the activity.

Tools Provided. The transcript grid provided to all the participants (in excel format) is composed of several categories which are themselves broken down into diverse exclusive criteria that can be redefined, completed or queried. A methodology guide is also made available to the participants, defining the various elements of the transcript grid. Automated formulae are introduced therein, thereby aiding the participants to rapidly detect coding errors.

3.3   Step 3: Coding and Processing the Data

Implementation. Once all the members of the group agree on the temporal description of the process in the form of actions (cf. step 2), they code the data relative to the completed categories and criteria in order to describe the evolution of the design project, the collective activity and the various analogical thoughts brought into play by the designers. These criteria and categories are the result of research and state of the art previously exposed to the learners as part of the theory taught in conjunction with this Workshop+.

Objectives. The step of processing the transcripts, bringing together the designers and observers, enables the participants to understand how to build links between the theory (lessons and models) on describing the collaborative design process, and their own observations. The objective of this task is that the student be able to take a step back from his or own activity and think about the knowledge acquired in the course. Incidentally, the learners may query the transcript grids and coding by redefining certain criteria or adding new criteria.

Tools Provided. For this step, three new categories are added to complete the transcript grid; these are relative to: the design (according to the degree of comprehension of the object versus the degree of abstraction of the object, collective actions [11], and analogies. Each category is composed of several criteria to more precisely specify collaborative activity in design. These criteria are the outcome of theoretical concepts introduced via lessons spread throughout the Workshop+ (taken from cognitive sciences, design research and CSCW [12].

3.4   Step 4: Analysis and Highlighting of the Results

Implementation. This final step marks the shift from description to interpretation. Here, the learners cross-reference the quantified data and choose the appropriate formalism to affirm or disconfirm their qualitative observations using the Common Tools tool (see below), made available to them as part of this Workshop+.

Objectives. The objective of this step is to link the quantified results from the students' coding with the research questions and qualitative observations that arose during the experiment. This step leads the group to asking themselves the following questions: what are our research questions? What do we want to showcase relative to the observed collective activity and design process? How can we enhance our results? How can we take a step back from what has been observed/experienced in our roles as designers and observers?

Tools Provided. Here, the learners shift from describing the facts to interpreting the results; by choosing relevant visual formalisms as support for data interpretation, they enhance the value of their results. In order to do so, a web platform - Common Tools - is made available to them, enabling them to transform the data from the transcript and coding grids into quantified data with a variety of visual formalism options (pie charts, stacked columns, time lines, crossing, clouds, etc.). Initiated within the context of the ARC Common project [13], and developed by LUCID (the University of Liège), this platform provides learners with a powerful and interactive data visualization tool for the analysis of collective design activities (Fig. 2).

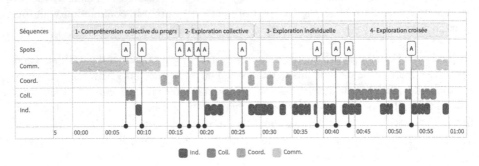

Fig. 2. Example of formalisms from Common Tools: timeline (of individual- /collective- /coordination- /or communication-actions).

4   Implementation Contexts

The described approach has been proposed and brought into play in the context of advanced training for students in master's or research master's programmes; the aim is to train them in reflective and shared analysis of their own collaborative design processes. It supports the training given in engineering, architecture, design, ergonomics and management programmes that we conducted on an international scale: architectural engineers at the Polytechnic Faculty of the University of Liège (B), ergonomists, designers and engineers at the University of Paris 8 (F), space, product and image designers from the ESSTED Tunis School of Design (TU), and architects from the University of Liège and the Université Libre de Bruxelles (Brussels) (B).

Two variations – short and long integration – are offered relative to the operational targets (time available to carry out the Workshop+) and the educational targets (relative to the educational objectives of the teachers wanting to apply this approach).

Short Integration. This short formula of the Workshop+ can be carried out in between ½ a day and two days. Only the assignment cards are used for "on the fly" note-taking. The objective of this formula is to (1) initiate the learner to the construction of an experimental protocol, and (2) begin the act of taking a step back and performing qualitative evaluation of the collective design activity and the querying of said design via the confrontation of diverse points of view.

Long Integration. This long formula of the Workshop+ can be spread out over 4 to 8 days. The assignment cards, the note-taking and transcript grids, and Common Tools are used. The objective of this formula is to (1) initiate the learner to scientific research and methods of data collection, processing and analysis, and (2) begin the act of taking a step back and performing qualitative and quantitative evaluations of the collective design activity.

5   Discussion

Integrating a Scientific Approach. As described above, the real challenge of this analytical approach is epistemological. It requires a dichotomy between the act of gathering data (which can only be carried out by the observers), and action research which claims to be collaborative in involving the designers in a global reflection process (with the observers of this process) in their collaborative design activities. To avoid this dichotomy while conforming to collaborative action research approaches, the Workshop+ proposed here implements several methodological, theoretical and analytical tools to serve in the shared collection, processing and analysis of the data gathered. These tools are defined in such a way that once the experiment stage has been completed, all the participants collaborate in the reflection stages. This approach seems to represent a shift from the classic conceptions of scientific work. Nevertheless, if the proposed approach is installed in parallel with the classic scientific approach (cf. Fig. 3), it is possible to show that one approach feeds the other, and they barely contradict one another.

The four steps described above strive to respect the demands of a classic scientific approach by allowing the various participants (researcher-guides, student-designers and student-observers) to begin the process of taking a step back from their work and querying the pre-requisites and theory they have been given. This functions via:

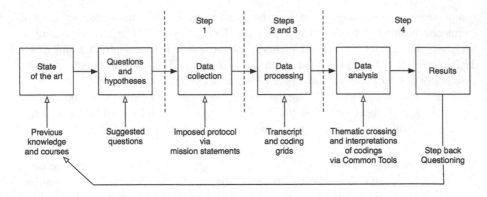

Fig. 3. Inscription of the Workshop+, regarding the principles of the scientific approach.

- the act of respecting an experimental objectified protocol that is rigorous and appropriate, and based on the definition of operational working hypotheses and the description of the facts as concerted actions: this first requirement enables better observation of the influence the situation and context have in the design and collaboration process between designers;
- the objectified description of the concerted actions via a pre-constructed transcript grid, (re)defined in accordance with the theory and the code of practise: because of its synergetic nature, this second requirement enables the objective cross-referencing of the observations, knowledge and skill of the participants, thereby producing meaning effects [8], and in doing so, combining individual reflections with that of the group;
- The cross-referencing of qualitative and quantitative analyses of the activity: this third requirement ensures that the data analyses are complementary, thereby facilitating the act of taking a step back from the task.

Enable Iteration. This approach is also introduced in such a way as to encourage reflection that is simultaneously progressive, self-confronted, co-evaluated and co-constructed. Actually, from step two ("transcript"), which serves as a reference for all the participants, a reflective and collaborative exercise is initiated in step three ("coding and processing the data"), and continues in step four ("analysis and highlighting of the results"). Describing the actions by collaborative coding of the imposed criteria incites the participants as a whole to consider the very activities of collaboration and design.

Via the interaction of diverse epistemological reflections, the participants are obliged to put their experience into words and communicate it objectively to the others in the group. This progressive strategy - a strategy that is in motion - ensures that the process of co-construction of meaning and the querying of the prerequisites remains active, while also ensuring triangulation between the transcript, analysis and interpretation of the data. Even if at first glance these steps appear to be perfectly locked (relative to the scientific approach described in Fig. 3), they influence one another, and moreover, they enable query and retrograde actions. The (anonymous) questionnaires given to the students to evaluate this Workshop+ clearly show the importance of this type of approach in a university course, and in the student's training: more than 80 % of them attributed a value equal to or higher than 4/5 for this criterion. This extract of written feedback from one of the groups on completing their first experience also testifies to this effect: *"we enjoyed this first research experience as it enabled us to highlight the importance of a clearly defined protocol, and it also made us aware of the importance of context in group work. It served as a reference in our attempts to objectify our observations"*. According to the students, this exercise was not only an opportunity to study the activities of collaboration and design, but also to collaborate with one another (researcher-guides, student-designers and student-observers) to develop a common meaning relative to the various concerted actions: *"the challenge became clear when the group had to agree on a sole description of the processes observed during the experiment and find a compromise to construct one reflection from several. Only this group reflection, based on the consensus and the search for a shared construction of the observable factors enabled us to maintain correct comprehension of the subject and progress in our research"*. The approach thereby clearly applies collective intelligence to the benefit of the analysis and interpretation of a complex assigned activity, as well as the act of taking a step back from said activity.

Providing the Tools for Analysis and the Act of Taking a Step Back. In addition, the students underline the synergy of the accompanying tools made available to them; the tools were provided to ensure the development of a common reflective area and the construction of this perpetually developing collective intelligence. Supported by an approach as qualitative as it is quantitative to analyse the complex activity, these unique accompanying tools open up a new area for reflection and negotiation at each step, thereby facilitating continuous interpretation of the highlighted results. The transcript grid, for example, enables the distancing and collective interpretation of a complex experienced/observed/analysed activity via the imposed criteria. Common Tools enable the rapid and quantitative illustration of the particularities of the observed process. This application requires the participants to hierarchize the processed data and choose the appropriate visual formalisms (step four). This step encourages them to specify their objectives once more and co-construct their research questions. They positively identify what should be accentuated in their results. The mediation provided by the tool therefore enables the rapid uprooting of points of view and shifts in meaning thanks to the visual formalisms which assist the objectification and co-construction of the interpretation. More than 70 % of the students highlighted how suitable the tool was when interpreting the data from the transcript grid. Certain learners even confirmed that, *"the fact of perceiving our own design and collaboration activities differently since this experience has generated a consciousness which pushes us to question our actions and regulate them"*. The participants not only understand the complexity of the situation, but also the involvement of the context, their individual roles, the communication strategies used and the very process of design in their manner of working together.

6   Conclusion

The analytical approach to the complex activity of design as described in this article and inspired by collaborative action research approaches, aims to bring practical work closer to research, and thereby exposing skills to knowledge. When applied to training provided at the end of the academic career in the field of design (second year of a master's or a research master's programme), the objective is to prioritise the sharing of the epistemological and didactic area:

- For the **teachers**, it allows to create courses about design learning using a « crossed point of view » approach;
- For the **learners,** it offers tools to (1) co-construct reflection on a skill (design), (2) structure and enrich management of this skill, (3) put the design into words, and work on how to do so, (4) develop critical thinking skills by confronting different points of view and initiate the act of taking a step back from one's work thanks to the introduction to the practice of design research;
- For the **researcher-guides**, the design and collaboration processes in diverse fields can be made explicit, and other approaches to comprehend design research can be tested.

However, it is not sufficient to share points of view in order to produce knowledge. This is the reason why this analytical approach implements several (methodological, theoretical and analytical) tools that promote the act of querying actions via the objectified co-construction of meaning relative to the activity studied.

References

1. Hmelo-Silver, C.E.: Problem-based learning: what and how do students learn? Educ. Psychol. **16**(3), 235–266 (2004)
2. Hubers, J.C.: Collaborative architectural design of buildings. The COLAB case. Int. J. Des. Sci. Technol. **16**(1), 61–72 (2009)
3. Dolbec, A.: La recherche-action. In: Gauthier, B. (ed.) Recherche sociale: De la problématique à la collecte des données, pp. 505–540. PUQ, Québec (2003)
4. Bourassa, M., Philion, R., Chevalier, J.: L'analyse de construits, une co-construction de groupe. Education et Francophonie **35**(2), 78–117 (2007)
5. Reason, P., Bradbury, H.: Handbook of Action Research: Participative Inquiry and Practice. Sage, London (2001)
6. Lavoie, L., Marquis, D., Laurin, P.: La recherche-action, théorie et pratique, manuel d'autoformation. PUQ, Sainte-Foy (2003)
7. Dubost, J., Lévy, A.: Recherche-action et intervention. In: Barus-Michel, J., Enriquez, E., Lévy, A. (eds.) Vocabulaire de Psychosociologie, Références et positions, pp. 391–416. Éres, Paris (2003)
8. Couture, C., Bednarz, N., Barry, S.: Multiples regards sur la recherche participative, une lecture transversale. In: Anadòn, M., Savoie-Zajc, L. (eds.) La recherche participative. Multiples regards, pp. 205–221. PUQ, Québec (2007)

9. Desgagné, S.: Le défi de coproduction de « savoir » en recherche collaborative, analyse d'une démarche de reconstruction et d'analyse de récits de pratique enseignante. In: Anadòn, M., Savoie-Zajc, L. (eds.) La recherche participative. Multiples regards, pp. 89–121. PUQ, Québec (2007)

10. Legendre, M.F.: Approches constructivistes et nouvelles orientations curriculaires: D'un curriculum fondé sur l'approche par objectifs à un curriculum axé sur le développement de compétences. In: Jonnaert, P., Masciotra, D. (eds.) Constructivisme Choix contemportains, pp. 51–91. Presses de l'Université du Québec, Québec (2004)

11. Ben Rajeb, S.: Conception collaborative distante: étude architecturologique pour la caractérisation des opérations cognitives. In: Angenot, V., Safin, S., Dondelero, M.G., Leclercq, P. (eds.) Interfaces numériques: Collaborer à distance, enjeux et impacts des interfaces numériques dans les pratiques collaboratives, vol 2, no. 3, pp. 509–530. Lavoisier (2013)

12. Gerson, E.: Reach, bracket, and the limits of rationalized coordination: some challenges for CSCW. In: Ackerman, M., Christine, H., Erickson, T., Kellogg, W.A. (eds.) Resources, Co-evolution and Artefacts: Theory in CSCW, pp. 193–220. Springer, London (2008)

13. Leclercq, P.: COMMON'14. Communication multimodale et collaboration instrumentée. Atelier des Presses de l'Université de Liège (2014)

Sentiment Analysis Based on Collaborative Data for Polish Language

Roman Bartusiak[✉] and Tomasz Kajdanowicz

Department of Computational Intelligence, Wrocław University of Technology,
Wyb. Wyspianskiego 27, 50-370 Wroclaw, Poland
roman.bartusiak@gmail.com, tomasz.kajdanowicz@pwr.edu.pl

Abstract. Due to the fact that majority of web content is provided within collaborative environments such as social media and social networks systems its complexity brings a new strong need for its accurate aggregation and understanding. Sentiment analysis (also known as opinion mining) is one of possibility to understand generated content that may brings an interesting summation in terms of attitudes expressed in texts. The paper proposes a new approach to sentiment analysis of polish language using machine learning approach.

Keywords: Sentiment analysis · Machine learning · Support vector machine · Classification

1 Introduction

Sentiment analysis is a relatively new and widely explored research area. It encountered its popularity by information explosion in social networks and other social media environments. Around 81 % of Internet users are publishing their opinion (Pang and Lee 2008) and such content can be used to draw interesting conclusions that can be utilised in many domains, e.g. in marketing, advertisement, investment, decision making in business, etc. It was proven that there existed a strong correlation between opinion about some brand and their stock status what allowed sucessfull stock investments (O'Connor et al. 2010).

Sentiment analysis aims at discovering the attitude of the text, which can be expressed in various scales. The most general one assumes that there are *positive* and *negative* statements accompanied by *neutral* ones. It can be also achieved using different contexts. For a short messages we can analyse contextual polarity of words, whole message polarity, or message polarity within given topic (Rosenthal et al. 2015). Sentiment analysis has been studied for many languages but mostly for English. Multiple interesting approaches to sentiment analysis in English has been proposed but due to the fact that it is a generous language, they cannot be applied to more complicated languages. Unfortunately, there are not much results in sentiment analysis for polish language, which requires specialised methods and algorithms.

© Springer International Publishing Switzerland 2015
Y. Luo (Ed.): CDVE 2015, LNCS 9320, pp. 216–219, 2015.
DOI: 10.1007/978-3-319-24132-6_27

2   Related Work

Sentiment has multiple meanings: emotions, opinion, tone. Opinion approach seams to be most useful in sense of commercial usage. Classes in that approach can be divided in three main groups: *Positive, Neutral* and *Negative*. Basically, sentiment analysis uses natural language processing tools and it have been shown, that automated sentiment analysis can be much more successful than manual based approach (Pang et al. 2002). Two main approaches to sentiment analysis be distinguished *knowledge base based* and *machine learning based*.

Quantity based approach is the easiest approach that can be applied. However, it requires a knowledge base, which for some languages can be really hard or even impossible to find. In that method the sentiment for each word from the text is discovered independently, and in order to classify the sentiment of whole document requires some aggregation. Most often the max operator is applied.

Algorithm 1. Quantity based sentiment analysis

1. **for** each word $w \in T$ **do**
2. $S_w \leftarrow FIND\_SENTIMENT(w)$
3.   **if** $S_w = POSITIVE$ **then**
4. $Sentiment[POSITIVE] + +$
5.   **else if** $S_w = NEGATIVE$ **then**
6. $Sentiment[NEGATIVE] + +$
7.   **else**
8. $Sentiment[NEUTRAL] + +$
9.   **end if**
10. **end for**
11. **return** $\arg\max_x Sentiment[x]$

The algorithm presented in Algorithm 1 takes as an input the text T and returns sentiment of it. $FIND\_SENTIMENT(w)$ is a method that retrieves sentiment of a word w from knowledge base. That approach is very straightforward, but in consequence not so perfect. In this approach the context of word is not taken into consideration and by that simple multi-word phrases will be not correctly processed. For example, if the word *nice* is present in the knowledge base as *positive* one, *not nice* will be classified as *positive*. It's caused by the fact that the negation is not detected here.

Machine learning based approach is based on supervised learning. Text corpora for witch we know sentiment is used to train model that will be used for classification. As a base classifier we can use any well known classifier: *Naive Bayes, C4.5, ILA*. Feature selection can case a problems in this approach. Some classifiers also require features that are numerical, for example *neural network*. Feature selection is very important, as in any other machine learning problem. For instance, correctly selected features allow to detect multi-word phrases.

3   Sentiment Analysis by Means of Classification Process for Polish Language

The proposed approach assumes that sentiment analysis is treated as a classification process. Correctly selected features will enable creation of very efficient classifier.

3.1   Problems

In supervised learning, a learning data that is classified must be provided. It does not exist any corpora for polish language, that can be used for sentiment analysis. However, thanks to tremendous volume of the data that is available online, in social networks, trading platforms etc. it is possible to extract appropriate learning data.

3.2   The Method

Polish language is quite complex when comparing to other languages. Many morphological forms of words can cause a lot of errors while building machine learning model. To avoid that problem, pre-processing phase is done accomplished before the model is build. Text is parsed and tokenized using NLP tools that are available for polish language (Piasecki 2007). Beside of that, also the base for of each word is extracted, so the inflection will not cause any problems.

In order to avoid the problem of not detecting the multi-word phrases, that is present in *quantity base* method, appropriate features were selected. From pre-processed text uni- and bi-grams are extracted. Unigrams are single words. Bigrams are continuous segments that contains two words from given text. Because of that, model will be able to recognise word phrases, for example negation.

3.3   Preliminary Results

The presented method is using SVM classifier. Because of its nature, features are numerical and it was achieved by bag-of-word method. Based on learning data, list of uni and bi-grams is extracted. Using that list, texts are vectorised. Each uni- or bi-gram from list has unique index. Vector that represent given text, has number of occurrences for each feature at appropriate index.

In order to handle large amount of data the experimental system was divided into multiple microservices. Each of them can be run separately and independently. Thanks to that, system is highly scalable. Single instance of sentiment analysis system, can be run cooperatively by multiple users from different part of word.

In order to acquire appropriate learning dataset Polish trading platform *Allegro* with its API was used. Each transaction in this platform can have a textual comment accompanied with one of labels: *positive* or *negative*. After appropriate pre-processing, those comments can be used as learning data.

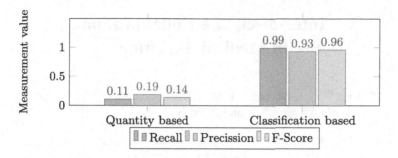

Fig. 1. Comparison of quality measures in sentiment analysis (Color figure online).

The proposed method was compared to quantity based approach, which was fed with knowledge base from early version of polish WordNet. In general, the words have sentiment annotation in the polish WordNet but the number of annotated words is quite small. Only 20000 words wear annotated during tests. Classification based method was trained on 400000 comments. Classes were distributed equally, there were 200000 *positive* and 200000 *negative* comments. For tests, separate set of 2000 comments was selected. Due to the fact that quantity method was tested on small knowledge base it returned unsatisfactory results. The proposed classification based method achieved clearly good results (Fig. 1).

4   Conclusions

It has been shown that SVM combined with natural language processing can perform sentiment analysis with very good results. Due to the fact, that received results were obtained on single dataset and can be contextually dependent, further work will be focused on validation of transfer learning approach.

References

O'Connor, B., Balasubramanyan, R., Routledge, B.R., Smith, N.A.: From tweets to polls: linking text sentiment to public opinion time series. ICWSM **11**, 122–129 (2010)

Pang, B., Lee, L.: Opinion mining and sentiment analysis. Found. Trends Inf. Retr. **2**(1–2), 1–135 (2008)

Pang, B., Lee, L., Vaithyanathan, S.: Thumbs up?: sentiment classification using machine learning techniques. In: Proceedings of the ACL-02 Conference on Empirical Methods in Natural Language Processing, vol.10, pp. 79–86. Association for Computational Linguistics (2002)

Piasecki, M.: Polish tagger takipi: rule based construction and optimisation. Task Q. **11**(1–2), 151–167 (2007)

Rosenthal, S., Nakov, P., Kiritchenko, S., Mohammad, S.M., Ritter, A., Stoyanov, V.: Semeval-2015 task 10: sentiment analysis in twitter. In: Proceedings of the 9th International Workshop on Semantic Evaluation, SemEval (2015)

Inter-discipline Collaboration
in Medical Teaching

S. Ubik[1(✉)], J. Navratil[1], J. Melnikov[2], J. Schraml[3], M. Broul[3],
and P. Pečiva[3]

[1] CESNET a.l.e., Prague, Czech Republic
ubik@cesnet.cz
[2] FIT Czech Technical University at Prague, Prague, Czech Republic
[3] MNUL Hospital KZ as., Usti nad Labem, Czech Republic

Abstract. High-speed networks together with visualizations in the highest resolutions enable new level of sharing visual perceptions. They can be used in interactive collaboration in real-time and in specialized training of professionals in many fields. In this paper we will focus on our practical experience in the medical field. We will present several scenarios for live surgery sessions and we will show the role of people who participate in it. The scenarios are different if the session is for a small or large group of attendees and if the session is a one way presentation of surgery techniques of famous surgeons or if it is an interactive session expecting high level of intercommunication including remote drawing into presented screens.

Keywords: Inter-discipline collaboration · E-learning · HD signal · 4K video

1 Introduction

Young doctors who grow up in the modern IT era, well understand both environments (medical and IT) and they are coming with many inspirational ideas how to use modern IT for improving medical practices. They use the Internet, video streaming and other real time applications since schools years. They expect that in the hospitals they will have similar or better conditions than in the university. The CESNET as an academic Internet provider which connect all research and teaching hospitals to one network is trying to help them. They do a lot of their education via the Internet, they collect and store clinical data for their future studies and they also store videos from their interesting surgeries. Live or recorded video transmissions of surgeries are becoming more and more popular as a form of teaching [1]. There is not much time to watch such educational videos in normal working days, but the good time for such education, exchange of knowledge and experiences are professional conferences at national or international levels. The situation is slowly changing and we collaborate with hospitals which are able to prepare locally (in the frame of the hospital) on-line live-surgery demonstrations to educate undergraduate students or their own staff several times per year.

The current reality is that teachers or speakers prefer to use pre-recorded video during their presentations. There are several simple reasons for that. The most important factor is that on-line broadcasting is more complicated and many hospitals

© Springer International Publishing Switzerland 2015
Y. Luo (Ed.): CDVE 2015, LNCS 9320, pp. 220–227, 2015.
DOI: 10.1007/978-3-319-24132-6_28

are missing the infrastructure (network connections between particular surgery rooms and lecture halls). The second factor is probably the effectivity of teaching (full operation is usually very long with many not interesting periods). Another issue is possible stress in direct broadcasting or the facts that only experienced surgeon-lectors are able to comment their work online for public. The sessions with on-line broadcasting are used mostly for cases, which are in some sense unique. For example, when a famous specialist or a visiting professor demonstrates his new techniques for a special group of specialists.

2   Live-Surgery Demonstrations

The live surgery demos are mostly connected with conferences, congresses and symposia. We implemented many different scenarios for such on-line sessions. Some organizers like to organize big virtual meetings of many specialists focused on one or similar type of disease (e.g., cataract). We have been participating on "surgery days" [2] when more than 20 patients were operated with similar diagnose on several clinics. The video images from all surgeries were transmitted to the conference venue where more than 300 specialists watched this event. Another example is when the organizers want to show in real-time two different methods of surgery for the same or similar diagnoses (e.g., robotic versus laparoscopy). Very effective from the education point of view are "Meetings with surgeon". In this scenario a pre-recorded video of surgery is used and the surgeon, who does the operation, comments his work on another screen. The attendees have a chance to communicate with the surgeon during this session. The video can be stopped or returned and the questions from public can be explained considering all details. Another interesting session was organized during an annual congress of gynaecologist. The visiting doctors could watch several surgeries executed in parallel in four different surgery theatres in three hospitals. Transmitted videos were projected in the venue on four big screens. The moderator (a recognized specialist) communicates with remote teams and adds his comments for the audience. The advantage of this scenario was in that the visitors could see the surgeries according to their own interests (Figs. 1 and 2).

The trend is that every year the doctors are coming with more sophisticated scenarios which represent challenges for technicians. Each such session needs a preparation phase (sometimes quite long) and during the event a close cooperation of several teams of specialists: medical staff, camera operators, networking and multimedia teams. It is similarly cooperative work as during making movies.

3   The Environment and the Roles of Individual Teams

We can generalize the examples described above. On one side there is a team of the medical staff and on the other side there are several hundred viewers sitting in a conference hall [8]. Between them is a network with many different devices located in different places sometimes many hundred miles away. We can talk about three fundamental parts which create a complex environment for these sessions: the surgery

Fig. 1. Meeting with surgeon

Fig. 2. Moderator in venue

theatre, the network and the presentation part. A typical technical setup for such a medical transmission is shown in Fig. 3. There is a daVinci Surgical System [5] or other medical equipment with a computer vision and a video camera in the surgery theatre. Video outputs from these devices are connected into transmission devices which convert video signals into networking packets and send them to remote sites via the network. On the remote site (e.g., conference venue) the network packets are converted back into video signals and projected onto walls. One or more pictures from surgery equipment can be complemented with a view to the surgery room or a commenting surgeon.

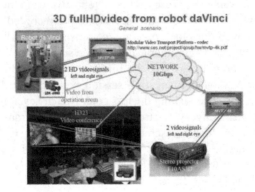

Fig. 3. An example for real-time medical video transmissions

In the following paragraphs we will discuss some typical cases for each element of this chain and we will also describe the roles of individual specialists who are involved in this process.

3.1   Surgery Theatre

The surgeon who decides to show his operating techniques and experience to public is a head of the medical team doing the surgery and he is also in contact with people who are working with the cameras and other technical devices in the room. He is also in remote contact with the conference venue. In some cases it can be a relatively small team, such as one or two persons during an eye surgery, but in other cases it can be a team of several specialists. For example, for the robot-assisted surgery (radical prostatectomy) it is a surgeon who sits behind a robotic console and an assistant who helps the surgeon. The assistant exchanges the robot tools and inserts them into the abdominal cavity suture. There are also a scrub nurse and the orderlies. Overall, a robotic surgery team presents 4–5 people. In execution of an open surgery for the same problem again a team of a surgeon, assistant, nurses and orderlies is needed (Fig. 4).

Fig. 4. Surgery theatres (robotic, cardio and eye laser)

Besides the medical team there must be people who ensure the video capture, filming or other types of visualizations. To present the work of a surgeon it is recommended to have several video sources. One source is a standard video camera which is scanning the operation space. The second camera is scanning the surgeon or his hand during important phases of his work and the third camera captures a general area of the operation room, see Fig. 5. For recording of surgeon comments we prefer to use a head microphone connected to a special sound system rather than a microphone on a video camera.

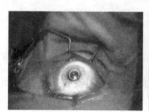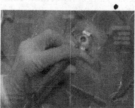

Fig. 5. Images from external cameras

In many cases, the images of the "operation space" are provided directly by special devices. For example, microscopes connected to lasers for eyes surgeries. The EKG, X-ray or ultrasounds for cardio surgery, etc. The laparoscopic towers or the daVinci robots use mini cameras which are located inside the patient body. The surgeon needs for his work inside the patient body to have stereo visibility. Therefore, these devices use 3D cameras with HD resolution. The video signal is zoomed and so the operational zone is visible with better resolution than the surgeon could see by his eyes. In Fig. 6 we show three types of images: microscope image (left), ultrasound image (middle) and image from the robot daVinci (right).

For robotic or laparoscopic surgery the surgeons use the special console to see 3D images or they use a 3D TV screen and stereoscopic glasses as it is shown in Fig. 7.

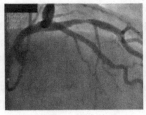

Fig. 6. Images of operational space from various devices

The same images as these devices provide to the surgeon can also be delivered to the audience which can be far away. A different situation is in the cases when we are scanning a classical "open surgery". In this case, the operation space is not well accessible for the cameraman. There are several ways to go over such obstacles. One of them is to use a crane for a camera as shown in Fig. 5 (right picture). In this case, we tested how 4K video can be used in medicine.

Fig. 7. Surgeons behind consoles

3.2   Networking Part

3.2.1   Technical Aspects of Video Transmissions

The video resolution was always a critical parameter for good visibility of medical images. A couple years ago, analog TV resolution (PAL or NTSC) was the norm. Nowadays most medical devices work with a HD resolution, starting to use a 4K resolution. For live transmissions in real-time to enable interactive discussions, we need to minimize the end-to-end delay. Therefore, we prefer to use uncompressed transmissions, which require significant network bandwidth, 1-1.5 Gbps per an HD channel.

Video transmission can be done in several ways. Videoconferencing tools or streaming technology (e.g., using RTMP) will deliver the video to anybody who connects to a video conferencing unit or to a streaming server. Current commercial videoconferencing devices use heavy compression so that they can work over inexpensive links with minimal bandwidth. Their required bandwidth for an HD channel is in the range from 128 Kb/s to 6 Mb/s, depending on the compression level. In our experience, 4 Mb/s is the lowest bandwidth for acceptable quality for medical transmissions. We do not recommend using this technology for purposes of medical on-line sessions.

The Internet streaming is another method to distribute video signals to the users. We usually use hardware H.264 encoders (e.g., Haivision Makito) to deliver the picture to a remote streaming server (such as Wowza). A web page then allows multiple users to individually connect using one of several distribution formats (FLASH video, HTML5) and resolutions. These encoders are small, very easy to use and compatible with common streaming servers. On the other hand, they introduce a very long latency, 5–10 s are not uncommon. Therefore, they are not suitable for cases when we need interaction with the surgeon.

In the past we successfully used DVTS (Digital Video Transport System) [3, 4] which was the first system which worked without compression. DVTS accepts image sources (e.g., digital camcorders, surgical instruments) over the IEEE 1394 interface and streams them over an IP network. The quality of the picture was mostly defined by the digital camera and lighting conditions. It was heavily used for live-surgery demos in Japan and based on their experiences we started to use it. The necessary bandwidth for this system was 30–35 Mb/s per channel including audio.

Currently, we are using more advanced systems which allow to transmit a wide spectrum of formats with resolutions from HD to 4K, including 3D formats and can transmit in uncompressed or compressed modes. The first one is the Ultragrid technology. It is a software tool publicly available from http://www.ultragrid.cz/en. For transmissions of multi-channel video signals, which are needed in complex surgery demos, CESNET has developed an FPGA-accelerated solution called Modular Video Transmission Platform (MVTP-4K) [7]. In the uncompressed mode, it can send and receive up to eight HD signals simultaneously, or up to two 4K signals. The processing latency on the sending and receiving device combined is as low as 3 ms. This functionality allows to combine several resources (different cameras and digital video devices) and to create an environment for a perfect illusion of presence in a surgery theatre.

3.2.2   Networks

The scientific conferences are nearly always part of the academic world, therefore for the connections we try to use the academic infrastructure as a primary. Since the beginning of the Internet the academic networking keeps a leading role in this field. The academic networks operate in each country as NREN (National Academic and Education Network). In the Czech Republic we have CESNET (see a map in Fig. 8) These NRENs are interconnected at the level of continents. In Europe we are integrated into the GEANT network (see Fig. 9), In the US, it is Internet2 and the network in Asia and Australia is called APAN. There is also a GLIF infrastructure [6], which represents a Global experimental facility (see Fig. 10). All networks together create a very flexible infrastructure, which can be used by academic communities.

During our international activity in the medical field we used all of them several times. A typical connection via these academic networks is demonstrated in Fig. 11. It shows how the path for the connection from Prague to Nantou University (Taiwan) venue of APAN38 meeting was created. The connection consists from several segments which were provided to us by the partners on the path (CESNET, GEANT, Internet2, KREOnet and TWAREN). In a similar way it worked for other paths: Prague-Hong Kong (APAN34 in 2011), Prague-Honolulu (APAN36 in 2013), etc.

Fig. 8. CESNET   **Fig. 9.** GEANT network   **Fig. 10.** GLIF

3.2.3   Connections to Hospitals and to the Venue

The difficult part of the connection is a link into the end points, a "last mile". One end is represented by the operational theatre and the second end is the venue. It is quite common that operating theatres are not connected at the requested capacity. But hospitals are usually located in cities where fiber infrastructure already exists, which can be extended to the hospital at a reasonable cost. The responsibility for the network on the other side (venue) is up to the organizers. Many conferences are organized in "interesting" places (big hotels, spa resorts, sport halls, etc.), which are not prepared for high speed transmission, needed for HD or 4K video. Large events are planned several months in advance so there is usually time to arrange a new link. A cost for a temporary fiber to a conference venue typically ranges from $1000 to $3000 in Czech Republic in 2014 prices for a one week conference. Sometimes fiber connection is not available and the venue must be connected via a satellite connection, which costs approx. $10000 for a conference. On the other hand, the advantage of a satellite connection is its flexibility. It can be in arranged in 2–3 days.

3.3   Presentations in Lecture Halls

The presentation system is the last element in the live surgery demo chain. Large conferences with several hundreds of participants need big screens with powerful projectors with high luminosity. Current large conferences sometimes become multimedia shows. They use several screens on which they can show different parts of presentations (surgeon/speaker, surgery zone, direct view or signals from medical devices, which are used for surgery, etc.) All this needs to use a mixing control console, which allows flexible switching of the signals, use methods, picture in picture, etc (Fig. 12).

Fig. 11. Connection from Prague (CZ) to Nantou (Taiwan)

Fig. 12. Large conferences (control console in the middle)

A special setup is needed for 3D video, when visitors should see the stereoscopic image same as it can be seen by the surgeon during his work inside the patient body. 3D glasses for all visitors must be used.

4 Conclusions

The preparation of special applications, experimental sessions or demos for doctors needs broad collaboration of many specialists from different fields of IT, good knowledge of existing e-infrastructures and provision of all necessary parts. CESNET and other international organizations such as Géant, Internet2 and APAN are open to such activities and support them. Our team has been active in this area for several years and in the past we provided several innovative presentations and specialized demos, which helped to rise up the user horizon in different areas not only in networking, but also in medical fields.

References

1. Augestad, K.M., Lindsetmo, R.O.: Overcomming distance: video-conferencing as a clinical and educational tool among surgeons. World J. Surg. **33**(7), 1356–1365 (2009). doi:10.1007/s00268-009-0036-0
2. Navratil, J.: CESNET Activities for Czech Medicine, 25th APAN Meeting, Hawaii, January 2008
3. Shimizu, S., Nakashima, N., Okamura, K., Tanaka, M.: One hundred case studies of Asia-Pacific telemedicine using digital video transport system over research and education network. Telemedicine e-Health **15**(1), 112–117 (2009). doi:10.1089/tmj.2008.0067
4. Ogawa, A., Kobayashi, K., Sugiura, K., Nakamura, O., Murai, J.: Design and implementation of DV based video over RTP. In: IEEE Packet Video Workshop, Cagliari, Italy (2000)
5. The da Vinci Surgical System, Intuitive Surgical. http://www.intuitivesurgical.com/products/faq/index.aspx
6. DeFanti, T., de Laat, C., Mambretti, J., Neggers, K., St. Arnaud, B.: TransLight: a global-scale LambdaGrid for e-science. Commun. ACM **46**(11), 34–41 (2003)
7. Halak, J., Ubik, S.: MTPP - modular traffic processing platform. In: IEEE Symposium on Design and Diagnostics of Electronic Circuits and Systems, pp. 170–173. Liberec (2009)
8. Navratil, J., Sarek, M., Ubik, S., Halak, J., Zejdl, P., Peciva, P., Schraml, J.: Real-time stereoscopic streaming of robotic surgeries. In: 13th IEEE International Conference on e-Health, Networking Applications and Services (Healthcom), 13–15 June 2011

Supporting Environmental Planning: Knowledge Management Through Fuzzy Cognitive Mapping

D. Borri[1], D. Camarda[1], I. Pluchinotta[1,2], and D. Esposito[1(✉)]

[1] DICATECh, Technical University of Bari, Bari, Italy
{dino.borri,d.camarda,dario.esposito}@poliba.it,
irene.pluchinotta@gmail.com
[2] LAMSADE-CNRS, Université Paris-Dauphine, Paris, France

Abstract. The inherently complex nature of the environmental domain requires that planning efforts become projects of participated, inclusive, multi-agent, multi-source knowledge building processes developed by the community. Knowledge is often hard to be processed, handled, formalized, modeled. Yet cognitive models are useful to avoid the typical unmanageability of domains with high complexity such as the environmental one, and enhance knowledge organization and management. We have investigated on the potentials of cognitive-mapping-based tools, particularly on cross impact evaluations, in the case study of Taranto (Italy). The process was aimed at building up future development scenarios in city neighborhoods, and fuzzy cognitive mapping were used to support decision-making by exploring cross impacts of possible policy perspectives. Although substantial results are rather general, the study proves to be interesting in enhancing the potentials of FCM-based approach to support decision-making, particularly when dealing with well-focused policy perspectives.

Keywords: Fuzzy cognitive mapping · Environmental planning · Decision support system · Multiple agents

1 Introduction

The environment is today firmly considered as a complex system by planning literature. In such conditions, planning initiatives affecting the environmental domain (i.e., environmental planning) are intrinsically knowledge demanding, in order to cope with such complexity and aim at effective future strategies. Yet, knowledge is nowadays considered as a multiform, multi-agent, dynamic disposition, being complex as it mirrors the phenomenological-relational complexity of the environment it refers to [1]. Environmental knowledge heavily depends on knowledge holders, i.e., all the community agents who use and/or build knowledge because of their study, their work, their behavior, their life. As a matter of fact, knowledge contents useful in planning efforts are not a

---

Within a common research work written and coordinated by D. Borri, D. Camarda wrote Chaps. 1 and 4, I. Pluchinotta wrote Chap. 3, D. Esposito wrote Chap. 2.

© Springer International Publishing Switzerland 2015
Y. Luo (Ed.): CDVE 2015, LNCS 9320, pp. 228–235, 2015.
DOI: 10.1007/978-3-319-24132-6_29

prerogative of traditional –rational- domain experts, i.e. scholars, professionals, researchers, technicians. Rather, knowledge is strictly connected to and reflecting on action, i.e., a prerogative of all expert and non-expert agents [2–4].

Planning efforts become projects of participated, inclusive, multi-agent, multisource knowledge, in which the community develops the building up of future visions and scenarios, as expert and non-expert agents [5]. Future scenarios are necessary substantial issues in this context, yet formal issues become particularly critical here, too. In fact, namely non-expert knowledge is often informal, puzzling, uncertain, and incomplete: complex, as mirroring the environmental complexity it refers to. As often reported by literature, social/environmental knowledge is often hard to be treated, handled, formalized, modeled. Yet cognitive models prove to be useful toward avoiding the typical unmanageability of domains with high complexity such as the environmental one, and to enhance knowledge organization and management [6]. Models are a basis for the building up of system architectures useful to support multi-agent interactions, decision-making, land use, policy-making and planning [7].

Therefore, a research question arises now, about how to build such a model that allows the management of complex environmental knowledge. Although qualitative knowledge contents are hardly manageable, strictly quantitative databases often imply rigid knowledge patterns, reductionist syntheses of phenomena and processes, often too deterministic and unable to represent the complex aspects they aim at investigating and measuring [8]. However, an ICT-based approach to knowledge analysis is able to enhance the possibility of handling both qualitative and quantitative data, formal as well as informal contents, through opportune modeling approaches.

Our research group has been deeply involved in such activity in the last decades. ICT-based, automatic as well as semi-automatic and hybrid (mixed) approaches have been carried out and accounted for in previous editions of CDVE Conferences. It has always been characterized as a case-based approach, in which experimentations were carried out where methodologies were tested and discussed in the real world (e.g., [5, 9, 10]). In recent years, the methodological focus has been slightly shifted from general, platform-oriented approaches to tools and methods. We have investigated on the potential of cognitive-mapping-based tools, particularly on cross impact evaluations. Fuzzy cognitive mapping (FCM) were dealt with in particular, as a great number of applications have been implemented with good significance [11, 12]. In our case studies, models based on FCM have allowed the use of local stakeholders' knowledge for ecological modeling and environmental management in participatory, interactive management schemes. As found out experimentally, FCMs could also be used as a qualitative tool for the stakeholder representation of environmental problems, with a multi-agent approach [13, 14].

The experimentation of the present paper is carried out in the scenario-building activity from the design process of the new master plan of Taranto (Italy). The Taranto case study is very intriguing for our aims, as it is a paradigmatic example of harshly decaying industrial community, today heavily fragmented with jobless redundancy and environment degradation [15]. A number of focus group sessions carried out among the community stakeholders represent the basis for a FCM-based analysis. They are aimed at modeling future visions and strategies, structuring environmental problems and analyzing the sensitivity of multi-agent-based policy-making decisions in planning strategies.

After the present introduction, Chap. 2 describes the experimentation layout, whereas Chap. 3 discusses the FCM-based outcomes. Brief remarks end up the work.

2   FC Mapper Application and Case-Study Description

Within the present case study, data analysis and processing is carried out by structurally and ontologically involving cognitive interactions with their inherent substantial contents and mutual connections, drawing on a fuzzy-logic based tool, called FCMapper. This is a soft-system modeling and mapping approach combining qualitative and quantitative methods, with a participative social–learning approach [14]. FCM is aimed at quantifying abstract concepts and turning them into data on which to build up future scenarios. It tries to reveal and structure emergent possibilities in complex systems such as urban settlements.

Concerning the case-study, this tool has been used to build a model of an environmental-urban system structure, by formalizing and explaining some causal links between the main elements. In particular, the nodes of maps represent system variables and weighted arcs represent causal dependencies among concepts. As a matter of facts, the interaction between concepts shows the dynamic of the system [16].

Indeed FCM approach was significantly affected by the work of Kosko [17]. He modified Axelrod's cognitive maps by applying fuzzy casual functions with real numbers (−1 to 1) to connections [18]. The positive sign indicates a positive causality, the negative one expresses a negative causality between nodes [19]. FCM simulations give structured hints on how the system will change over time, analyzing how the implementation of a specific policy affects some variables and consequently causes changes in the entire map. Therefore, in the scenarios analysis phase, FCM expresses the effects on the system by a certain policy implemented as a change of a particular node strength or of a certain value of causal relationship.

In this study, the aim of FCM is to support the decision-making process in the field of urban empowerment and improvement. Specifically, FCM is applied to single out major problems affecting the city of Taranto based on the distributed knowledge of people, in order to design and evaluate policy possibilities to minimize their negative effects and improve city livability.

In 2014, a number of meetings with citizens took place in Taranto neighborhoods. Three of those interaction sessions are taken into account in this study, aiming at comparing situations in different environmental contexts. Therefore, we started from three different cognitive maps built on the information statements collected. These maps are designed through a process of participatory knowledge interaction based on scenario-building methodologies and slightly modified from Khakee et al. [20]. The maps are named according to the neighborhood location in which the meetings took place: *Città Vecchia, San Vito* and *Torretta*. Each neighborhood represents specific points of view on city problems even if they are often in the same problem field.

People attending the meetings were first grouped around tables. Afterwards, they entered their views (under the form of written statements) about their neighborhood on graphical cognitive maps, displayed on the available laptops for this task.

Many problem statements expressing similar meanings were clustered according to the evaluations of expert agents into twenty-five summary items (symbolized by A1 to E3 letters), representing the core concept of each problem field. Furthermore, these twenty-five items are used as input variables in the FCM matrix, aggregated into five general areas, i.e., *(A) Community security, (B) Natural environment, (C) Infrastructures, (D) Urbanized and cultural environment, (E) Economy and society.*

Subsequently, these items are organized into adjacency matrices, one matrix for each chosen neighborhood is composed. Thus, the expert agents use a direct fuzzy linguistic weight function to define the value of the reciprocal causal influence for each couple of variables on the matrix [17]. Therefore they assign a positive or negative sign and a value of 0, 5 or 1 to express the grade of casual relationship among concepts [14]. It is important to note that the causal relationship is not necessarily reversible. A confronting round among expert agents is used to choose final, shared values for each matrix cell.

After applying the *Pajek* visualization tool to the FCM matrices, the maps are shown in 2D projection. Main concepts are presented in circles with different colors, one for each general area, and the causal links between the main variables are shown through oriented arcs among nodes. The three maps are examined individually and also compared with each other, in order to find out similarities and differences. After a detailed comparison, only the two city contexts of *Città Vecchia* (CV, inner city) and *San Vito* (SV, a seaside neighborhood) proved to be suitable for further analysis (Fig. 1).

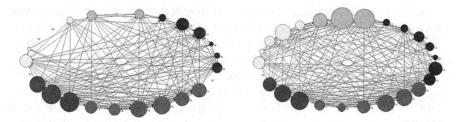

Fig. 1. Views of *Città Vecchia* and *San Vito* fuzzy map projections – circular layout.

Therefore, map structures are observed to investigate the outcomes of different policy choices through the comparison of alternative future scenarios. These scenarios are obtained by artfully influencing certain variables, broadly following a sensitivity-analysis approach. This methodology produces a rearrangement of each map structure, showing the effects that the alternative choices could induce in relation to the other system's variables. The next chapter illustrates this process.

3   Discussion

In two different case studies, we analyzed variables values, corresponding to specific attributes of the adjacency matrix: high centrality, *outdegree* and *indegree*. Specifically,

Papageorgiou and Kontogianni [18] define *outdegree* and *indegree* as the cumulative strengths of connections respectively as row and column sums of absolute values. Instead, *centrality* measures map complexity and shows how one variable is connected to other variables and what is the cumulative strength of these connections.

In particular, in *San Vito* high values of centrality are visible in items B2, B3 (environment protection), E1, E2 (planning and design), D1, D2, D3 (building and natural decay), ranging from 22.50 to 14.00. In *Città Vecchia*, the centrality of items D1, D2, D3, D4, E1, E2, E3 is significantly high (28.00–19.50), whereas the centrality of B3 is lower (13.00) and B2 is an unconnected item. In this case-study, variables A1 (vandalism), C2, C3 (infrastructure) are also meaningfully high (18.00–17.00).

In both case studies we worked out and compared two similar scenarios. On the one hand, scenario A simulates the results of implemented policies. It concerns active/ proactive actions in a frame of medium/long term planning and oriented to the protection and enhancement of local resources. On the other hand, scenario B focuses on a dual active/reactive and long/short time perspective. This scenario is more general then the first one and is clearly characterized by difficult interpretation and higher level of ambiguity.

The aim of this effort is to compare the effects of similar policies in the two different contexts. The modification of specific initial vectors has been done in order to show the evolution of the map according to clusters. This type of analysis allows investigating "what-if" scenarios by performing simulations of a given model from different initial state vectors. Each vector is a matrix item with high values of centrality, associated with the concepts identified by suggestions and available local knowledge elicited during the focus group sessions.

Using the *Pajek* visualization tool, four maps have been made (the size of the vertices is linked to the input file and represents centrality). In the scenario analysis, the graphical tool allows to understand the positive or negative changes in the map through the different colors and positions that are linked to the input file (deriving from the adjacency matrix elaborated with *FCMapper*). In particular, scenario A maps were drawn using the partition derived from the modification of vectors (value = 1) B2, B3, E1, E2 in San Vito, B3, E1, E2, E3 in *Città Vecchia* and without the modification (value = 0) of vectors D1, D2, D3 and D4. In both case studies, scenario B maps are built through the modification of all the previous vectors.

FCM has been used to explore the values in a group of individuals in order to improve the understanding of a multiple stakeholder decision problem. Starting from the comparison of type-A scenarios (Fig. 2), we can see that the map 'reacts' to changes consistently with centrality values. The general areas are certainly comparable, and changes in item are specific and can be fairly singled out.

Let us deal with a certain policy aimed at preserving and enhancing ecology and natural environment (B2, B3). The policy is using planning actions stimulating local-based economic development (E1, E2) and is drawing also on cultural and artistic heritage, where available (E3). Fuzzy cognitive maps change as follows.

In SV, the only positive –even if "low positive"- change impacts on infrastructures, particularly enhancing slow mobility, whereas in CV it enhances urban security. This difference reflects the context of the maps in the two case studies.

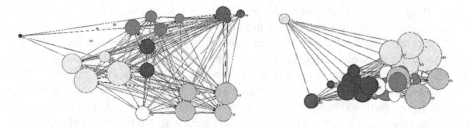

Fig. 2. Scenario A of Città Vecchia and San Vito maps according to the cluster.

"High negative changes" in CV map are connected to urban and cultural environment, particularly to the possibility/need of public good privatization. Moreover, in SV the items relating to security and the involvement of citizens show negative effects. This evolution of the map of SV seems to confirm that a policy attentive to the natural environment but excluding the urban environment, the community and the care of public spaces, may cause negative dynamics.

Furthermore, we can notice that SV and CV show up as areas quite sensitive (with "medium negative changes") to the presence of pollution (air, water, soil) in case of policies not specifically attentive to that issue.

Both B-type scenarios (Fig. 3) show a map with homogeneous changes: in this case the individuality and the specificity of items is lost. Negative (light grey) "strong changes" and positive (medium grey) "very weak changes" are visible, but maps are far more ambiguous and hardly interpretable. This may suggest that the FCM-based model is unsuitable to the analysis of policies that are not focused on specific themes.

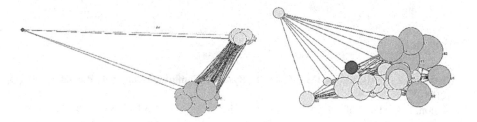

Fig. 3. Scenario B of Città Vecchia and San Vito maps according to the cluster.

4   Conclusions

The present paper aims at exploring the potentials of fuzzy cognitive maps to support decision-making in urban management processes. FCMapper software tool has been used to simulate and possibly evaluate the possible impacts of policy decisions concerning the futures of a number of areas inside the town of Taranto. The software typically carries out iteratively a simulation process, so as to foster a sort of sensitivity analysis, based on the previously collected knowledge, within the general system architecture (Borri and Camarda [10], p. 131, Fig. 1). The model works on a scenario building process embedded in the making up of the Master Plan of Taranto.

As a general outcome, the study raises interesting yet mixed results. After processing data inputs, the FCM model delivers scenario alternatives to be used in a decision support model. However, from the two scenarios depicted by the analysis, only one seems to be somehow coherent in the two neighborhoods analyzed, whereas the second one induces too much ambiguity and interpretation, thus preventing an effective support to decisions. From the substantial point of view, when compared with the outcomes of a previous experimentation in microclimate management case study [13], such results are significantly less coherent and useful as a whole. This may be due to the set of items analyzed, which was more focused on few concepts, rather than scattered throughout a large number of different problems -inherently characterizing scenario building activities.

Nevertheless, some further considerations can be carried out beyond substantial issues. As a matter of fact, the effort of raising common, informal knowledge from community interaction needs to be complemented by setting up suitable models and architectures for knowledge management. However, ICT-based integrated systems often either work as black boxes, preventing an aware management of data, or tend to synthesize the complexity of the knowledge at hand, so losing the reliability of analyses [20]. The use of FCM-based models provides interesting clues in this concern, as it is located in that area of hybrid, semi-automatic systems providing support and suggestions while leaving more control on the process. This increased reliability is typically obtained to the detriment of times and costs, which rise significantly, lowering the appeal of such models to decision-makers.

Implicitly, research perspectives on how to improve these aspects are wide and interesting, and represent a fair stimulus to enhance and enrich the overall research effort for the future.

References

1. Bossomaier, T.R.J., Green, D.G.: Complex Systems. Cambridge University Press, Cambridge (2000)
2. Schön, D.A.: The Reflexive Practitioner. Basic Books, New York (1983)
3. Friedmann, J.: Planning in the Public Domain: From Knowledge to Action. Princeton University Press, Princeton (1987)
4. Fischer, F.: Citizens, Experts, and the Environment: the Politics of Local Knowledge. Duke University Press, Durham (2000)
5. Borri, D., Camarda, D., De Liddo, A.: Envisioning environmental futures: multi-agent knowledge generation, frame problem, cognitive mapping. In: Luo, Y. (ed.) CDVE 2004. LNCS, vol. 3190, pp. 230–237. Springer, Heidelberg (2004)
6. Sawyer, R.K.: Social Emergence: Societies as Complex Systems. Cambridge University Press, Cambridge (2005)
7. Wierzbicki, A., Makowski, M., Wessels, J.: Model-Based Decision Support Methodology with Environmental Applications. Kluwer Academic Publishers, Dordrecht (2000)
8. Faludi, A.: A Decision-centred View of Environmental Planning. Pergamon, Oxford (1987)

9. Borri, D., Camarda, D.: Visualizing space-based interactions among distributed agents: environmental planning at the inner-city scale. In: Luo, Y. (ed.) CDVE 2006. LNCS, vol. 4101, pp. 182–191. Springer, Heidelberg (2006)

10. Borri, D., Camarda, D.: Planning for the environmental quality of urban microclimate: a multiagent-based approach. In: Luo, Y. (ed.) CDVE 2011. LNCS, vol. 6874, pp. 129–136. Springer, Heidelberg (2011)

11. Ozesmi, U., Ozesmi, S.L.: Ecological models based on people's knowledge: a multi-step fuzzy cognitive mapping approach. Ecol. Model. **176**(1–2), 43–64 (2004)

12. Giordano, R., D'Agostino, D., Apollonio, C., Lamaddalena, N., Vurro, M.: Bayesian belief network to support conflict analysis for groundwater protection: the case of the Apulia region. J. Environ. Manage. **115**, 136–146 (2013)

13. Borri, D., Camarda, D., Pluchinotta, I.: Planning for the microclimate of urban spaces: notes from a multi-agent approach. In: Luo, Yuhua (ed.) CDVE 2014. LNCS, vol. 8683, pp. 179–182. Springer, Heidelberg (2014)

14. Borri, D., Camarda, D., Pluchinotta, I.: Planning urban microclimate through multiagent modelling: a cognitive mapping approach. In: Luo, Y. (ed.) CDVE 2013. LNCS, vol. 8091, pp. 169–176. Springer, Heidelberg (2013)

15. Camarda, D., Rotondo, F., Selicato, F.: Strategies for dealing with urban shrinkage: issues and scenarios in Taranto. Eur. Plan. Stud. **23**(1), 126–146 (2014)

16. Ozesmi, U., Ozesmi, S.: A participatory approach to ecosystem conservation: fuzzy cognitive maps and stakeholder group analysis in Uluabat Lake, Turkey. Environ. Manage. **31**(4), 518–531 (2003)

17. Kosko, B.: Fuzzy cognitive maps. Int. J. Man-Mach. Stud. **24**(1), 65–75 (1986)

18. Papageorgiou, E., Kontogianni, A.: Using fuzzy cognitive mapping in environmental decision making and management: a methodological primer and an application. INTECH Open Access Publisher (2012)

19. Din, M.-A., Moise, M.: A fuzzy cognitive mapping approach for housing affordability policy modeling. Latest Adv. Inf. Sci. Circuits Syst. **4**, 262–267 (2012)

20. Khakee, A., Barbanente, A., Camarda, D., Puglisi, M.: With or without? Comparative study of preparing participatory scenarios using computer-aided and traditional brainstorming. J. Future Res. **6**, 45–64 (2002)

Ranking of Collaborative Research Teams Based on Social Network Analysis and Bibliometrics

Menglei Zhang[⊠], Xiaodong Zhang, and Yang Hu

Donglink School of Economics and Management,
University of Science and Technology Beijing, Beijing, China
cherryzhang97@163.com, xdzhang@manage.ustb.edu.cn

Abstract. How to discover and rank the scientific research team from the huge amount of literatures is a hard challenge for scientific researchers. Therefore, based on social network analysis with bibliometrics, a comprehensive method to discover and rank collaborative research teams is proposed in this paper. With the data from 2010–2015 in *CIMS* as the sample, of a Chinese journal of CIMS as the samples, n-clique and snow ball sampling method is used to identify collaborative research teams. Then, the research teams are ranked using indexes which include both scientific research outcomes and the close degree of Co-author networks. Case study shows that the method is more comprehensive than the ranking method which considers bibliometrics or network properties only.

Keywords: Social network analysis · Team discovery · Team ranking · Co-author network

1 Introduction

With the increasing complexity and professional of the scientific research, research cooperation has become a very important working style. The discovery and analysis of collaborative scientific research teams from the huge amount of literatures has become a necessary task. As the same time, the discovered teams should be ranked in order to know the influence of these teams on the research field. With the knowing of the ranking of the teams, researchers can follow these teams and then enhance their own researches. Meanwhile, team discovery and ranking are also very important in the scientific project application and evaluation. As a result, scientific research team discovery and ranking have been a hot research point in recent years in the field of collaborative working and big-data mining.

There are a lot of method about research team ranking, Huang [1] have used peer review method to evaluate the performance of cooperated universities teachers. In addition, evaluation index based on post and citation index (H - index, G - index, etc.) have also been used by Waltman [2] to set evaluation system. However, peer review, and other similar expert evaluation may exist subjectivity or prejudice. [3] Some scholars pointed out that the evaluation results of peer review and expert opinions may only be set in a series of positive and negative opinions [4]. On the other hand, some

© Springer International Publishing Switzerland 2015
Y. Luo (Ed.): CDVE 2015, LNCS 9320, pp. 236–242, 2015.
DOI: 10.1007/978-3-319-24132-6_30

scholars think that the existence of the self-citation has negative influence on the validity of H - index and G - index [5].

Bibliometrics is widely used in evaluation due to its objectivity. Researchers had used this kind of indexes to prove the effectiveness of the research teams [6]. But only use the output of the team as the judgment is not comprehensive, for the cooperation relationship of team members is also an important aspect to reflect the team's competitiveness. Jesue et al. [9] showed that the member in the solid team has better performance then who is not. And with the development of social network analysis technology, it's possible to establish a social network with a large number of nodes and calculate the network properties. Researchers have tried to apply index of social network analysis to scientific research team's discovery and evaluation [10], and they also pointed that the evaluation system combined with network index and bibliometric can be more convincing.

According to the analysis above, this article aims to discover and rank the collaborative research teams scholars of a Chinese journal based on the cooperation network of authors. First, the method of condensing subgroup combined with snowball method is used to identify the research team. Then a new way proposed to rank the teams based on social network analysis and bibliometrics. The evaluation indexes are set up which include team's output, team's influence and team's close degree of cooperation.

2 Methods

Social Network Analysis (SNA) is a quantitative analysis method applied to the study of social relationships. The study of objects and the relationships is showed by nodes and edges. This method is used to analyze the relationship between the nodes and study the network's structure, properties and characteristic. The overall properties of the network including the analysis of the small world effect, small group study, cohesive subgroups. Properties can represent the connectivity of the network. Indexes such as density, clustering coefficient, the average path length are used to evaluate the degree of aggregation and to analyze the relationship among nodes and edges.

3 Data Source and Team Discovery

3.1 Data Source

In this study, data come from articles published in the journal of computer integrated manufacturing system in 2010–2014. Record each paper's title, authors, keywords, fund number, references, and authors of references are extracted and a database is established. The reason of select ing CIMS is that computer integrated manufacturing is an emergent research field which needs multi-subject collaboration of manufacturing automation, information technology, and system integration.

By retrieving articles, the established database got 1668 articles, and 3380 Authors. After initial calculation we found that the partnership among the authors is very clear.

93.64 % of the papers are in collaboration with 2–5 authors. 3 and 4 in the form of cooperation is most common and the proportion is more than 30 %. The average number of authors per paper is 3.5 people. This shows that the size of the cooperative network is larger and the authors have high cooperation level, which is conducive to the establishment of cooperative networks.

3.2   Team Discovery

The discovery of team is based on the foundation of the whole network. Firstly, the whole cooperation network diagram of the author is built. If two or more authors published a paper together, there is a partnership between them, and can be expressed by Cooperation Matrix, pick up literature writer and literature information from sample data. Regard the 3380 authors with different relationship as vertices to establish co-occurrence matrix. The overall cooperation network is generated by Software Ucinet, shown in Fig. 1.

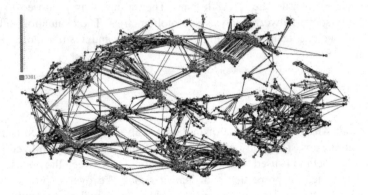

Fig. 1. The overall cooperation network

Cohesion subgroup is a common method to discover team. Generally, this method is often used when the size of network is relatively small, and not suitable for analysis of network structure. Since this study has many nodes, so cohesion subgroup combines the "snowball" method to determine the individual team members is more effective, the research team is structured into team leaders, core members and non-core members. The final establishment of eight research teams is shown in Fig. 2.

4   Comprehensive Ranking of Teams

4.1   Team Evaluation System

(1) The ranking indexes

In this study, combined social network analysis method with traditional citation analysis and bibliometrics, we proposed a more comprehensive evaluation system.

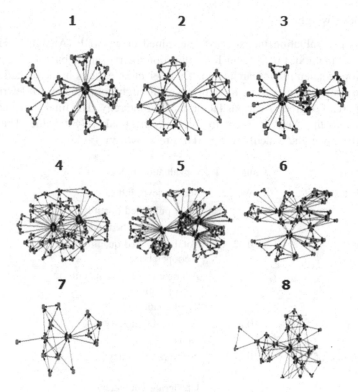

Fig. 2. Cooperative network of each team

The evaluation system consists of two levels, the first level includes scientific research, literature influence and the close degree of cooperation, the second level includes 9 indexes.

(2) Indexes description

Team output: We chose total published quantity, average published quantity, total published quantity in cooperation and average published quantity in cooperation as the second level index. Documents published with the involving of the members in the team will be regarded as team documents. Because of the good cooperation with the periodical there is a situation that one thesis belongs to some different teams, thus we create a concept "documents published in cooperation", representing all the authors belongs to a same team.

Team influence: In this part, the second level index consists of total citations and average citations. Citation evaluation is an objective factor to represent team influence as well as a most widely adopted index for team evaluation.

The close degree of cooperation: These indicators built on the basis of social network. Density, network efficiency and clustering coefficient are chosen as indexes, which can be used to reflect the relationship between nodes in the network.

(3) The index weight

The weights of evaluation indexes are determined using AHP (Analytical Hierarchy Process, AHP) method. First establish the question matrix on the basis of the results of the evaluation of scientific research team. Then select 30 experts in the related field and ask them to score the questions in same level through comparison, to determine the relative important degree of various factors in the hierarchy. The final statistical results will be put into the AHP software to calculate the final weight value. The ranking indexes and the weights calculated by AHP are shown in Table 1.

Table 1. Team evaluation indexes

First level indexes	Weight	Second level indexes	Weight
		Total published quantity	0.41
		Average published quantity	0.15
Team output	0.42	Total published quantity in cooperation	0.32
		Average published quantity in cooperation	0.12
		Total citations	0.61
Team influence	0.34	Average citations	0.39
		Density	0.21
The close degree of cooperation	0.24	Network efficiency	0.38
		Clustering coefficient	0.41

4.2 Empirical Analysis of the Evaluation Team

(1) Index calculation

Bibliometric indexes can be achieved through statistical tools, as it shown in Table 2. Each team's network attribute index calculated by the Ucinet, as shown in Table 3.

Table 2. Index calculation based on bibliometrics

No.	Total published quantity	Average published quantity	Total published quantity with cooperation	Average published quantity with cooperation	Total citations	Average citations
1	63	2.333333	9	0.333333	30	1.111111
2	44	2.2	13	0.65	11	0.55
3	41	1.708333	14	0.583333	15	0.625
4	41	0.931818	29	0.659091	12	0.272727
5	80	1.230769	31	0.476923	104	1.6
6	41	0.953488	22	0.511628	10	0.232558
7	21	1.5	7	0.5	77	5.5
8	31	1.24	15	0.6	7	0.28

Table 3. Index calculation based on social network analysis

No.	Density	Network efficiency	Clustering coefficient
1	0.2391	0.498256	0.929
2	0.2125	0.504286	0.833
3	0.1913	0.446628	0.87
4	0.1591	0.429369	0.88
5	0.27	0.481464	0.943
6	0.8791	0.594884	0.863
7	0.4842	0.588235	0.872
8	0.48	0.543478	0.827

The impact of the three network indicators, is positively related to each other. The higher these indexes are, the closer the network is. Under ideal circumstances, a higher degree of close cooperation of the research team should have a high network density, network efficiency values and the clustering coefficient.

(2) Team Sorting

Each team's index data will be normalized. According to the expert scoring, the weights of various levels are calculated. The calculated results are shown in Table 4.

It is seen that after introducing the index of close degree of cooperation, the ranking result is no longer simply depend on the team output. Since the members in team No. 7 and No. 4 cooperated more frequently, the network of the team has a more stable structure. These teams got relatively high scores.

Table 4. Comprehensive evaluation of team

Number	Comprehensive score	Ranking
5	0.798827	1
7	0.674721	2
1	0.54047	3
2	0.508887	4
4	0.505838	5
3	0.476506	6
6	0.451397	7
8	0.434092	8

5 Conclusion

In this paper, a method to discover and rank the collaborative research team is proposed using the data of a Chinese journal "Computer Integrated Manufacturing Systems" as the samples. To discover collaborative research team, the method that combine cohesion subgroup and the "snowball" method is used. It is found that the cooperation rate in this research field is high, the phenomenon of inter cooperation is significant. Based on the team discovery, a new way to rank the team is put forward, which combines social network analysis and bibliometrics together. Case study shows that the method is more comprehensive than the ranking method which considers bibliometrics or network properties only.

Acknowledgments. This work is based upon research work supported by the National Natural Science Foundation of China under grant No. 71171019 and No. 06198040; the Fundamental Research Funds for the Central Universities under grant FRF-SD-13-004B and FRF-TP-14-055A2; and the Program for China Postdoctoral Science Foundation under grant No. 2013T60064.

References

1. Huang X L, Liang Y B. Peer evaluation used in colleges and universities about performance evaluation. Wuzhou Univ. J. **5** (2014) (in Chinese)
2. Waltman, L., Van Eck, N.J.: The inconsistency of the h-index. J. Am. Soc. Inform. Sci. Technol. **63**(2), 406–415 (2012)
3. Sandström, U., Hällsten, M.: Persistent nepotism in peer-review. Scientometrics **74**(2), 175–189 (2008)
4. Južnič, P., Pečlin, S., Žaucer, M., et al.: Scientometric indicators: peer-review, bibliometric methods and conflict of interests. Scientometrics **85**(2), 429–441 (2010)
5. Schreiber, M.: Self-citation corrections for the Hirsch index. EPL (Europhys. Lett.) **78**(3), 30002 (2007)
6. Schreiber, M.: The influence of self-citation corrections on Egghe'sg index. Scientometrics **76**(1), 187–200 (2008)
7. Jiancheng, G., Junxia, W.: Evaluation and interpretation of knowledge production efficiency. Scientometrics **59**(1), 131–155 (2004)
8. Martín-Sempere, M.J., Garzón-García, B., Rey-Rocha, J.: Team consolidation, social integration and scientists' research performance: an empirical study in the biology and biomedicine field. Scientometrics **76**(3), 457–482 (2008)
9. Rey-Rocha, J., Garzón-García, B., Martín-Sempere, M.J.: Scientists' performance and consolidation of research teams in Biology and Biomedicine at the Spanish Council for Scientific Research. Scientometrics **69**(2), 183–212 (2006)
10. Chen, H.: Popular social networking services cause analysis. News World **5**, 114–115 (2009)

A Solution of Collaboration and Interoperability for Networked Enterprises

Chengwei Yang[1,2,3] and ShanShan Gao[4(✉)]

[1] College of Management Science and Engineering,
Shandong University of Finance and Economic, Jinan, China
yangchengwei2006@163.com
[2] Shandong Provincial Key Laboratory of Software Engineering, Jinan, China
[3] CVIC Software Engineering Co., Ltd, Jinan, China
[4] College of Computer and Science, Shandong University of Finance and Economic, Jinan, China
gsszxy@aliyun.com

Abstract. The cross-enterprise business process is different from the common business process. More issues of level interoperability must be defined and differentiated. The enterprise interoperability framework has been proposed by five levels. And a novel method of cross-enterprise process collaboration is presented. In order to enhance the capability of process reengineering and change, the services composition strategy which is based on SCA components have been proposed. An example of cross-enterprise business of cloth-order in textile industry is illustrated and analyzed as well.

Keywords: Networked enterprise · Collaboration · Interoperability

1 Research Background

Today's Enterprises face many challenges especially related to lack of interoperability. Enterprises need to adapt more quickly to changes in the business and economic market. It is required to become more responsive to customer's needs. The operational ability to collaborate is a key success factor for networked enterprises, and interoperability is the target result for the enterprises involved in long established as well as ad-hoc or occasional forms of collaborations [1–3].

Meanwhile, the integrated technologies for some legacy systems under object web environment is confronted with challenges. Most of the application systems in the enterprises are Un-Web service application should be encapsulated as Web services and deployed by ESB tools. However, In order to adjust the business process on the demand of business change, the associated services need to be banded according to these different conditions.

The service components in legacy system must be encapsulated. SCA is the most basic structural unit component. There may be a number of candidate mapping services, so the key issue of service selection is to choose the most appropriate service among those candidate services.

© Springer International Publishing Switzerland 2015
Y. Luo (Ed.): CDVE 2015, LNCS 9320, pp. 243–249, 2015.
DOI: 10.1007/978-3-319-24132-6_31

The rest of the article is organized as follows. Section two compares some other related works. The third section briefly introduces the enterprise interoperability framework. Section four portrays an approach of cross-enterprise process collaboration. It presents the approach of layered integration aiming at achieving seamless interoperability. The composition process using the XML format document to achieve the business process with loose coupling mode. In section five, an application example is presented and the approach are analyzed. The paper concludes with section six addressing the needs for future research.

2   Rated Works

The LISI (levels of information systems interoperability) approach in the goal of providing a maturity model and a process to detect joint interoperability needs, evaluate the capability of the systems to meet those needs, select pragmatic solutions and transition path to achieve higher states of capability and interoperability for the US Department of Defense (DoD), is developed by C4ISR Architecture Working Group (AWG) during 1997 [1]. Other frameworks such as IDEAS interoperability framework [2], European Interoperability Framework (EIF) [3] and the ATHENA interoperability framework (AIF) [4] also have deep influence.

A process describes the collaboration for mutual or automated activities which have a common blueprint [5]. A process uses a meta-model to define the concepts and notations concerning process description and activities expression. Considering process level interoperability, an approach using E-mails communication to realize process interoperability is given in [6, 7]. In this approach, process interoperability is subdivided into one Build-Time component and four Run-Time components. The authors in [8] propose a solution in interoperability of Process-Sensitive Systems (PSSs). The main idea of the solution is a virtual PSS independent of PSSs used to guarantee interoperability. The solution is efficient but costs much.

3   Enterprise Interoperability Framework

The interoperability and collaboration problem in a holistic way come from different perspectives of the enterprise. For this reason, the enterprise interoperability framework has been proposed by five levels, which include presentation level, service level, business level, process level and data level.

1. **Presentation interoperability** needs to respect the personalized demands in those aspects such as the enterprise interface design, the retrieval and safety strategy, the setting of personal collections, etc. At the same time, it also has the ability of quickly and easily providing different kinds of enterprise with the appropriate bindings between the services and different interfaces.
2. **Service interoperability** refers to discover, composite different kinds of functions or services for well collaborative work. WS also provides another capability of aggregate them into Composite Web Services (CWSs).

3. **Process interoperability** is the capability to make various processes work together. That is to say, it characterizes as the ability of business activities of one party to interact with those of any other party, whether these business activity or not belongs to different units of the same business or to different businesses.
4. **Business interoperability** is the ability of an enterprise to cooperate with other. The organizational structures and business requirements can change flexibly and adaptability. The cross enterprise process composition policy and modeling technology become more and more concerned.
5. **Information/data interoperability** is related to the management, exchange and processing of different documents, messages and/or structures by different collaborations. Data synchronization engine is responsible for data migration under the circumstance of cross-enterprise. In order to solve the embarrassment of semantic interoperability a knowledge library of SMEs oriented should be set up.

4   An Approach of Cross-Enterprise Process Collaboration

The enterprise business process aims at enabling flexible adaptation to change business needs. In the enterprise, the business processes are often changed with the growing of the enterprises. Unfortunately, the business processes at the circumstance of cross-enterprise are very differences. More issues of cross-organization enterprise collaboration must be defined and differentiated.

Cross-organization collaborative mainly occurs in the interoperability levels of service, business and process. As it shown in Fig. 1, service level interoperability has encapsulated the service components. In order to adapt the needs of presentation and process level interoperability, the service level is divided into atom service components (ASC), compound service components (CSC), process service components (PSC), and other service components (OSC). Business process modeling has the ability of describing the enterprise business process with defined language. A general policy is to make the modeling tools with the same language. The collaborative process engine is only responsibility for compositing the process, including process activity analysis, interoperability point test, business process compositing execution and process executing monitor.

The process composition can be described as follow: Process activity analysis is used to identify requested and responded information for all the activity nodes including start and end of the process models. For two activity nodes, if one's requested information is corresponding to the other's responded information partly or completely, interoperability point testing can decide that interoperability exists between them. Then, the interoperability point will be checked though compositing logs or the references of service interface information. After finishing the test of interoperability point, business process composition is driven by the process executing engine. The cross-enterprise business process is set up. It is called build-time of process. When the process starts, the process executing monitor begins to record the situations of process executing.

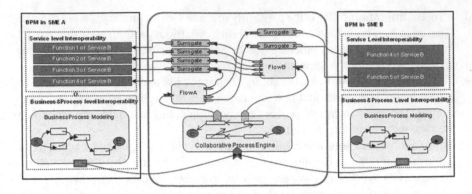

Fig. 1. Enterprise collaboration and interoperability model

5   Implements of Interoperability Based on SCA

The cross-enterprise business process composition policy is different from the common business process. More issues of process level interoperability must be defined and differentiated. The cross enterprise process composition policy can be described as follows: Firstly, analyze the business process including the organization structure, node definition, execution role, allocation resource and application, etc. On the condition that inter-enterprise interoperability, most of processes have existed in the standalone enterprise. Therefore, the aim of step must take these factors into account. Some research of process modeling tools start to support cross-enterprises business model. Unfortunately, due to the more complication of the cross-enterprise process collaboration rather than single process modeling, the definition of enterprise ontology in the process level interoperability paid close attention. Secondly, the service components in legacy system need to be encapsulated. SCA is the most basic structural unit component. Modeling tools support the composition strategy to simulate the implementation on the service model, which achieve pre-inspection. The process of modeling service selection phase implements the mapping to service of each activity. There may be a number of candidate mapping services, so the key issue of service selection is to choose the most appropriate service among those candidate services. The instances of candidate services are distributed and dynamic, so it is not reliable to choose the best appropriate service instance in the service selection process. The dynamic service binding strategy is to dynamically select the best process branch and the most appropriate service instance to implement according to the conditions and limitations.

In SCA programming model, service components will be combined in accordance with business groups. As it shown in Fig. 2, component A and component B utilizes service surrogate to encapsulate resource and build a service composition process.

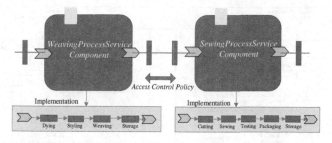

Fig. 2. The service composition of interoperability model

The following XML code is the definition for the extended SCA component and the composition process.

```
<composite xmlns="..." targetNamespace="..." xmlns:hw=...
                name="explosion_service">


        <component name=" DyingProcessService ">
    <implementation.java class="cn.sdu. DyingProcessService "/>
                    </component>
        <reference name="DyingProcessService" promote="
                DyingProcessService ">
    <interface.java interface=" cn.sdu. DyingProcessService " />
                    <binding.ws ....../>
                    </reference>
        <component name=" StylingProcessService ">
    <implementation.java class="cn.sdu. StylingProcessService "/>
                    </component>
            <reference >......</reference>
    </composite>
```

As growing complexity of WS compositions, exactly this information of composition performance is needed to access and used in the process of composite web service. For this reason, the management of web services at runtime becomes more and more important. However, the most of existing solutions, which were focus on monitoring the quality (QoS) provided by each single WS. Typically, composition structure and dependencies between services are not taken into account.

6   Case Study and Design

As we all know, textile industry is different from the general discrete manufacturing industry production management features. There are many small and medium enterprises

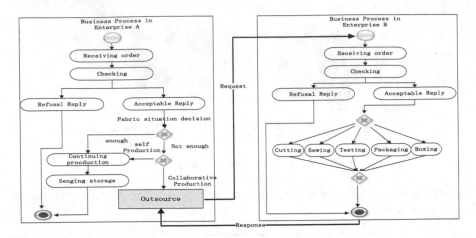

Fig. 3. An enterprise collaboration example

in textile industry of China. We illustrate a Chinese textile industry business of cloth-order collaborative and interoperability for instance in Fig. 3.

When an enterprise A receives a new order, it firstly does a checkup for the new order. If the new order does not pass the checkup, the enterprise will send a refusal to the source of the order and the process is ended. Otherwise, the enterprise will send an acceptable reply to the order source and then contracts with it. After the contract becomes effective, enterprise A begins to produce. Before producing products, the number of cloth in storage is checked. If cloth used in this order is enough, the cloth can be removed from the storage and be made into products. When the products are finished, they will be stored into the storage and then be sent out. Later, enterprise A receives a goods arrival reply and goes into the phase of financial settlement. After financial settlement, the whole process comes to a finished end. There is also another situation that the cloth is not enough for the order. In this situation, enterprise A will decide to whether the cloth is produced by itself according to its own production capability or assignment quantity. If it can finish the cloth producing by itself, materials out of storage will be weaved into cloth. Then the cloth is stored in the storage for the use of producing products. If enterprise A can't finish the preparation of the cloth, it will send a cloth order to an enterprise B, which is eager to producing cloth for A. After receiving an acceptable reply, enterprise A reaches a cloth agreement with enterprise B. When the cloth produced by enterprise B arrives, the production will be continued. Besides, the procedure of producing products in enterprise A includes five phases: cutting, sewing, testing, packaging and boxing. Compared to enterprise A, enterprise B has a simple way of business. After contracts become effective, enterprise B will directly begin to produce and then send goods. Finally, enterprise B does financial settlements.

7   Conclusion

The interoperability and collaboration problem becomes more and more common and importance for networked enterprises. According to the function, the enterprise interoperability framework has been proposed by five levels. And a novel method of cross-enterprise process collaboration is presented in this paper, which includes the description of a process composition. a cross-enterprise business of cloth-order collaborative and interoperability example is illustrated and analyzed as well. Furthermore, the detailed collaborative modeling, algorithm, and application are in future research progress. In addition, the definition of enterprise ontology in the process level interoperability paid more close attention.

Acknowledgement. This paper is supported in part by Natural Science Foundation of China under Grant 61303088 and 61402261, and part by the Natural Science Foundation of Shandong Province (Doctoral Foundation) under Grant BS2015DX013, and part by A Project of Shandong Province Higher Educational Science and Technology Program under Grant J14LN19, and part by the Fundamental Research Funds for Shandong Provincial Key Laboratory of Software Engineering under Grant 2013SE05, The second author is the corresponding author, and his e-mail address is gsszxy@aliyun.com.

References

1. The C4ISR Architecture Working Group (AWG) (CAWG): Levels of Information Systems Interoperability (LISI) (1998)
2. IDEAS: Interoperability Development for Enterprise Application and Software—Roadmaps, Annex 1—Description of Work (2002)
3. EIF: European Interoperability Framework, White Paper. Brussels (2004)
4. Guglielmina, C., Berre, A.: ATHENA, "Project A4" (Slide Presentation). In: ATHENA Intermediate Audit, Athens (2005)
5. Conradi, R., Fernstrom, C., Fuggetta, A., Snowdown, B.: Towards a reference framework for process concepts. In: 2nd European Workshop on Software Process Technology, Trondheim (1992)
6. Burkhart, T., Werth, D., Loos, P.: Realizing process interoperability using E-Mail communication. In: 1st International Conference on the Applications of Digital Information and Web Technologies, pp. 579–583. IEEE Press, Ostrava (2008)
7. Burkhart, T., Werth, D., Loos, P.: Process interoperability through proactive e-mail annotations. In: 2st International Conference on the Applications of Digital Information and Web Technologies, pp. 175–180. IEEE Press, London (2009)
8. Estublier, J., Barghouti, N.S.: Interoperability and distribution of process-sensitive systems. In: International Symposium on Software Engineering for Parallel and Distributed Systems, pp. 103–114. IEEE Press, Kyoto (1998)

A Novel Automatic Process for Construction Progress Tracking Based on Laser Scanning for Industrial Plants

Jian Chai[1], Hung-Lin Chi[1(✉)], and Xiangyu Wang[1,2]

[1] Australasian Joint Research Centre for Building Information Modelling,
Curtin University, Perth, Australia
jian.chai@postgrad.curtin.edu.au,
{hung-lin.chi,Xiangyu.wang}@curtin.edu.au
[2] Department of Housing and Interior Design, Kyung Hee University,
Seoul, South Korea

Abstract. As-built modelling has potentials in progress tracking and quality control in industrial plants construction. Although noted work has been conducted, there remain gaps in sophistication of automation and the extent of recognition for semantic information during the process is low. This paper developed a new modelling process for industrial components to fill in these gaps by incorporating 3D object recognition and graph matching techniques. The new process firstly groups the point cloud data of industrial components into geometric primitives. The process is also developed to recognize industrial components by matching connection graph, which is retrieved from geometric primitives, of as-built model with that of as-designed model. Furthermore, the tracking process is able to identify schedule delays by deviation analysis between as-built and as-designed model. A pilot study is carried out and proves that the developed process enables as-built modelling with semantic information and automatic construction progress tracking. Results show that the developed method is promising in saving time and labor cost during construction.

Keywords: As-built modelling · Construction progress tracking · Laser scanning · Graph matching · 3D object recognition · Total life cycle support

1 Introduction

As-built modelling is the process of creating actual model of a facility as what it is built. The current status is of vital importance for construction management, such as progress tracking and quality control. At present, as-built information are mainly captured through manual inspection. Those traditional approaches are time consuming and labor cost is high. This paper investigates approach of automated as-built modelling through laser scanning so as to improve speed and reduce cost.

Laser scanning is capable of rapidly producing large volume of measurements of construction site with high accuracy. Figure 1 is an example of point cloud of an industrial facility that is acquired by a territorial laser scanner. The point cloud can describe major information of the facility. However, it lacks of construct-related

© Springer International Publishing Switzerland 2015
Y. Luo (Ed.): CDVE 2015, LNCS 9320, pp. 250–258, 2015.
DOI: 10.1007/978-3-319-24132-6_32

Fig. 1. Point cloud of an industrial facility acquired by a laser scanner (The point cloud consists of more than 7 million points with millimeter accuracy)

information and recognized primitives for the use of the construction management. Despite many manual or semi-automatic approaches exist for the integration, automated as-built modelling from point cloud is challenging due to the following reasons: It is difficult to recognize objects from whole point cloud given similarity of points and repeatability of various objects; Furthermore, there is merely geometry information and little semantic information can be effectively retrieved from point cloud.

The goal of this research is to propose approaches of automated retrieve information from the point cloud for as-built modelling and investigate methods of progress tracking using as-built models. Contributions of this paper are as followings:

1. A fully automated process of construction progress tracking using laser scanning technology;
2. An automated as-built modelling process of industrial components by referencing with as-designed models;
3. Robust progress tracking with more details using state-of-the-art 3D object recognition methods.

2   Related Works

Modelling and recognition from point cloud have been widely studied in fields of computer vision, remote sensing and construction.

Various methods of reconstructing geometric model from point cloud have been proposed. A geometric reconstruction method of industrial instrumentation from point cloud was proposed by [1, 2]. The method used an improved Hough transform algorithm to detect geometric primitives including cylinder, sphere, and plane, and then fit CSG (Constructive Solid Geometry) objects by manual selection [3]. Kawashima et al. [4, 5] proposed methods to detect piping system from point cloud and reconstructed parameterized model. Xiong et al. [6] introduce context-based modelling algorithm to identify and model planar structures of an indoor environment from laser scanned data.

Different approaches of object recognition from point cloud have also been investigated [7]. A free-form shape detection approach is proposed in [8] by matching local 3D features to accumulate evidence in a 3D Hough space. A pose clustering strategy is developed to recognize an object and determine its pose [9]. Geometric consistency constraints are used to detect an object based on local feature correspondences [10].

Related works have been conducted to track construction progress via 3D measurement technology given high efficiency and reliability. The main strategy is through identifying differences between progressive point cloud data and existing planned models. The feasibility of progress tracking via fusing time-stamped point cloud data and CAD (Computer-Aided Design) model is investigated and results show that tracking performance is related to recognition rate of 3D objects [11]. A fully automated method of registering point cloud with CAD model to perform project progress monitoring is developed in [12]. Son and Kim [13] presented a method of assessing structural component progress by creating as-built models from image and point cloud data. Even though these researches prove it is promising to monitor construction progress using 3D data, there still remains significant work to improve robustness and performance. It is of critical importance to create detailed and accurate as-built model given that tracking performance relies on successful recognition and modelling of point cloud.

3 Modelling Process of Industrial Components

A fully automated process of construction progress tracking using laser scanning technology is proposed in this paper. As shown in Fig. 2, there are mainly three phases during this process:

1. Geometric modelling is to reconstruct geometric models of objects from point cloud;
2. Object recognition is to recognize type and identity information of a certain object;
3. Progress identification is to determine the current status of construction compared to planned schedule of the construction.

Inputs of this process include as-designed 4D (and P&ID) models and progressive point cloud which can be captured by a laser scanner at different stages of the construction. Outputs are as-built model of the construction facility and actual construction progress.

3.1 Industrial Component Recognition from Point Cloud

The above clustering step segments point could to various segments, each of which potentially corresponds to an industrial component. This step is to recognize which industrial component each segment is and determine its pose.

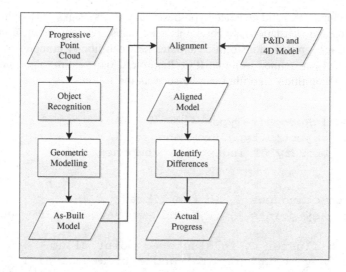

Fig. 2. Flowchart of proposed framework for construction progress tracking

Recognition is the process of finding a given object from a scene and estimating the object's pose. Given that there are noise and occlusion in point cloud and segmentation maybe inaccurate, the recognition in this step should be robust in dealing with noise and incompleteness. This paper implements local feature based 3D object recognition approach to find industrial components from laser scanning data [7].

A point cloud library of industrial components is created where there is a corresponding point cloud model for every type of industrial component. Some components in the library for industrial plants are shown as Fig. 3. Since models not contained in the library will not be recognized, it is of vital importance to build complete and typical representation for a target scene.

Key points and feature descriptors are estimated both for industrial components library and scene point cloud. 3D SIFT (Scale Invariant Feature Transform) features, which are invariant to scale and rotation, and are capable of being used to recognize objects with occlusion and noisy data [14]. They are chosen in this work. As shown in Fig. 4, the approach recognizes objects by matching and clustering local feature correspondences between a library and point cloud. Hough voting strategy is used to

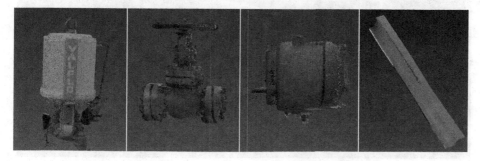

Fig. 3. Component examples of the library for industrial plants

cluster correspondences and generate hypothesis candidates. Peaks in Hough parameter space (rotation and translation) are chosen as candidates. To improve the accuracy and robustness of recognition, transform candidates between library component and point cloud is verified and refined using an IPC (Iterative Closest Point) algorithm [15].

The type recognition algorithm can be seen as the follows:

Algorithm 1 *RecognizeTypes()*:
Recognize object's type from the scene.
$\{I_j\}$ is a library of industrial components

Begin
1. **Foreach** component I_i in the library $\{I_j\}$
   Detect key points $K_i=\{P_j\}$ and estimate 3D SIFT features

2. **Foreach** cluster C_i in clustered point cloud
   Detect key points $KP_i=\{Q_j\}$ and estimate 3D SIFT features

3. **Foreach** component I_i in the library $\{I_j\}$
   a. Match key point correspondences $\{<P_i, Q_j>\}$ between $K_i=\{P_j\}$ and $KP_i=\{Q_j\}$ using SIFT features
   b. Hough vote to cluster feature correspondences and generate candidates from point cloud
   c. Refine with IPC algorithm to verify hypothesis transform

End.

Fig. 4. Results of point correspondence clustering

Above recognition process enables identification of the type information of an item. However, there are many components which have the same type in an industrial plant. A further step is conducted to distinguish items belonging to the same type. In this work, a graph matching method is proposed to further determine identity of an item. A graph of a scene can be built with each component as a node and their connection as edges. By matching graph between a scene and designed model, components can be identified as corresponding component in designed model. Compared to common methods which directly align as-designed 3D model with point cloud, this recognition method can deal with facilities without 3D model, given that a graph can be extracted from not only 3D models but also P&ID drawings. The algorithm and result to identify specific item can be seen as the follows (Fig. 5):

Algorithm 2 *IdentifyItem()*:
Determine identities of each component.
G_{model} is graph from as-designed documents
G_{scene} is graph from clustered point cloud of construction site

Begin
1. Create a graph from clustered point cloud
   Foreach cluster C_i in clustered point cloud
        Create a Node N_i with position, type, and size of the object and add to graph G_{scene}
   Foreach Node N_i in Graph G_{scene}
        Search neighborhood around cluster C_i and find subset of clusters $\{C_j\}$ that are connected to cluster C_i
        IF $\{C_j\}$ is not empty
             Create an edge E_{ij} between corresponding nodes N_i and N_j

2. Build a graph from point cloud of a model
   Repeat Step 1 to create a graph G_{model} from as-designed Model

3. Graph match between G_{scene} and G_{model}

4. **FOREACH** node correspondence after matching
        Assign identity of a node from G_{model} to the corresponding node in G_{scene}

   End.

Fig. 5. Results of component recognition

3.2 Geometric Modelling of Components

Geometric modelling is to create parametric models of industrial components from point cloud. Given that most components in an industrial plant are man-made objects and can be represented by combinations of geometric primitives, such as cylinder, sphere, box etc. [1]. A strategy of detecting and fitting primitive shapes is adapted in this paper. Primitive shapes composing an industrial scene are inferred from existing documents, such as P&ID and detected with an efficient RANSAC approach. The approach is adopted due to its efficiency and robustness to noise or outliers. This enables successful modelling even in scene with scatter or occlusion, which is common for an industrial plant because of its complexity.

3.3 Progress Identification

This stage is to identify actual progress of construction by comparing time-lapsed as-built models from above steps with 4D as-designed model. Through analyzing differences between as-built and as-designed models, components already installed or delayed are identified. Tasks are color coded with respect to "on time" or "delayed".

With laser scanned data at a given time, all installed components in plant are created and recognized through as-built modelling methods described in the above sections. Meanwhile, according to tasks scheduled at given time, all components should be finished are retrieved from 4D model. Ideally, for each item due at specific time, there should be a corresponding one in as-built model. Thus, actual progress is identified by checking whether there is a correspondence in as-built model. For better interpretation, actual progress is visualized through color coded status of installation including "on time", "delayed" or "ahead of time". The algorithm for progress identification can been seen as the follows:

Algorithm 3 *ProgressIdentify():*
Find out actual progress of construction.
$C_t=\{I_j\}$ is components installed subject to schedule at given time t
$BM_t=\{I_j\}$ represents as-built model at given time t

Begin
1. Given time t, retrieve collection of components $C_t=\{I_j\}$ that should be installed from schedule

2. **Foreach** component I_j in C_t
      Check if there is component I_iof the same identity in as-built model $BM_t=\{I_j\}$
   IF EXIST I_i
      Mark I_j as installed on time
   ELSE
      Mark I_j as delayed
   END IF

3. Color coding as-designed model to visualize current progress

   End.

4 Conclusion

In this research, a fully automated process of construction progress tracking using laser scanning technology is proposed. Related algorithms have been implemented and demonstrated through a module of industrial plant as a pilot study. A library containing regular industrial plant components is established and 3D SIFT features are used for matching and clustering local feature correspondences between a library and point cloud. Once the component type is confirmed, a further step, through graph matching, is conducted to distinguish components belonging to the same type. In this work, construction progress is identified by comparing the created time-lapsed as-built models with 4D as-designed model. The demonstrations in this paper show that the developed process enables as-built modelling with semantic information and automatic construction progress tracking. It is worthy conducting future evaluations in collecting the quantitative results for saving time and labor cost during construction.

Acknowledgement. This research was undertaken with the benefit of a grant from Australian Research Council Linkage Program (Grant No. LP130100451).

References

1. Rabbani, T.: Automatic reconstruction of industrial installations using point clouds and images. Ph.D. thesis, Delft University of Technology, Delft, the Netherlands (2006)
2. Rabbani, T., Van Den Heuvel, F.: 3D industrial reconstruction by fitting CSG models to a combination of images and point clouds. In: International Archives of the Photogrammetry, Remote Sensing and Spatial Information Sciences (ISPRS), vol. 35, p. B5 (2004)
3. Schnabel, R., Wahl, R., Klein, R.: Efficient RANSAC for point-cloud shape detection. Comput. Graphics Forum. **26**(2), 214–226 (2007)
4. Kawashima, K., Date, S.K.H.: As-built modeling of piping system from terrestrial laser scanned point clouds using normal-based region-growing. J. Comput. Des. Eng. **1**(1), 13–26 (2014)
5. Son, H., Kim, C., Kim, C.: Fully automated as-built 3D pipeline extraction method from laser-scanned data based on curvature computation. J. Comput. Civil Eng. **29**(4) (2014). B4014003
6. Xiong, X., Antonio, A., Burcu, A., Daniel, H.: Automatic creation of semantically rich 3D building models from laser scanner data. Autom. Constr. **31**, 325–337 (2013)
7. Yulan, G., Bennamoun, M., Sohel, F., Min, L., Jianwei, W.: 3D object recognition in cluttered scenes with local surface features: a survey. IEEE Trans. Pattern Anal. Mach. Intell. **36**(11), 2270–2287 (2014)
8. Tombari, F., Di Stefano L.: Object recognition in 3D scenes with occlusions and clutter by hough voting. In: Fourth Pacific-Rim Symposium on Image and Video Technology (PSIVT) (2010)
9. Mian, A., Bennamoun, M., Owens, R.: On the repeatability and quality of keypoints for local feature-based 3D object retrieval from cluttered scenes. Int. J. Comput. Vis. **89**(2–3), 348–361 (2010)
10. Johnson, A., Hebert, M.: Surface matching for object recognition in complex 3-D scenes. Image Vis. Comput. **16**(9), 635–651 (1998)
11. Bosche, F., Haas, C., Murray, P.: Performance of automated project progress tracking with 3D data fusion. In: CSCE 2008 Annual Conference, pp. 10–13 (2008)
12. Kim, C., Son, H., Kim, C.: Fully automated registration of 3D data to a 3D CAD model for project progress monitoring. Autom. Constr. **35**, 587–594 (2013)
13. Son, H., Kim, C.: 3D structural component recognition and modeling method using color and 3D data for construction progress monitoring. Autom. Constr. **19**(7), 844–854 (2010)
14. Rusu, R.B., Cousins, S.: 3D is here: point cloud library (PCL). In: IEEE International Conference on Robotics and Automation (ICRA) (2011)
15. Besl, P.J., McKay, N.D.: A method for registration of 3-D shapes. IEEE Trans. Pattern Anal. Mach. Intell. **14**(2), 239–256 (1992)

An Integrated Approach for Progress Tracking in Liquefied Natural Gas Construction

Jun Wang[1(✉)], Wenchi Shou[1], Xiangyu Wang[1,2], and Hung-Lin Chi[1]

[1] Australasian Joint Research Centre for Building Information Modelling, Curtin University, Perth, Australia
{jun.wang15,wenchi.shou}@postgrad.curtin.edu.au,
{xiangyu.wang,hung-lin.chi}@curtin.edu.au
[2] Department of Housing and Interior Design, Kyung Hee University, Seoul, South Korea

Abstract. Progress tracking is an essential management function for successful delivery of Liquefied Natural Gas (LNG) projects. It relies on accurate and prompt data collection from construction sites and project participants, which is then used to early detect actual or potential schedule delay. Currently, many Information Technology (IT)-supported methods have been implemented to improve progress tracking. However, none of them has been able to deliver satisfactory and reliable information. This paper aims to develop an integrated approach for construction progress tracking by integrating laser scanning, Building Information Modeling, mobile computing and Radio Frequency Identification. The approach consists of three modules: milestone progress tracking, onsite activity/Task progress tracking, and supply chain tracking. Finally, a pilot LNG project was selected to validate this approach.

Keywords: Building information modeling · Information integration · Cooperative visualization · Progress tracking

1 Introduction

Australian economy has benefited and will continue to benefit significantly from Liquefied Natural Gas (LNG) investments committed in the past. There are many projects on the drawing board, representing an investment exceeding AUS$180 billion. However, the cost of building new LNG projects has increased tremendously in the past decade and is now about 20–30 % higher than that of the competition in North America and East Africa [1]. Early detection of actual or potential schedule delay or cost overrun in field construction activities is vital to project management [2]. Several methods of automated construction schedule generation [3], and progress tracking [4, 5] have been investigated. A common method of as-built data collection is the use of cameras or laser scanners [6, 7]. Obviously this method could not be applied to obscured/concealed works. The use of Radio Frequency Identification (RFID) technology can facilitate tracking and locating of large prefabricated steel components. However, it cannot be used in many other trades such as painting. In order to overcome these problems, this paper aims to develop an integrated approach for progress tracking in LNG projects by

© Springer International Publishing Switzerland 2015
Y. Luo (Ed.): CDVE 2015, LNCS 9320, pp. 259–267, 2015.
DOI: 10.1007/978-3-319-24132-6_33

integrating laser scanning, Building Information Modeling (BIM), mobile computing and RFID technologies. Project progress tracking in this paper is divided into different levels, such as milestone progress tracking, activity progress tracking, and task progress tracking. Moreover, project resources are also tracked so as to improve supply chain management.

2   Related Works

Typical practice for progress tracking mostly depends on site workers' daily or weekly reports which involve intensive manual data collection and entail frequent transcription or data entry errors [4]. This requires a significant amount of manual work that may impact the quality of the progress estimations [8]. In contrast to manually based quantity collection efforts, a number of researches concentrate on developing integrated systems for automated project progress tracking. Azimi et al. [9] developed an automated and integrated project monitoring and control framework to facilitate decision making. Dong et al. [3] had proposed an Automated Look-ahead Schedules Generation method and developed a software prototype to implement this method into practice. Song and Eldin [10] had demonstrated an adaptive real-time tracking solution for look ahead scheduling during construction field operations. Nowadays, web-based systems are becoming the main stream and proven to be an effective solution to aggregate scattered information and share information across different applications. Cheng et al. [11] had prototyped a service oriented, web-based system to facilitate the flexible coordination of construction supply chains by leveraging web services, web portal, and open source technologies. Moreover, Web-based system offered construction personnel a simple and flexible method of tracking, modifying, and updating cost and time-based project data [12].

Due to the dynamic nature and complexity of most construction operations, there is a significant need for a method that combines the capabilities of traditional modeling of engineering systems and real time field data collection. Akhavian and Behzadan proposed an integrated framework of data collection and analysis for remote monitoring and planning of construction operations [13]. El-Omari and Moselhi [5] presented a control model that integrates different automated data acquisition technologies to collect data from construction sites. The users could move with a tablet in the construction site and record, take snapshots and also hand written comments about activities on site. Work-packaging model was also designed to enable project managers to acquire and process data for progress management at various levels of detail [14].

In summary, construction information related to both safety and activity in field operations can be automatically monitored and visualized [15]. Up-to-date technologies for progress assessment, such as four-dimensional (4D) BIM, RFID, laser scanning, photogrammetry and video tracking, are reviewed and analyzed so that we can select appropriate technologies which are suitable for LNG project. Due to the page limitation, the detailed review and evaluation of each technology is not included in this paper.

3   Integrated Approach for Progress Tracking in LNG Construction

This section describes an integrated approach for progress tracking (Fig. 1). All modules within the approach are based on the same 3D model.

3.1   Module 1: Milestone Progress Tracking

This module focuses on milestone schedule tracking which is critical in LNG project because of its impact to system commissioning. Laser scanning is a measurement technology that enables rapid and reasonably accurate representation of the 3D surface of an object, in the form of a point cloud [7]. A 4D BIM model results from the linking of 3D model to the fourth dimension of time [16]. Previous research had demonstrated significant benefits of BIM in architectural visualization [17], decisions-making, project constructability assessment, and space constraint identification [18]. In order to obtain precise as-built 3D data, this research utilizes laser scanning to measure the actual progress. 3D registration is implemented to align the as-built 3D point cloud data with the as-planned 4D BIM model. After registration, differences between these two models can be automatically detected.

3.2   Module 2: Onsite Activity/Task Progress Tracking

The complicated nature of LNG activities makes the detailed progress monitoring challenging. Current LNG project progress monitoring methods involve submission of periodic reports and are constrained by their reliance on manually intensive processes and limited support for recording visual information. Recent advances in image-based visualization techniques enable reporting construction progress using interactive and visual approaches. However, analyzing significant amounts of as-built construction photographs requires sophisticated techniques. To overcome limitations of existing approaches, this module focuses on developing an integrated onsite progress monitoring system for activity and task. Various technologies, such as wireless communication, barcode reading, and client-server database, were utilized to efficiently manage, transfer, and visualize project information on a mobile computing platform. The proposed module is expected to assist construction engineers in achieving a high level of productivity and efficiency.

3.3   Module 3: Supply Chain Tracking

Construction project control attempts to effectively obtain real-time information and enhance dynamic control and management via information sharing and analysis from involved participants of the projects to reduce construction conflicts and project delay. However, extending the construction project control system to job sites is considered inefficient since construction sites are unconventional practice. Integrating promising information technologies such as barcode, QR code and RFID technology can help improve the effectiveness and convenience of information flow in construction supply chain control systems [19]. A typical RFID system includes an antenna, a transceiver (RFID reader) and a transponder (Radio Frequency tag). The antenna generates an electromagnetic zone where the tag detects the activation signal and responds by sending the stored data from its memory through radio frequency waves. This module explains the tracking materials that deliver to site. It will track the materials onsite and determine the correct usage of the materials as well.

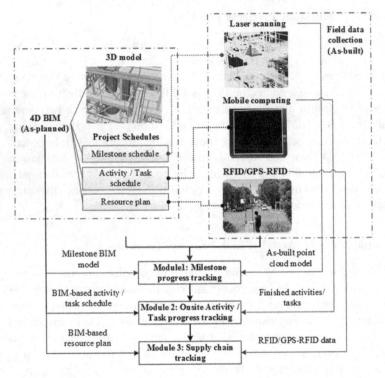

Fig. 1. Integrated approach for progress tracking in LNG construction

4   Pilot Case Study

In order to validate the proposed approach, a pilot LNG case was selected. Four types of technologies are utilized to perform data collection and analysis: (1) laser scanning is used to capture as-built model at project milestones so as to track milestone schedule; (2) mobile computing is used to collect information of activities so as to assess percentage completion of each activity; (3) RFID is used to real-time track construction resource including materials, equipment and tools. In addition, GPS-based RFID is used to locate the resource during transportation stage; and (4) BIM is used to check and visualize the comparative results between as-built and as-planned model.

4.1   Laser Scanning for Milestone Schedule Tracking

Figure 2 illustrates the integrated model of point cloud and BIM model. Firstly, the point cloud data acquired from a construction site is processed to eliminate the irrelevant components to progress measurement such as heavy equipment, materials and surroundings. Then, the coordinate system of the as-built data is changed to align to the as-planned BIM model. Thirdly, as-built data and as- planned BIM model are integrated into one platform to extract the features of the as-built data that correspond to those in the BIM model. Finally, a matching process uses the extracted features to calculate the actual progress of each LNG system.

Fig. 2. BIM integrated point cloud model

4.2   Mobile Computing for Activity/Task Tracking

Figure 3 shows the tracking methods for activity and task. For instance, there is an activity named install pressure regulator, which contains four tasks: search in warehouse, deliver to laydown area, install and bolt in position, and inspection. For activity tracking, it consists of four steps: (1) create activity list; (2) define status of each activity, such as start, finish and percentage completion; (3) workers input actual status onsite; and (4) calculate actual percentage completion. For task tracking, it also includes four steps: (1) create task list; (2) define task list in mobile application; (3) use barcode to record progress information; and (4) workers choose task and scan barcode to send progress information to system.

Since different mobile users have different requirements. The module 2 can define different roles and their access control. For instance, a project manager needs software functions including reviewing 4D BIM, monitoring progress, updating schedules and

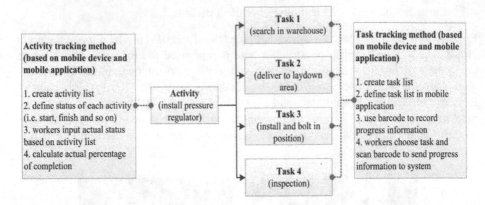

Fig. 3. Tracking methods for activity and task

distributing records, and a site engineer may need different software functions such as the as-built data input and review up-to-date activity list and task list. Therefore, the role of a user decides the selection and implementation of mobile application software for the specific information requirements. Mobile users need to have essential computer skills to operate mobile computers and use mobile application software. If users lack the required computer skills and knowledge, training and education are necessary for them before the use of relevant mobile computing technologies. In order to retrieve and transfer information on work sites, this module uses Wireless Local Area Network to transfer and update data.

4.3   RFID for Materials Tracking

In the field study, material tracking is divided into three phases. In phase 1, RFID and barcode are used to track material status (i.e. order, preparation, production and inspection) in manufacturing stage for decision-making. In phase 2, GPS-based RFID is used to track locations of LNG construction resource so as to assess how long they will arrive at construction site. In phase 3, RFID and barcode are used to track resource onsite, such as where they are? How many/much is left? Figure 4 illustrates the overall process of the GPS-based RFID for resources tracking at the construction site.

4.4   Benefit Assessment

Several questions have been raised when performing the proposed framework in the pilot case study in order to assess its value. Four key questions are identified by [20] so as to determine whether new technologies are providing apparent improvement for industry.

Are we doing the right things?
The first thing we do is to examine empirically how production is controlled at the moment in LNG industry, especially concentrating on the root causes for failing to

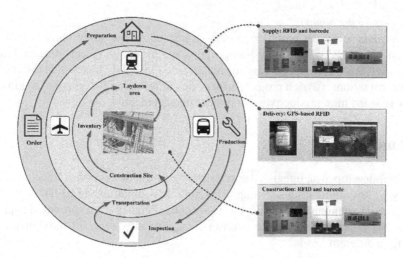

Fig. 4. GPS-based RFID for resources tracking

implement schedules as planned and the interrelationships between various LNG systems. Progress tracking is an essential management function for successful delivery of LNG projects. It relies on accurate and prompt data collection from construction job sites and project participants, which is then used to early detect actual or potential schedule delay. Currently, many IT-supported methods have been implemented to improve progress tracking. However, none has been able to deliver satisfactory and reliable information, for instance, data collection from laser scanning and camera cannot be applied to obscured/concealed works.

Are we doing them the right way?
The empirical research is carried out by using laser scanning, BIM, RFID, mobile computing and AR as the underlying technical model. To achieve real-time progress tracking and cost effectiveness, four level-of-detail schedules are defined in this research: milestone schedule, activity schedule, task schedule and resource supply chain. Therefore, we can use laser scanning to track milestone schedule, mobile computing to activity and task schedule, RFID & GPS-based RFID to resource supply chain. Data collecting from these technologies is effective and efficient, and give rich information for project manager to make a high quality and quick decision in this pilot case study.

Are we getting them done well?
A standard production control process based on the proposed system is developed, and the project teams are trained using the model process. In addition, a number of work packages are created to give a step-by-step guidance for workers and progress checkers. The organizational capability, resources availability and supporting infrastructure required to work with the proposed progress tracking system are also be assessed regularly.

Are we getting the benefits?

When implementing the proposed system in this pilot case study, three benefits are achieved: (1) timely and visually show progress against planning, calculate the forecast based on actual production rates, and to prevent potential delays by reacting to deviations with control actions; (2) rich project performance information for decision-making; and (3) low risk and high productivity for project management.

5   Conclusions

This paper developed an integrated approach for construction progress tracking in LNG industry by leveraging laser scanning, BIM, mobile computing and RFID. A pilot case was selected to demonstrate the effectiveness and efficiency of the proposed approach. The results reveal that schedule overrun is significantly reduced through progress tracking in different levels.

Acknowledgement. This research was undertaken with the benefit of a grant from Australian Research Council Linkage Program (Grant No. LP130100451).

References

1. Ellis, M., Heyning, C., Legrand, O.: Extending the LNG boom: improving Australian LNG productivity and competitiveness. McKinsey Global Institute, Report (2013)
2. Halpin, D.W.: Construction Management. Wiley, Hoboken (2010)
3. Dong, N., Fischer, M., Haddad, Z., Levitt, R.: A method to automate look-ahead schedule (LAS) generation for the finishing phase of construction projects. Autom. Constr. **35**, 157–173 (2013)
4. Turkan, Y., Bosche, F., Haas, C.T., Haas, R.: Automated progress tracking using 4D schedule and 3D sensing technologies. Autom. Constr. **22**, 414–421 (2012)
5. El-Omari, S., Moselhi, O.: Integrating automated data acquisition technologies for progress reporting of construction projects. Autom. Constr. **20**(6), 699–705 (2011)
6. Chi, H.-L., Wang, J., Wang, X., Truijens, M., Yung, P.: A conceptual framework of quality-assured fabrication, delivery and installation processes for liquefied natural gas (LNG) plant construction. J. Intell. Rob. Syst. 1–16 (2014)
7. Wang, J., Sun, W., Shou, W., Wang, X., Wu, C., Chong, H.-Y., Liu, Y., Sun, C.: Integrating BIM and LiDAR for real-time construction quality control. J. Intell. Rob. Syst. 1–16 (2014)
8. Kiziltas, S., Akinci, B.: The need for prompt schedule update by utilizing reality capture technologies: a case study. In: Proceedings of Construction Research Congress, San Diego, CA (2005)
9. Azimi, R., Lee, S., AbouRizk, S.M., Alvanchi, A.: A framework for an automated and integrated project monitoring and control system for steel fabrication projects. Autom. Constr. **20**(1), 88–97 (2011)
10. Song, L., Eldin, N.N.: Adaptive real-time tracking and simulation of heavy construction operations for look-ahead scheduling. Autom. Constr. **27**, 32–39 (2012)
11. Cheng, J.C., Law, K.H., Bjornsson, H., Jones, A., Sriram, R.: A service oriented framework for construction supply chain integration. Autom. Constr. **19**(2), 245–260 (2010)

12. Chou, J.-S., Chen, H.-M., Hou, C.-C., Lin, C.-W.: Visualized EVM system for assessing project performance. Autom. Constr. **19**(5), 596–607 (2010)
13. Akhavian, R., Behzadan, A.H.: An integrated data collection and analysis framework for remote monitoring and planning of construction operations. Adv. Eng. Inform. **26**(4), 749–761 (2012)
14. Yang, Y.-C., Park, C.-J., Kim, J.-H., Kim, J.-J.: Management of daily progress in a construction project of multiple apartment buildings. J. Constr. Eng. Manage. **133**(3), 242–253 (2007)
15. Cheng, T., Teizer, J.: Real-time resource location data collection and visualization technology for construction safety and activity monitoring applications. Autom. Constr. **34**, 3–15 (2013)
16. Koo, B., Fischer, M.: Feasibility study of 4D CAD in commercial construction. J. Constr. Eng. Manage. **126**(4), 251–260 (2000)
17. Wang, J., Wang, X., Shou, W., Xu, B.: Integrating BIM and augmented reality for interactive architectural visualisation. Constr. Innov. **14**(4), 453–476 (2014)
18. Shou, W., Wang, J., Wang, X., Chong, H.Y.: A comparative review of building information modelling implementation in building and infrastructure industries. Arch. Comput. Methods Eng. **22**(2), 1–18 (2014)
19. Hou, L., Wang, X., Wang, J., Truijens, M.: An integration framework of advanced technologies for productivity improvement for LNG mega-projects. J. Inf. Technol. Constr. **19**, 360–382 (2014)
20. Thorp, J.: The Information Paradox – Realizing the Business Benefits of Information Technology. McGraw-Hill, Toronto (2003)

A Min-cost with Delay Scheduling Method for Large Scale Instance Intensive Tasks

Chengwei Yang[1,2,3] and Sumian Peng[1(✉)]

[1] College of Management Science and Engineering,
Shandong University of Finance and Economic, Jinan, China
yangchengwei2006@163.com, psml61913@sina.com
[2] Shandong Provincial Key Laboratory of Software Engineering, Jinan, China
[3] CVIC Software Engineering Co., Ltd, Jinan, China

Abstract. With the emergence of cloud computing paradigm, it provides a promising new solution for sophisticated instance intensive applications. However, the reliability and response speed begins to be suffered because of the limitation of the Hadoop's FIFO scheduling model. It becomes unacceptable to execute the large scale instance intensive tasks under such conditions. In order to enhance the system resource utilization, we propose a solution in this paper. We use a delay scheduling algorithm to determine the scheduling opportunity and reduce the cost. Delay scheduling can ensure that the current scheduled tasks can make full use of the physical resources, raise resource utilization, and reduce the probability of failure scheduling. The experimental evaluation illustrates that the large scale instance intensive tasks can benefit from the Min-cost delay scheduling algorithm presented in the paper.

Keywords: Instance intensive tasks · Delay scheduling · Min-cost

1 Research Background

Cloud computing is a promising solution to provide the resource dynamical scalability [1, 2]. Cloud-based platform uses the distributed collection of computation and storage facilities. Another feature of cloud computing is use of virtual resources for task execution. When we start to review existing solutions for instance intensive tasks, the limitation becomes unacceptable with respect to the scheduling scalability and response speed. The scheduling method becomes a critical problem for many current sophisticated applications.

Besides, when we began to build the big data analysis and execution platform based on Hadoop, it was found that the data consolidation provided by a shared cluster was highly beneficial. Nevertheless, the response time started to suffer from Hadoop's FIFO scheduler. This is unacceptable to execute large scale instance intensive tasks under cloud computing environment [3, 4]. In order to improve the performance, we present a new solution which raises the resource availability according to the conditions of physical loading. It determines the best opportunity to execute the task from the scheduling queues.

© Springer International Publishing Switzerland 2015
Y. Luo (Ed.): CDVE 2015, LNCS 9320, pp. 268–277, 2015.
DOI: 10.1007/978-3-319-24132-6_34

The issues for a dynamic optimization scheduling model to facilitate large scale instance intensive tasks are discussed in our previous short paper [13]. In this paper, we extend this work and demonstrate the detailed results of our experiments. The contributions are as follows:

(1) A novel Min-cost with delay scheduling algorithm is presented to satisfy the requirements of large scale instance intensive tasks. This method can make full use of the physical resources, raise resource utilization, and reduce the probability of failure scheduling.
(2) The focus on the improved genetic evolution method, which is proved that this method is better than traditional sequence and even greedy methods.
(3) The presentation and analysis of our experiments demonstrate the global mapping algorithm effectively, and prove the Min-cost delay scheduling algorithm is more suitable for a large scale cloud environment.

The remain part of the paper is organized as follows. In the next section, we survey the representative related work for comparison. Section three presents a delay-based load optimized scheduling model, the core design and its components. In section four, a detailed dynamic scheduling algorithm called Min-cost with delay scheduling algorithm is proposed. Section five illustrates the primary experimental results. Finally, section six concludes the paper and overlooks the future research.

2 Related Works

Dynamic Resource Management Strategies for Distributed Environment: In paper [10] presents a resource management solution which includes the user's QoS volunteer resources collection, dynamic resources provision, and service resources migration. When the QoS violation occurs, the engine will deal with a conflict according to the configuration which is set up before. A resource management of YML system is proposed in the paper [8, 9], which uses volunteer resources for heterogeneous environment. If the resources provided by service providers are not able to satisfy the user's QoS requirements, the user can have the chance to replace the original service by selecting other services. Paper [11] proposes a new dynamic resource extension model. It has a negotiation mechanism among multiple third party service providers and automatic chooses the best matching resources. Paper [14] presents a service migration method. When a server loading is overweight, it will move parts of the request to the other idle servers for the purpose of reducing the server pressure.

The above methods need to provide sufficient service resources for computing environment. The differences among them are the resource selection, allocation and recovery strategy.

Scheduling for Instance Intensive Cluster Application: Paper [15] presents an algorithm for instance intensive tasks scheduling (MCUD). The algorithm specifies a deadline assigned to each task to optimize additional execution time. It can dynamically adjust follow-up task scheduling time at the running time. Paper [7] pays close attention to the intensive scheduling problem of the community cloud in order to solve the problem of the cloud cooperation with community members. The USS -I scheduling strategy has proposed. This strategy consists three components: cloud scheduling algorithm among members of the community (QCOAL), cloud scheduling algorithm in members of the community (QCPCSA) and QoS decomposition algorithm (QD). For the problem of instance intensive tasks scheduling, the preview of scheduling algorithm (PCSA) is presented in paper [16]. The main characteristic is that the tasks are ranked by the degree of urgency. The idle computing resources are chosen to carry out, and the execution results will be approximate optimal.

The reference scheduling method we have talked above tackles the conflict scheduling between locality and fairness. Paper [12] point out the scheduling as an optimization problem, which is very close to our work. The difference is that tasks must be matched to nodes and different assignments have different cost based on locality and fairness that is concerned by us. Besides, delay scheduling is relative simpler method than the other works [5, 6], and it is more suitable to use under the cloud environment.

3   A Dynamic Delay Optimization Scheduling Model

As shown in Fig. 1, dynamic delay optimization scheduling model is composed by two core parts, they are analyzer and scheduler. Analyzer is mainly responsible for the task priority scheduling according to user's QoS constraints, select the best scheduling strategies, and determine the mapping between task allocation and distributed resources. Thus, the design of analyzer is to guarantee the performance of global optimization scheduling. Scheduler gets the current load of the available resources, computes the current scheduling cost and determines the executing time in the phase of local execution.

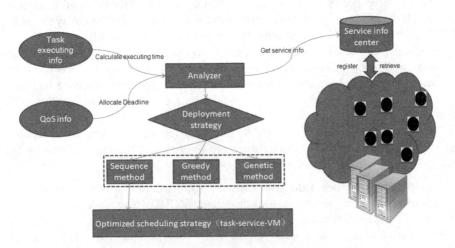

Fig. 1. A dynamic delay optimization scheduling model

To reduce the cost, we use delay scheduling algorithm to determine the scheduling opportunity. Delay scheduling ensures that the current service can make full use of resources, raises resource utilization, and reduces the probability of failure scheduling.

4 Min-cost with Delay Scheduling Algorithm

4.1 Genetic Based Min-cost Loading Mapping

Genetic evolution algorithm runs through the fitness function and evolution of the next generation. We assign a task through two steps: First, we create a sort list of tasks according to our hierarchical scheduling policy. Second, we scan the list to find a task which launch a task from, applying delay scheduling to skip jobs which do not have data on the node being assigned in a limited time. And then, it begins to execute the current schedule instance or waits for the next, analyzing scheduling cost, which can be calculated at time of the instance creation. We assume cloud jobs $J = \{j_1, j_2, ..., j_n\}$, n is the number of jobs, set $G = \{g_1, g_2, ..., g_m\}$ is the execution nodes, $T = [t_i]$ is the execution time matrix. Let $P = \{p_1, p_2, ..., p_M\}$ denote the price set, $D = \{d_1, d_2, ..., d_n\}$ is the deadline set.

This algorithm is shown below:

Algorithm 1: Genetic based Min-cost Loading Mapping

Input: Integrated Task-to-VM list Tasks ; Virtual machines(VMj,Pricej,Speedj)
Output: Optimised task-level scheduling plan
Get ready status tasks list of cloudlets and VMs;
do genetic encoding and init Population of fixed size;
for condition of convergence is not met do
   select the next pops;
   calculate the fitness value ;
   do crossover pops and setting the crossover rate equals 25%
   execute mutation pops operation;
   replacement pops before;
end for
   record the fitness result;
   deployment of the tasks ;

The fitness function directly affects the convergence speed. Based on the definition of total execution cost, the fitness function can be defined as:

$$fi = (t_{ij}p_j + \max(0, li(s_i + t_{ij} - d_i))) \tag{1}$$

In order to select the next generation individual, c probability must be choose as the probability of individual selection. By this selection, individuals in a population with shorter completion time will be evolved as the next generation, and it can provide good genes. So, we set P_{ii} is:

$$P_{ii} = f(i)_j = 1SCALEf_i(j) \tag{2}$$

Crossover mutation imitates natural biological principle of genetic recombination. It will pass the good genes to the next generation, and generate a new individual. We assume the biggest fitness value is f_{max}. Then, in order to cross the larger one of the two individual fitness values, we set k1, k2 as individual of fitness value of crossover probability and mutation probability.

$$Pcross = k_1(fmax - f')/(f_{max} - f_{avg}) \tag{3}$$

$$Pmutation = k_2(fmax - f')/(f_{max} - f_{avg}) \tag{4}$$

The sequence strategy and greedy strategy have also been implemented for the experimental comparison in Sect. 5. We want to prove that the improved generation strategy is more fitness for the scheduling of large scale instance intensive tasks.

4.2   Delay Scheduling Opportunity Selection

In this section, we consider a new delay scheduling which is called Min-cost with Delay Scheduling. Noting the core of this algorithm is to determine Min-cost scheduling under system loading. We have explained the rationale for this design in our analysis of delay scheduling. As a result, when the $\Delta F_{r,M} \geq 0$, the request r is delay scheduled, or if $\Delta F_{r,M} < 0$, the request will be scheduled at once. Pseudo code for this algorithm is shown below:

Algorithm 2: Mini-Cost with Delay Scheduling
---
1) For all the ready scheduling instance ti{
2) For all the task requests from ready scheduling instance {
3) For all the ready scheduling machine m{
4) Compute value ofFMstart, FMwait and ΔFr,M}
5) If(ΔFr,M<0) {
6) minr,M={r,M};
6)If(Fr,Mpenalty<minCost){
7)minCost=Fr,Mpenalty ;
}
8) Assign task request to miniumCost VM;
}

Note that the core of this algorithm is to determine min-cost scheduling under system loading. We have explained the rationale for this design in our analysis of delay scheduling. Therefore, we give the formula directly. At the time t_i, set scheduling cost of a request r* is:

$$FM_{start} = r \in M \cup \{r*\} F_{wr}(f^\wedge w(r) + \Delta t_{start}(1_{estart} - 1_{ewait}) - d_{w(r)} d_{w(r)} - b_{w(r)}) \quad (5)$$

At the time t_i, set delay scheduling cost of a request r^* is:

$$FM_{wait} = F_{wr*} f_{\wedge wr} + \Delta t_{wait} - d_{wr*} d_{wr*} - b_{wr*} + r \in F_{wr}(f_{\wedge w(r)} - d_{w(r)} d_{w(r)} - b_{w(r)})$$

$$(6)$$

For any request r and candidate machine M, the total scheduling cost is:

$$\Delta F_{r,M} = FM_{start} - FM_{wait} \quad (7)$$

As a result, when the $\Delta F_{r,M} \geq 0$, the request r is delay scheduled, or if $\Delta F_{r,M} < 0$, the request will be scheduled at once.

5 Experiments and Evaluation

5.1 Experimental Environment

In this section, two types of primary experiments are made to evaluate the algorithm strategies that proposed in first phase and the system performance evaluation with Delay based on load optimization in the second phase. The deployment environment is depicted in Table 1.

Table 1. Parts of computing resources used in our experiments

Characteristics	Master/worker	Workflow engine
OS	Windows 2000 Server	Windows 2000 Server
Runtime platform	Nuts-platform	Nuts-platform
Database persistence	MySQL 5.5	MySQL 5.5
CPU	P8700 2.53 GHz	P8700 2.53 GHz
Memory	2 GB	4 GB
Instance storage	80 GB	120 GB
Number of instances	3	1
Application server	Microsoft.Net Framework 2.0	Tomcat 6.0
Bandwidth	100 Mbit/s	100 Mbit/s

5.2 Experimental Evaluation

In the first experiment, the experiment algorithm selected three kinds of typical scheduling strategies, including sequential scheduling method, greedy scheduling method, and genetic scheduling method. We let MI (Million Instruction) denotes the length of task and the MIPS (Million Instruction Per Second) denotes the capacity of VM requesting service.

As it shown in Fig. 2, we take the service resources quantity as 5, the tasks number as 10, 15, 20, 25, 30(×100) cases. We select the proposed scheduling strategy and the genetic algorithm to get the best performance. At the same time, the greedy scheduling algorithm and genetic scheduling algorithm is very closed on the condition of task number less than 30(×100). However, with the increase of these numbers, the efficiency of genetic scheduling optimization is better than others.

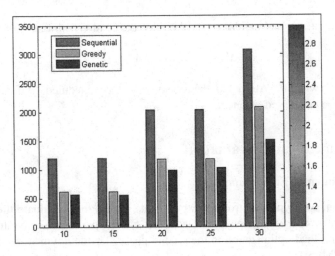

Fig. 2. Algorithm performance comparison (service quantity unchanged)

As it shown in Fig. 3, we take the tasks number as 50 (×100), service resources quantity as 2, 4, 6, 8, 10 (×1) cases. While increasing the number of resources, the genetic algorithm to optimize scheduling strategy has obvious advantages. This shows the similar results with the previous experiment. However, when the number of service resources is 8, using genetic scheduling algorithm, the resource consumption slightly

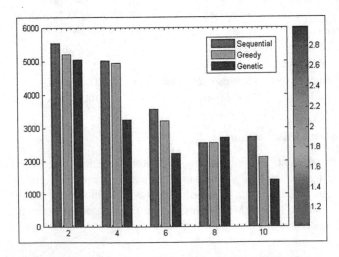

Fig. 3. Algorithm performance comparison (tasks number unchanged)

more than the other two algorithms at the condition of service resource unchanged. The reason for this phenomenon also shows the weaknesses of uncertainty for the genetic algorithm.

In this experiment, the initial jobs are 10000, and the mean scheduling queue length and the CPU Utilization is shown in Fig. 4. Delay scheduling can ensure that the current scheduled tasks can make full use of the resources, rase resource utilization, and reduce the probability of failure scheduling.

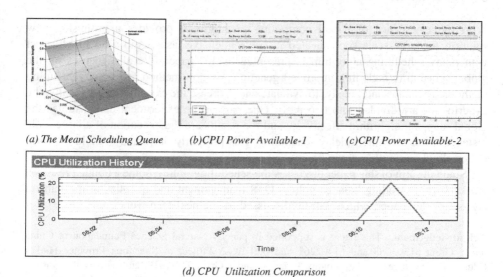

(a) The Mean Scheduling Queue   (b)CPU Power Available-1   (c)CPU Power Available-2

(d) CPU Utilization Comparison

Fig. 4. The mean scheduling queue and CPU utilization

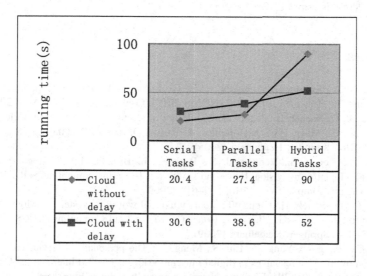

	Serial Tasks	Parallel Tasks	Hybrid Tasks
Cloud without delay	20. 4	27. 4	90
Cloud with delay	30. 6	38. 6	52

Fig. 5. Instance intensive scheduling with or without delay

In Fig. 5, the experimental result illustrates that in a instance intensive tasks, the number of tasks and the task types have influence on the executive efficiency. Less quantity or simple tasks are more suitable for running in cloud environment without delay scheduling. In contrast, the complicated and large scale instance intensive tasks will be benefit from the Min-cost delay scheduling algorithm which is proposed in the paper.

6 Conclusion

With the emergence of Cloud computing paradigm, it provides a promising new solution for large scale sophisticated instance intensive tasks. And a novel Min-cost with delay scheduling algorithm is presented in this paper. We also focuses on the global scheduling including improved genetic evolution method and other scheduling methods (sequence and greedy) to evaluate and decrease the execution cost. Finally, the experiments are divided into two parts. One part of the experiment demonstrates the global mapping algorithm effectively, and the results are the execution of a large scale instances with or without delay scheduling. It is primarily promoted to build platform under cloud computing environment.

Since the aim of this paper discusses the scheduling policy, some extended research works such as loading balance policy, QoS management and negotiation mechanism are out of this paper, which will be discussed as the next step work.

Acknowledgement. This paper is supported in part by Natural Science Foundation of China under Grant 61303088 and 61402261 and part by A Project of Shandong Province Higher Educational Science and Technology Program under Grant J14LN19, and part by the Natural Science Foundation of Shandong Province (Doctoral Foundation) under Grant BS2015DX013, and part by the Fundamental Research Funds for Shandong Provincial Key Laboratory of Software Engineering under Grant 2013SE05. The third author is the corresponding author, and his e-mail address is psm161913@sina.com.

References

1. Andrzejak, A., Kondo, D., Anderson, D.P.: Exploiting non-dedicated resources for Cloud computing. In: The 12th IEEE/IFIP (NOMS 2010), Osaka, Japan, 19–23 April 2010
2. Bowers, S., Ludäscher, B.: Actor-oriented design of scientific workflows. In: Delcambre, L. M.L., Kop, C., Mayr, H.C., Mylopoulos, J., Pastor, Ó. (eds.) ER 2005. LNCS, vol. 3716, pp. 369–384. Springer, Heidelberg (2005)
3. Buyya, R., Yeo, C.S., Venugopal, S., Broberg, J., Brandic, I.: Cloud computing and emerging IT platforms: vision, hype, and reality for delivering computing as the 5th utility. Future Gener. Comput. Syst. 25(6), 599–616 (2009)
4. Zhang, C., De Sterck, H.: CloudWF: a computational workflow system for clouds based on hadoop. In: Jaatun, M.G., Zhao, G., Rong, C. (eds.) Cloud Computing. LNCS, vol. 5931, pp. 393–404. Springer, Heidelberg (2009)
5. Yang, C., Wang, L., Yang, C., Liu, S., Meng, X.: The personalized service customization based on multimedia resources in digital museum grid. In: The 3rd International Conference on U-media, pp. 298–304. Zhejiang Normal University, China, June 2010

6. Zaharia, M., Borthakur, D., Sen Sarma, J.: Delay scheduling: a simple technique for achieving locality and fairness in cluster scheduling. In: EuroSys 2010 (2010)
7. Grounds, N.G., Antonio, J.K., Muehring, J.: Cost-minimizing scheduling of workflows on a cloud of memory managed multicore machines. In: Jaatun, M.G., Zhao, G., Rong, C. (eds.) Cloud Computing. LNCS, vol. 5931, pp. 435–450. Springer, Heidelberg (2009)
8. Pandey, S., Karunamoorthy, D., Buyya, R.: Workflow engine for clouds. In: Cloud Computing: Principles and Paradigms. Wiley, New York (2011)
9. Cunsolo, V.D., Distefano, S., Puliafito, A., Scarpa, M.: Cloud@home: bridging the gap between volunteer and cloud computing. In: Huang, D.-S., Jo, K.-H., Lee, H.-H., Kang, H.-J., Bevilacqua, V. (eds.) ICIC 2009. LNCS, vol. 5754, pp. 423–432. Springer, Heidelberg (2009)
10. Li, W.: Research on instance intensive workflow scheduling for community cloud. Shandong Univ. (2010)
11. Liu, X., Yuan, D., Zhang, G., Chen, J., Yang, Y.: SwinDeW-C: a peer-to-peer based cloud workflow system. In: Furht, B., Escalante, A. (eds.) Handbook of Cloud Computing, pp. 309–332. Springer, New York (2010)
12. Shang, L., Petiton, S., Emad, N., Yang, X.: YML-PC: a reference architecture based on workflow for building scientific private clouds. In: Antonopoulos, N., Gillam, L. (eds.) Cloud Computing, pp. 247–252. Springer, London (2010)
13. Yang, C., Guo, J.-D., Chi, J.: A dynamic delay optimization scheduling model. In: Luo, Y. (ed.) CDVE 2014. LNCS, vol. 8683, pp. 68–71. Springer, Heidelberg (2014)
14. Ju, J., Buyya, R.: Scheduling scientific workflow applications with deadline and budget constraints using genetic algorithms. Sci. Program. 14(3-4), 217–230 (2006)
15. Yan, J., Wu, G.: Scheduling algorithm for instance intensive workflow. Comput. Appl. 11, 2864–2866 (2010)
16. Liu, K., Jin, H., Chen, J., Liu, X., Yuan, D., Yang, Y.: A compromised-time-cost scheduling algorithm in SwinDeW C for instance-intensive cost-constrained workflows on cloud computing platform. Int. J. High Perform. Comput. Appl. 24, 445–456 (2010)

Author Index

Printed in the United States
By Bookmasters